Nobility and the Making of Race in Eighteenth-Century Britain

Nobility and the Making of Race in Eighteenth-Century Britain

Tim Mc Inerney

BLOOMSBURY ACADEMIC
LONDON • NEW YORK • OXFORD • NEW DELHI • SYDNEY

BLOOMSBURY ACADEMIC
Bloomsbury Publishing Plc
50 Bedford Square, London, WC1B 3DP, UK
1385 Broadway, New York, NY 10018, USA
29 Earlsfort Terrace, Dublin 2, Ireland

BLOOMSBURY, BLOOMSBURY ACADEMIC and the Diana logo are trademarks of
Bloomsbury Publishing Plc

First published in Great Britain 2023
This paperback edition published in 2025

Copyright © Tim Mc Inerney, 2023

Tim Mc Inerney has asserted his right under the Copyright, Designs and Patents Act, 1988,
to be identified as Author of this work.

For legal purposes the Acknowledgements on p. ix constitute an extension
of this copyright page.

Cover image © Slipper, England, 1720/30s. Heritage Image Partnership Ltd/
Alamy Stock Photo.

All rights reserved. No part of this publication may be reproduced or transmitted in any
form or by any means, electronic or mechanical, including photocopying, recording, or
any information storage or retrieval system, without prior permission in writing from the
publishers.

Bloomsbury Publishing Plc does not have any control over, or responsibility for, any thirdparty
websites referred to or in this book. All internet addresses given in this book were
correct at the time of going to press. The author and publisher regret any inconvenience
caused if addresses have changed or sites have ceased to exist, but can accept no
responsibility for any such changes.

A catalogue record for this book is available from the British Library.

A catalog record for this book is available from the Library of Congress.

Library of Congress Cataloging-in-Publication Data

Names: McInerney, Tim, author.
Title: Nobility and the making of race in eighteenth-century Britain / Tim McInerney.
Description: New York, NY : Bloomsbury Academic, 2023. | Includes bibliographical
references and index. | Summary: "Examines how race theory was created and
established in 18th-century Britain and Ireland"– Provided by publisher.
Identifiers: LCCN 2023022780 (print) | LCCN 2023022781 (ebook) | ISBN
9781350346369 (hardback) | ISBN 9781350346390 (paperback) | ISBN
9781350346376 (epdf) | ISBN 9781350346383 (epub)
Subjects: LCSH: Race–History–18th century. | Great Britain–Race
relations–History–18th century.
Classification: LCC HT1521 .M3765 2023 (print) | LCC HT1521 (ebook) |
DDC 305.800941–dc23/eng/20230525
LC record available at https://lccn.loc.gov/2023022780
LC ebook record available at https://lccn.loc.gov/2023022781

ISBN: HB: 978-1-3503-4636-9
PB: 978-1-3503-4639-0
ePDF: 978-1-3503-4637-6
eBook: 978-1-3503-4638-3

Typeset by Deanta Global Publishing Services, Chennai, India

To find out more about our authors and books visit www.bloomsbury.com and sign up for
our newsletters .

For Emma

Contents

List of figures		viii
Acknowledgements		ix
Note on translations		x
1	Introduction	1
2	The noble paradigm	13
3	The race myth in retrospect	43
4	Human hierarchy and the Great Chain of Being	59
5	Civilized anatomies in eighteenth-century human-variety theory	73
6	Superior blood: Horses, ethno-histories and hereditary disease	97
7	Mankind's new nobility: The rise of genealogical race theory	121
8	Ireland's imposter aristocrats	139
9	The South Seas: Laboratory of the noble physique	157
10	'Royal slaves': Abolitionism and fantasies of slave nobility	175
11	Noble race in a time of revolution	195
12	Conclusion	211
References		221
Index		241

Figures

1	Court dress, made in England *c.* 1750	34
2	Outdoor pattens for high-heeled shoes 1700–1800	36
3	Nineteenth-century engraving of the Viscount Pitt porcelain figure group	38
4	*A Marquis in His Parliament Robes,* from Francis Nichols (1729)	40
5	*The Manner how the Whole Earth was Peopled by Noah and his Descendants after the Flood,* from the *Universal Magazine* (1749)	54
6	'Pedigree of Wingfield, of Wingfield, Letheringham, &c' (*c.* 1712–99)	55
7	*Integrae Naturae* from Robert Fludd (1617)	62
8	*The Laplander,* from Oliver Goldsmith (1774)	90
9	*The Duke of Newcastle upon Tyne, with Page* from William Cavendish (1743)	100
10	'Paddy on Horseback' by James Gillray (1779)	149
11	*A Young Woman of Otaheite Bringing a Present* from James Cook and James King (1784)	164
12	*Omai, a Man from the Island of Raiatea* by Joshua Reynolds	170
13	*Elihu Yale, William Cavendish, 2nd Duke of Devonshire, Lord James Cavendish, Mr. Tunstal and page* by unknown artist (*c.* 1708)	178
14	'The Duchess of Queensbury playing at foils with her favourite lapdog Mungo after expending near 10,000 to make him a — ', by William Austin (1773)	180
15	*Bust of a Man* by Francis Harwood (*c.* 1758)	183

Acknowledgements

This book would not exist without the wisdom and guidance of Professor Isabelle Bour of the Université Sorbonne Nouvelle. Professor Bour's invaluable direction during my doctoral thesis provided the bedrock for this study, and for that I will forever be grateful. I am also deeply indebted to my exceptional colleagues at the Université Paris 8 Vincennes-Saint-Denis, alongside whom I have had the honour of working during the production of this monograph and especially to those at the TransCrit research unit who work so tirelessly to support and elevate our research. I also owe a debt of gratitude to my parents and grandparents, who always valued learning and education above all and whose unconditional support will ever be a source of inspiration. This monograph is dedicated to my best and oldest friend, who, on a sunny afternoon long ago, made me promise to mention her in my first book. Emma, I am happy to finally oblige.

Note on translations

Where possible this study uses contemporary translations of eighteenth-century texts, which are frequently examined in their own right. In some instances, where the contemporary translations have significantly abridged or modified their sources, the original texts are referenced alongside them. I have provided my own translation for certain texts, in which case the original versions have been included in footnotes.

1

Introduction

Something extraordinary took place in the field of natural history towards the end of the eighteenth century. Until this point, the study of human diversity had revolved primarily around ideas of environmental influence: the body was seen as a decidedly malleable subject, responsive to the influences of nutrition, sunlight, altitude and civil society and was thus innately capable of comprehensive transformation. Natural historians in Europe and America had generally approached the anatomical variation they observed in different parts of the world as a question of bodily potential; it was commonly held that, given enough time, the human body could adapt to match the environment in which it was placed. From the 1770s onwards, however, these theorists increasingly turned towards an alternative model of human classification: race. In doing so, they were making use of a concept that had previously held little association with ideas of human phenotype or skin colour. 'Race', for most of the eighteenth century, had constituted a discourse of lineal family. It was rooted most firmly in the ancient traditions of hereditary nobility, which disseminated the notion that one's natural place in the order of the universe was intricately bound up with bloodline and descent. Race, in this capacity, formed part of a strategic paradigm which not only protected and maintained hereditary elites in positions of sociopolitical authority but also perpetuated spirals of descent-based hierarchy that ultimately served to sustain a greater illusion of natural order in all levels of society. Through race, in other words, hereditary elites were able to present themselves as naturally, inimitably excellent while simultaneously framing those around them according to various degrees of non-excellence based on descending grades of lineage. By the later decades of the century, this ancient language of 'race' was progressively being deployed to reimagine the entire global population in terms of blood purity rather than climatic adaptation. According to the emerging doctrine of race theory, mankind could be divided up into a handful of lineal families, each perpetuating a certain set of physical and mental characteristics through their bloodlines. A 'major human race', like a noble lineage, became something that could be tarnished or contaminated through admixture with another line of descent. Bodily potential was swapped in for bodily destiny, and the infinite possibilities of the environment were exchanged for the ineluctability of heredity. The following study argues that natural history's shift towards blood hierarchy at the end of the eighteenth century was by no means arbitrary or incidental. On the contrary, it represented the integration of a tried and tested collection of highly successful power strategies that had been refined by hereditary elites over millennia. These same power strategies fundamentally influenced the structure of race as it came to exist in subsequent years. By reframing global populations in terms of purity and impurity and by recasting whiteness in terms of genealogical excellence that automatically defined the nature of non-excellence, white Europeans were able to use the ancient paradigm of nobility to portray themselves as the natural aristocracy of mankind.

Focusing primarily on Britain and Ireland, this book examines the web of interlaced relationships that existed between nobility and race thinking over the course of the eighteenth century and demonstrates how both can be considered as part of a common hierarchal discourse. The period under examination falls primarily between 1735, when the Swedish natural historian Carolus Linnaeus first created the revolutionary genus *Homo*, and 1795, the year in which the German physician Johann Friedrich Blumenbach published his seminal treatise on major human races, the *De generis humani varietate nativa*. This represents a time frame wherein the vocabulary and methodology of race theory had yet to be firmly established, and before the word 'race' itself had fully come to represent the idea of major divisions within the human species. Nevertheless, it was during this same period when some of the most important building blocks of modern race thinking were positioned. Both race and nobility, this study argues, exist primarily within a discourse of inference and intimation, which seamlessly permeated a remarkable range of disciplines and contexts at this time. The primary sources examined in this book therefore include a selection of both well-known and much lesser-known texts, from fields as diverse from one another as natural history, philosophy, political theory, travel writing, medical tracts, literature, drama and poetry. They do not attempt to exhaustively catalogue the structural relationships between nobility and race but rather to identify a consistent set of patterns that underpinned the very idea of hierarchy and natural order in early modern Britain and Ireland. They also demonstrate that these influences were not always of the 'top-down' variety, proliferating instead within a complex matrix of assumption and prejudice which constantly reinforced fundamental paradigms of excellence at all levels of society. The first seven chapters of the book break down the major narratives of eighteenth-century human hierarchy, examining the foundational paradigm of nobility in Britain and Ireland (Chapter 2), the development of race as a discourse of genealogical gradation (Chapter 3), the 'Great Chain of Being' world view of universal hierarchy (Chapter 4), the dynamic evolution of heredity as an agent of human type (Chapters 5 and 6) and the steady entry of race-based identity into theories of human classification (Chapter 7). From there, the shared paradigmatic codes of nobility and race are explored more closely through a selection of more specific analyses: the example of multiple, ethnically based nobilities in Ireland (Chapter 8), the projection of noble rank onto racialized groups in the South Seas (Chapter 9), the confrontation of inherited nobility with inherited slavery (Chapter 10) and the re-imagining of noble race in the turbulent 1790s (Chapter 11).

It goes without saying that this is a study that builds on an extensive critical and historiographical tradition, which has long endeavoured to delineate the complex origins and structure of race. That critical tradition is, in fact, as old as race theory itself. Even during the heyday of racial pseudoscience in the early twentieth century, scholars such as the American anthropologist Franz Boas (1912: 530) or the German political philosopher Eric Voegelin (1933: 12) railed against the doctrines of racialism, denouncing its plethora of internal contradictions and glaring dearth of empirical evidence. When an international committee of anthropologists came together to definitively renounce race theory after the Second World War (see Chapter 3) and when their condemnation was subsequently vindicated by the steady advancement of molecular genetics, questions about the origins of race became all the more urgent. If the so-called major races were not grounded in any scientific reality, why had so many people come to accept them as a self-evident element of the natural world? Why did this particular model of human stratification achieve such ubiquity and so quickly? Why has race continued to proliferate for so long after its scientific basis was debunked? Why, indeed, have we felt such a powerful desire to stratify human anatomy in the first place? The acceptance of race as social construct, notes Ron Mallon, involves the recognition that 'race is real, but not a biological kind', thereby opening up a whole host of new metaphysical questions about the nature of its construction (2004: 644). Kwame Anthony Appiah, for instance, distinguishes 'racialism' (by which he means the belief that humanity is divisible into a small number of heritable phenotypes) first against an 'extrinsic racism' which makes moral distinctions between those groups on account of their supposed differences in behaviour or mindset, and second against an 'intrinsic racism' which holds that those groups should be treated differently merely by virtue of being different (1989: 44–6). George Fredrickson similarly points out that racism as well as race has historically manifested itself in extremely diverse ways, both before and after the inception of racial pseudoscience, and that these manifestations rarely map perfectly onto one another (2002: 79). Jean-Frédéric Schaub has drawn attention to the political and geographical contextuality of any such questions: the race concept has manifested itself remarkably differently in different parts of the world, and thus determining the precise moment that a 'modern' notion of race emerged often holds specific political and cultural implications in different geopolitical contexts (2015: 77–95). Indeed, notes Stuart Hall, speaking of race in terms of 'transcultural or transcendental' categories can miss out on the 'extraordinary diversity of subjective positions, social experiences and cultural identities' composing individual racialized categories (1996: 444). The very word 'race', Michael Banton has demonstrated, can hold very different significance in different languages; concordantly, the use of a particular vocabulary of race, such as 'coloured' or 'mixed race', often reinforces a set of racial idioms that are specific only to a certain place and time (1998: 1–2). To begin to understand race, then, suggests Joshua Glasgow, we must accept that the reality of race is itself contingent on what racial terms purport to refer to – so that it is often most important to 'empirically identify the folk theory of race' in a given cultural context (2008: 334). It is the multifaceted 'folk theory' of race, and its various influences, with which this study is mainly concerned.

One problem faced by any historian of race in the pre-modern world, notes Andrew Wells, is that the modern concept of race always 'lurks in the background' of its pre-modern antecedents (2015: 427). When discussing the rise of race theory at the end of the eighteenth century, therefore, it is essential to appreciate the myriad and often disparate contexts in which it was conceived. Bancel et al. point out that a 'deep epistemological change' took place in the domain of natural history towards the end of the century, 'enabling the strict separation of human groups' through the use of new techniques in taxonomic classification and anthropometry (2014: 1–3). Joyce Chaplin, meanwhile, has argued that race as we know it is 'a specific product of Atlantic history', designed to uphold systems of human inequality that were moulded by the international slave trade (2009: 173). At the same time, this developing vision of race was predicated on much older hierarchical tropes, which often continued to exist alongside the doctrines of race theory. Hannah Arendt's highly influential observation that there exists a phenomenon of 'race thinking' – which always undermines the unity of mankind by asserting the existence of a superior kind of human being – highlights how the power dynamics underpinning race and racism can proliferate quite independently of any specific race ideology (1951: 160–1). Michel Prum has relatedly asserted that to study race is not to study differences within a particular template of human type but ultimately to study social 'alterization' – the fabrication of an other (2012: 7). In fact, suggests Tzvetan Todorov, racial pseudoscience could be seen as 'a way of responding with biological data to what is actually a question of social psychology' (1993: 92).

Further distinctions must be made between race as a lineal family, race as a fully realized model of human taxonomy, and the various historical discourses that we might consider racialized from a modern standpoint. Robert Bernasconi, for example, points out that the blood-purity statues of early modern Spain and Portugal, which were deployed against Jewish and Muslim *conversos* even after their conversion to Christianity, can be identified as a case of 'racism' while not being 'sustained by a scientific concept of race' (2009: 83). Bernasconi also earmarks the significance of the seventeenth-century physician François Bernier's ambivalent human taxonomy in the *Nouvelle Division de la Terre* (1684), which used the French terms *race* and *espèce* interchangeably to describe an indefinite number of human varieties (Bernasconi 2009: 84; see Chapter 5). Staffan Müller-Wille and Hans Jörg Rheinberger, meanwhile, pinpoint the *casta* system in sixteenth-century Latin America as an early building block of race, because it assigned legal and social status to individuals not only based on their skin colour but also according to the minute details of their parentage (2012: 66). Francisco Bethencourt, on the other hand, stresses that while such systems likely influenced the classifications of natural history, they were local by nature and never pretended to represent a universalist scheme of racial type (2013: 171; see Chapter 7).

Racial categories are also deeply embroiled with ideas of nation. Nicholas Hudson has highlighted the interplay of race and nation during the eighteenth century in the context of the transatlantic slave trade, which systematically stripped enslaved people of signifiers of national difference and instead projected racialized identities onto the commoditized body (1996: 251–2). Paul Stock notes how eighteenth- and early nineteenth-century encyclopaedias often emphasized linguistic differences as markers of perceived race groups, indicating a kind of heredity of mores and national character that maintained a specific identity over time (2011: 26–8). Some historians, such as Benjamin Isaac, have identified 'sets of ideas' they equate with 'proto-racism' in the Ancient Greek and Roman world (2004: 1–2). Ian Hannaford, in his landmark study *Race: The History of an Idea in the West*, also recognizes these modes of thinking dating to antiquity while cautioning against ascribing modern ideas of race to constructs which appear familiar but which are actually built around entirely different criteria from our own (1996: 6, 21). For the modern concept of race to exist, Hannaford asserts, Man must first be understood as a biological subject, removed from ethics, morality and history, and comprising a global network of categories and subcategories (1996: 57–8). Effectively, this interpretation of mankind would not be fully refined until the inception of the genus *Homo* in 1735 (see Chapter 5).

The argument presented in this book is indebted to the work of scholars who have already interrogated the intriguing overlaps between race thinking and noble tradition in the early modern world. Étienne Balibar and Immanuel Wallerstein have highlighted the existence of an 'aristocratic racism', which delineates racial categories 'by elevating the group which controls the discourse to the status of a "race"' (1991: 208). That is to say that the isolation and self-definition of a hereditary caste marked out as superior creates a prototype of race and in turn shapes the parameters of those who will be understood as 'racially' inferior (1991: 207–8). Jenny Davidson's study of 'breeding' among the upper orders charts how a combination of blood lineage, high civility and animal husbandry often informed understandings of human nature and perfectibility during the eighteenth century, helping to blur distinctions between innate and environmental influences on the body and mind (2009: 1–4). Nicholas Hudson has likewise noted that race was an especially convenient term for eighteenth-century natural historians, precisely because it originally pertained to both animal husbandry and noble genealogy. In the context of human-variety theory, Hudson claims, race could therefore be invoked to dehumanize ostensibly inferior groups while conveying a sense of dynastic dignity in the case of white Europeans (1996: 253–4). Roxann Wheeler has highlighted the steady development of skin colour as a component of developing race discourse in the eighteenth century, notably pointing to marriage plots in mid-century fiction wherein complexion is sometimes deployed as a symbol of inherited social rank (2000: 153–75). Jean Feerick, meanwhile, claims that noble blood allowed hereditary elites in the early modern period to define their physical bodies first and foremost in terms of rank distinction. The noble body itself provided evidence of metaphysical separation from social inferiors while intimately linking each individual noble with a wider network of noble families (2010: 9–14). Race, Feerick stresses, was originally a quality of the upper ranks alone; it was the absence of documented bloodlines that characterized the greater population (2010: 9). Claude-Olivier Doron has written about how the 'genealogical reasoning' of race – which he characterizes as an exclusively cultural discourse based on 'nobiliary discourses', 'breeding practices' and 'spiritual status' – began in the eighteenth century as largely incompatible with the 'logico-classificatory style of reasoning' deployed by natural historians. Yet, Doron notes, over the course of the century this language of family and blood can be seen to permeate the realm of natural philosophy, altering the shape and sense of emerging taxonomies (2012: 75–82).

The idea of nobility is in many ways just as nebulous as that of race. In eighteenth-century Britain and Ireland, nobility officially indicated membership of the peerage – a precise legal status granted to the (primarily male) heads of the kingdoms' most powerful landed families. From this simple legal standpoint, standards of nobility were changing all the time and often quite dramatically. Yet, the titled peers of Britain and Ireland, comprising only a few hundred individuals, do not come close to encapsulating the reach of noble authority at this time. As discussed in Chapter 2, nobility must at the very least include the close-knit circle of families who overwhelmingly dominated the peerage throughout the eighteenth century and not simply their titled patriarchs. Even more importantly, we must take into account the implications of nobility as an idea at this time. Legally recognized titles were, after all, contingent on a much broader understanding of nobility as a part of the universal order. Arlette Jouanna has pointed out the unique and quasi-mystical nature of noble status, which marries recognized hereditary privilege with a metaphysical idea of the most perfect specimen within a given classification (1981: 125). By virtue of this greater idea of nobility, an English lord could be compared to a Spanish *señor* or a French *baron*, even though each of those titles depended on a different legal framework. In Scotland the inherited chiefdoms of Highland clans were understood as an alternative form of nobility and were accordingly entwined with the honours of Scottish peerage and royalty. The Dukes of Argyll, for instance, were also the hereditary *Tòisichean* (chiefs) of the *Clann MacCailean Mór* (Clan Campbell), while the Earls of Seaforth also formed part of the *Clann MacCoinneach* (Clan Mackenzie). In Ireland, the beleaguered lords and ladies who held legally recognized titles of nobility were widely ridiculed as fatuous *arrivistes*, while Gaelic and Hiberno-Norman dynasties with their avowed genealogical mandates remained the only true nobles in the eyes of many (see Chapter 8). Princely visitors from far-flung lands frequently made appearances at the London court, in the understanding that they represented an exotic state of nobility, comparable to that of the courtiers who clamoured for their attentions (see Chapters 9 and 10).

More than this, nobility had been associated with ideas of bodily difference for centuries. H. C. Baldry has noted that even Homeric poetry regularly recognized 'a hereditary physical difference between nobles and the multitude, a natural division separating them in bodily physique as well as spirit and way of life' (1965: 15). Certain low-born characters in the *Iliad* and the *Odyssey*, he points out, are berated as ugly, or deformed, while those titled *basileis* ('kings') are commonly described as 'more delicate and beautiful than ordinary people' (Baldry 1965: 15; Starr 1992: 8). Anatomical difference was no less relevant to noble tradition in the eighth-century CE when the Venerable Bede recounted the story of Imma – an Anglo-Saxon nobleman who tried to evade capture by disguising himself as a peasant, but whose high birth was revealed when no fetters could bind his feet ([*c.* 731 CE] 1907: 4.22, 268). In medieval chivalric romances, notes Lawrence James, attention is constantly drawn to the 'fine features and complexions' of the hereditary elite, while medieval funerary effigies in England frequently represented them as markedly taller, more muscular and more physically robust than other people (2009: 25; 2004: 118). Such representations may have partly reflected contemporary health inequalities and their effects on physical stature. Even by the late eighteenth century, note Jaadla et al., an analysis of Dorset's militia ballot lists shows a 'clear wealth gradient in height', with an average difference of 2–3 centimetres between recruits drawn from the highest and lowest economic brackets (2021: 390). The cultural trope of the superior noble body certainly remained resilient throughout the eighteenth century, constantly blurring the lines between fantasy, expectation and reality, and frequently manifesting itself in the more 'serious' fields of medicine, history and taxonomic classification (see Chapters 5–7). For the New England theologian Samuel Stanhope Smith, enigmatic accounts of the superior noble body throughout history were not necessarily confined to the realm of fantasy. 'The tales of romances that describe the superlative beauty of captive princesses' he wrote in his *Essay on the Causes of Variety of Complexion and Figure in the Human Species* (1787),

> are not to be ascribed solely to the venality of writers prone to flatter the great, but have a real foundation in nature ... [L]anguage, which is borrowed from nature, vindicates this criticism. A *princely* person, and a *noble* thought, are usual figures of speech. (Stanhope Smith 1787: 74)

The resulting understanding of noble difference is now so tightly woven into cultural narratives of social hierarchy that today we can often fail to notice its decidedly strange premise. Modern readers will probably not find it particularly unusual that Hans Christian Anderson's fairy-tale princess should detect a handful of peas secreted beneath her tower of mattresses, while her non-noble rivals – though posing as high-born pretendants to the prince's hand – cannot. She, we already understand, is different from the other women; she is a *real* princess and thus bestowed with some additional, ill-defined quality that allows her to achieve super-human feats. The very fact that noble difference, from Homer's *Odyssey* to Anderson's *Princess and the Pea*, lends itself so readily to fantasy and folktales is revealing in itself. Much like race theory, nobility is a discourse that revels in superstition, flourishing on its own fanciful logic whereby bloodlines are neatly arranged on a predetermined hierarchy, and wherein every individual's position on that hierarchy has a meaning. The internal logic of nobility, it must be remembered, functions no differently in the pages of a children's storybook than it does within the present-day halls of Westminster. In both instances, though it might be all too easy to forget, it is equally fictional.

It is this greater idea of nobility that I have called the noble paradigm: a set of basic tenets without which nobility loses all coherence. The noble paradigm contends that a special brand of excellence can be passed down through lineal families, who must reperform the virtues of their ancestors and defend the purity of their bloodlines in order to maintain the integrity of their 'race'. As will be discussed in Chapter 2, this basic structure of nobility is built around a number of highly successful power strategies, which have been refined over the centuries to make this model of hereditary governance one of the most enduring in European history (Leonhard and Weiland 2011: 6). Moreover, these power strategies constantly endeavour to render themselves invisible, instead presenting paradigmatic nobility (and the various states of non-nobility which are essential for its existence) as a reflection of the natural order of the world. The same power strategies can be seen to percolate through the discourse of human variety at the end of the eighteenth century alongside the language of 'race' and descent. By reframing human variety through the prism of the noble paradigm, natural historians were able to reconceive entire global populations according to a familiar and even intuitive hierarchy that had bolstered ideas of natural superiority and inferiority for as long as anyone could remember.

In the historiographical fields of both nobility and race, terminology can be misleading. As mentioned, nobility as an idea extended far beyond the peerage, and thus the term 'nobility' is used in this study not only in reference to titled peers but also to denote the multiple incarnations of nobility that competed with or complemented this institution. As for the peerage itself, it should be appreciated that there were originally three peerages on the islands of Britain and Ireland, representing the distinct nobilities of England, Scotland and Ireland, which were only merged in 1707 and 1801, respectively, into a 'Peerage of Great Britain and Ireland'. Since Ireland was not incorporated into this system until the beginning of the nineteenth century (and since its elite ranks were in countless ways incomparable with those of Britain), the terms 'British peerage' and 'British nobility' are used deliberately to refer to groups in Scotland, Wales and England. Likewise, 'Britain' and 'Great Britain' are used as retrospective geographic terms for the island of Great Britain before and after the 1706–7 Acts of Union. The term 'elite' is frequently used when discussing involvement from both the nobility and those loci of power outside the main noble spheres of influence (top-tier income families who had few direct connections to the peerage, for example). This last term is important since, as will be seen in Chapter 2, one of the main power strategies of paradigmatic nobility involves the management and potential assimilation of non-noble power.

Most importantly, it is crucial to appreciate that the English word 'race' has undergone multiple and almost uninterrupted semiotic shifts since the eighteenth century. Despite the landmark taxonomical texts of the late eighteenth century, the definition of human races as 'major groupings of mankind' did not begin to gain widespread acceptance until many decades later. Moreover, race held enormous figurative potential – it was a term that could be employed to frame nations, cultures and almost any given group in terms of lineal family. In this respect, race could easily be used to categorize populations, divided up, among other things, on account of physical appearance. Thus, while it should be presumed unless otherwise stated that the term 'race' in this text refers to the broad and capacious concept as it existed in the eighteenth century, it must also be appreciated that all these applications ultimately fed into the later idea of discrete and immutable human races. The terms 'heredity' and 'blood' must also be understood in their contemporary sense. In an age before molecular genetics or reproductive biology, noble blood did not necessarily correlate with a tangible physical liquid, nor was that liquid commonly understood to 'reproduce' traits in the next generation (see Chapters 3, 6 and 7). Ideas of 'unmixed' or 'pure' blood, likewise, generally implied a complex process of breeding, which incorporated active virtue, environmental influences and careful cultivation of civility over multiple generations. All this meant that eighteenth-century ideas of heredity, or rather 'the hereditary', did not form a single unified concept as we would understand it today (see Chapter 6). To complicate matters further, these terms could hold a metaphorical dimension: to speak of 'inherited' traits was to borrow from a language of intergenerational property transfer and did not always reference direct transmission of material from one body to the next. That considered, we should remember that the modern construct of pure blood is still a metaphor. There is not, and never has been, any such thing as blood purity from the point of view of genetics. While eighteenth-century commentators did not interpret genealogical purity in the same way as, say, early-twentieth-century eugenicists, that does not mean that their understanding of hierarchized bloodlines did not contribute to those subsequent ideas. If anything, the racial pseudoscientists of the nineteenth and twentieth centuries built their discourses of pure and impure bloodline on the 'metaphorical' biases of their forbears.

In all, this book argues that the noble paradigm was fundamental to the development of race and racism as we know them today. Eighteenth-century noble tradition, it suggests, promoted a seminal template of heritable superiority that could be cultivated over successive generations within individual bloodlines, asserting that these bloodlines thereafter needed to be protected from contamination from inferior inherited traits, and consolidating the idea that the human body itself was an expression of social and political rank. The noble paradigm's projected ladder from *demoi* to *aristoi*, from lowly servitude to anatomical and moral excellence, thereby informed a wider system of social order, which provided the conceptual framework for a scale of excellence from the Black to the white body, from the non-European to the European and from the savage to the civilized. Just beneath the surface of those fanciful tales of prodigious kings and slumbering princesses, this is a tradition that vaunted a brutal form of human hierarchy based around the protection and maintenance of those who had decided, for themselves, that they were born to rule.

2

The noble paradigm

In 1968, the eminent social historian Harold Perkin extolled the merits of eighteenth-century Britain's singularly open aristocracy. 'France', he pronounced confidently, 'where social climbing was frustrated, had a political revolution. Britain, where it was not, had an industrial one' (1968: 137). For Perkin, Britain simply boasted the 'right king of society' for industrial expansion, being centred around an 'open aristocracy based on property and patronage' (1968: 127). Younger sons of 'aristocratic' families, he explained, 'had to compete with those below them for positions in the professions and in trade and industry', thus establishing 'that two-way flow of men and wealth so characteristic of English as distinct from continental society' (1968: 130, 136). His is a familiar nationalistic fantasy: Britain's nobility, gentry and middling sorts alike are portrayed as a pugnacious band of businessmen, hard-wired towards economic success and ever ready to choose mercantile pragmatism over the foppery and effeminacy of the mainland. Even the monarch, according to Perkin, was little more than 'the greatest property-owner, the first of the borough-mongering country gentlemen of England' (1968: 130). Indulgent as such a narrative may seem, it had already dominated historiographies of British nobility for over a century and a half before Perkin put pen to paper. In the wake of the French Revolution, notes Amanda Goodrich, the postulation that British peers were more level-headed, more meritocratic and more industrious than their freshly deposed cousins across the Channel was carefully crafted and disseminated by anti-radicals, who at once sought to defend 'the supremacy of hereditary aristocracy and its superior education and culture' and to distance the peerage from the French *noblesse* (2005: 102). Unsurprisingly, the historiographical myth of an open aristocracy in eighteenth-century Britain quickly collapses under interrogation, but its legacy has nevertheless rendered the power structures upholding British nobility particularly surreptitious. First, it is a story that has always taken a curiously English perspective on the kingdoms' noble institutions. It is rather unlikely, for instance, had Harold Perkin thought to consider Britain's colonial aristocracy in Ireland, that he would have judged it 'the right kind of society to generate a spontaneous industrial revolution' (1968: 127). Moreover, it has meant that Britain and Ireland's nobilities have all too often been studied in starkly economic or political terms, while the phenomenon of nobility itself has been treated as a merely superficial detail. The rituals and customs of Britain's hereditary elite, we might easily understand, represented little more than a colourful but harmless legacy of feudal rule – nobles were simply gentlemen with bigger homes and nicer titles. What this historiographical perspective tends to overlook is the fundamental *idea* of nobility. The state of being noble was certainly not incidental, nor irrelevant, nor superficial. It was the product of a carefully tended set of political strategies, which had successfully protected schemas of hereditary power since antiquity. This chapter examines that paradigm of nobility in eighteenth-century Britain (Ireland will be explored in a separate chapter). Through a review of noble privileges, noble display and noble self-presentation, we will see how its power strategies – the same strategies which would eventually come to uphold race theory – actually worked.

* * *

All manifestations of nobility can be seen to rely on the same basic paradigm, whose shape, form and function are designed to preserve the illusion of its reality. What I have called the 'noble paradigm' refers to a set of self-sustaining power strategies which endeavour above all to control and define what human excellence looks like. Through maintaining authority over the discourse of human excellence, the noble paradigm not only harnesses the ability to fashion that excellence in its own likeness but simultaneously defines non-excellence according to descending degrees of adherence to those arbitrary parameters. It follows that entire spectrums of superiority and inferiority, sophistication and vulgarity, and civility and barbarism rely on how closely one can approach the parameters of excellence set down by those who have defined the nature of excellence itself.

The noble paradigm, I propose, can be summarized in six basic tenets:

1. Some people are naturally excellent.
2. This excellence can be transmitted genealogically.
3. This familial excellence naturally gives rise to cultural and economic dominance.

4. Inherited excellence must be re-performed in each generation.
5. The noble body is both an expression and a tool of inherited excellence.
6. Integrity of genealogical, cultural, economic, performative and corporeal excellence – called 'true nobility' – is essential for the continuance of inherited excellence in future generations.[1]

These ideas are extraordinarily insidious. The strategy of the noble paradigm is not, as one might expect, to convince everyone to revere titled nobles. If that were the case, it would have failed at the outset: for as long as nobility has been recorded, its representatives have been met with satire, ridicule and mockery as much as (and sometimes more than) they have enjoyed respect and deference. Rather, the core strategy of the noble paradigm relies on three ostensible truisms. The first of these is that something called nobility exists in the first place. The tenets listed earlier are articulated around the idea of individual nobles gaining access to a common well of natural excellence. Some or even many might fail in this endeavour, it is understood, but at no point is the existence of that well of excellence called into question. Thus, no matter how much nobles might be derided or denounced, they nevertheless preserve and promote a particular idea of human hierarchy. 'Bad' nobles call attention to the absence of noble excellence, while 'good' nobles confirm expectations of what noble excellence looks like. Either way, the existence – and, by implication, the necessity – of true nobility is constantly reinforced. The second ostensible truism is that nobility is transmissible between generations. True nobility is distinct from other forms of excellence because it is always anchored to genealogy: a born noble's excellence is the expression of virtues handed down through generations; a non-noble who has attained noble excellence likewise warrants ennoblement, so as to immediately establish a new genealogical line of transmission. The noble paradigm allows, as it must, for the inevitable failures along the way: deficiencies of noble excellence can be blamed on the insufficient performance or embodiment of inherited virtues; individual nobles may fail to live up to the great deeds of their ancestors, but their bloodline continues unscathed – taking up where it left off in subsequent generations. The transmissible nature of noble excellence, in turn, casts a genealogical lens on the various degrees of non-excellence against which it is defined. The third ostensible truism is that what nobles *do* is noble. In other words, noble excellence always revolves around attributes that nobles themselves have defined as excellent, thereby controlling

---

1 These tenets notably reflect and build upon Arlette Jouanna's four precepts of the 'noble race' concept as it stood in sixteenth- and seventeenth-century France (see Jouanna 1981: 24).

the parameters of their own excellence and ensuring that to be non-noble is to be non-excellent. Horsemanship, say, or decorum; breeding, or deportment; grace, or countenance, are only marks of nobility in so far as nobles themselves affirm them to be and only for as long as they remain effective signifiers of the specific brand of excellence the nobles wish to promote. Noble identity, in short, is at the centre of a solar system of its own creation – orbited by infinite cycles of value and hierarchy that are always directly relative to the cardinal star.

In his discussion of the British upper orders between 1780 and 1820, David Cannadine remarks that 'one of the greatest strengths of the British aristocracy has been to present itself as venerable, while constantly evolving and developing' (1994: 2). The same, in fact, can be said of the noble paradigm in every age. The capacity to adapt to new social, economic and political contexts while maintaining the illusion of constancy is essential to the survival of nobility as a concept. Nobility can be at once a legal status, a cultural motif and a metaphysical representative of ordered hierarchy in the world. It has been granted to social-climbing commoners and has been fiercely protected by haughty ancient lines. It has been portrayed as a quality of military prowess and of parliamentary perspicacity, of the battlefield and of the court; it has been the position of laymen and churchmen, of Christian and heathen, even of rich and of poor. The historiographical label of 'nobility' can be applied to groups as different from one another as the senatorial Patricians of Ancient Rome and the warring *taoisigh* of Gaelic Ireland, the feudal chevaliers of medieval Paris and the modernizing grandees of eighteenth-century London. Hereditary elites – be they courtly, military, senatorial, clerical, parliamentary or otherwise – have consequently resurfaced with striking regularity in European history, almost always maintaining the same base template of descent-based exclusivity and constituting one of the most recognizable 'longue durée' elements of the European hierarchical tradition (Leonhard and Weiland 2011: 6).

In the process, noble tradition has fashioned a curious discourse of real-world power based on quasi-mystical allusions. As Arlette Jouanna has pointed out, nobility can never represent just another 'normal' aspect of government because it always evokes both an imagined reality and a social reality that interact to varying degrees:

> Nobility does not identify beings of a different nature; it serves to determine the most perfect, those who possess the defining quality of their 'kind' [*espèce*] to a more eminent degree. . . . [T]hus, the idea of nobility features as just one category in an imagined framework, which allows for a hierarchy of created beings: this category corresponds with the notion of the most perfect within

each kind; it is the opposite of another category corresponding to the idea of the least perfect. (Jouanna 1981: 125)[2]

Any manifestation of nobility, thanks to the noble paradigm, can be equated with any other manifestation of nobility, as all are immutable reflections of the ordered universe. The sixteenth-century English diplomat Thomas Smith, for instance, defended the rank distinctions of early modern England on the basis that hereditary elites across the ages had all been expressions of the same, divinely chosen, ruling caste. England's gradation of 'dukes, marquises, erles, vicountes and barrons', he explained in 1583, 'doeth answere to the dignitie of the Senators of Rome, and the title of our nobilitie to their *patricij*'. Untitled gentlemen, for their part, represented 'those whom their blood and race doth make noble and knowne, εὐγενής [*eugenes*] in Greeke, the Latines call them all *nobiles*' (Smith 1583: 38).

In many ways, Thomas Smith was not wrong. Nobles in eighteenth-century Britain and Ireland relied on the very same paradigmatic code as their distant predecessors. The foundation stones of that code are largely contained in two seminal concepts from the ancient world, which Smith also duly referenced: *eugeneia* and *nobilitas*. Most important was the ancient idea of *eugeneia*, meaning 'good birth'. As early as the sixth century BCE, notes Paul Cartledge (2009: 48), strict Athenian aristocracies were governed by a hereditary cabal of *Eupatridai*, or 'descendants of good fathers', who styled themselves as *aristoi* (the 'best people'). The term '*aristos*', in turn, shared etymological roots with the concomitant concept of *arete* – describing a sort of essential excellence present in every entity: speed in a horse, for example, or graceful flight in a bird (Jaeger 1944–5: 1.6). It must be remembered that this model of natural superiority functioned within the parameters of a slave-owning society. Aristotle's famous dictum of the fourth century BCE, to become a favourite among advocates of the slave trade in the eighteenth century, vindicated the social function of birth-right hierarchy. 'For that some should rule and others be ruled is a thing not only necessary, but expedient'; he claimed, 'from the hour of their birth, some are marked out for subjection, others for rule' ([*c*. 335–323 BCE] 1921: 1254a). For Aristotle, indeed, there was little doubt that a nobleman's *arete* befitted him

---

2 My translation: '[l]a noblesse ne distingue pas des êtres qui seraient d'une nature différente ; elle sert à discerner les plus parfaits, ceux qui possèdent en un degré plus éminent la qualité qui caractérise leur «espèce» . . . [L]a notion de noblesse apparait comme l'une des catégories d'une grille mentale permettant d'établir une hiérarchie au sein des êtres crées : cette catégorie correspond à la notion de plus parfait selon l'espèce ; elle s'oppose à une autre catégorie correspondant à la notion de moins parfait' (Jouanna 1981: 125).

perfectly for his social function. 'The noble are citizens in a truer sense than the ignoble', he asserts in the *Politics*, 'those who are sprung from better ancestors are likely to be better men, for nobility is excellence of race' (Aristotle [*c*. 335–323 BCE] 1921: 1283a).

Eugeneia holds a clear political function. It provides ruling elites with a core strategy for maintaining power within an exclusive family line. For one thing, it promotes the idea that human excellence is transmitted from parent to child. The maintenance of power and influence among a small, interfamilial elite can thereby be granted immediate and relatively unquestioned justification. Furthermore, *eugeneia*'s insistence on untainted bloodline renders nobility effectively inimitable: as a genealogical discourse it is inseparable from the human body and cannot simply be aped by the non-noble. This, in essence, is one of the most potent aspects of paradigmatic nobility. Even when removed from political authority or material wealth, one's nobility remains legitimate; the prince might become a pauper, but he will always be the *real* prince. As such, *eugeneia* acts as a highly effective barrier to would-be usurpers while simultaneously serving to protect the sociopolitical superiority of elite families even in the face of economic or political shifts. By proclaiming and promoting their eugeneic exclusivity, the *aristoi* could ensure that they would always be the 'best people', regardless of their competitors' claims to power. *Eugeneia* was the definitive watermark of exclusivity because good birth was beyond comparison: not only could true nobility never be performed by the non-noble, but those possessed of this enigmatic quality could claim a natural aptitude for rulership that the low-born, ostensibly, could not even comprehend. In the face of the Athenian statesman Solon's constitutional reforms in the sixth century BCE, notes Chester G. Starr, which aimed to undermine the link between heredity and rulership by opening up prominent offices on the basis of wealth rather than rank, the *aristoi* increasingly emphasized the unique excellence that could only attend true-born nobility (Starr 1992: 23–4). By the end of the following century, notes Walter Donlon, claims of 'mental and moral superiority' had become a regular feature of noble self-presentation, while the *aristoi* 'increasingly and explicitly asserted that those who were not members of their class were incapable of high ethical behaviour or refinement of thought and feeling' (1999: 143). This, he adds, worked to maintain a profound sense of separation between the noble and the non-noble, which would endure even under democratic systems of government (Donlon 1999: 143).

The second elemental building block of the noble paradigm was the Ancient Roman code of *nobilitas* (signifying 'renown, or distinction'), which addresses one of the inbuilt challenges of eugeneic tradition: in order for nobility to exist, it is not enough to simply attain power – that power must be retained within a family line over multiple generations. This presents a quandary for the noble paradigm. How can nobility encourage an institutional framework which vaunts the exclusivity of ruling families while accommodating the inconvenient realities of non-noble power all around it? What exactly renders nobles worthier than non-nobles, some of whom might wield greater economic or social influence than themselves? What, in a word, proves that they are *different* from anyone else? *Nobilitas* works not only to overcome these obstacles but also to render them invisible.

For much of Rome's Republican period, the most prominent eugeneic distinction was that which existed between the Patricians and Plebeians – a split once described by the eighteenth-century English historian Edward Gibbon as 'the proudest and most perfect separation which can be found in any age or country, between the nobles and the people' (1787: 3.87). The Romans believed this divide to date back to the days of Romulus, who had designated a number of *Patres* among the city's leaders (Beck 2022: 350). In fact, the fifth-century BCE 'Law of the Twelve Tables', which appears to have codified a set of much older traditions, forbade intermarriage between this group and the Plebeians below them (Spurr 2014: 576). The Patricians, in turn, were further refined into those with the oldest family lines (*gentes maiores*) and the newer, less venerable dynasties (*gentes minors*) (Spurr 2014: 576). Plebeians, meanwhile, constituted the greater body of non-Patrician Roman citizens and were effectively defined by their exclusion from eugeneic patriciate. *Nobilitas*, however, was an informal and conveniently ambiguous rank which could be shared by both major factions under the Roman Republic (Brunt 1982: 1–2). It was not granted on the basis of birth or wealth alone but often depended on the bearer's ancestor having attained a consulship (Brown 2012: 95–6). That is to say that *nobilitas*, once attained, became hereditary. Though rare, a Plebeian *novus homo* could, by way of a consulship, introduce a new line of *nobilitas* to his family. By consequence, a *nobile* 'could never be talked about only as wealthy', notes Peter Brown, '[t]hey were *nobiles* . . . they had to shine in the proper Roman style' (2012: 95).

Here we see two parallel notions of hereditary privilege: the eugeneic patriciate, based around the blood of the 'first fathers', and a more practical foil in the *nobiles*, who included this patriciate but also defined a larger hereditary sphere of influence. The distinction between a primary (eugeneic) and secondary (nobiliary) form of hereditary privilege forms an abidingly valuable element of the noble paradigm, for it essentially creates a self-sustaining noble hegemony.

In a Roman context, the *eugeneia* of inimitable bloodline is maintained by the existence of a Patrician rank, while *nobilitas* permits the integration of new power – immediately inducting it, in its turn, into an exclusive hereditary line. A rank of *nobiles* constitutes a sort of secondary eugeneic unit, apparently based on merit but actually forming a wider spiral of hereditary privilege. On closer inspection, the significance of *nobiltas* as a hereditary quality is in every way predicated on the template of eugeneic excellence espoused by the patriciate, and in this way it always surrounds and protects the primary eugenic powerbase. In other words, by acknowledging the existence of genealogical excellence according to the parameters set down by the eugeneic patriciate and by participating in a pastiched version of this template, a rank of *nobiles* automatically reinforces the legitimacy of the top eugeneic group. Their claim to power is dependent on the condition that its form, shape and validity in every way defers to the primary power above.

It is perhaps unsurprising, then, that the existence of a *petite noblesse*, or secondary rank of hereditary elites, has become a recurrent feature of nobilities throughout European history. In early modern Britain, one might identify an analogous dynamic underlying the hegemonic relationship between nobility and gentry. Eighteenth-century gentility, like *nobilitas*, was a quality shared by noble and non-noble alike: all noblemen were gentlemen, while only some gentlemen were noble. The gentry, while being non-noble by legal definition, nonetheless participated in the tradition of genealogical hierarchy; this, in turn, was bolstered by the fact that their socio-economic *nobilitas* constituted a secondary adherence to parameters of *eugeneia* set down by the nobility. In many ways, the bulk of the gentry could be seen as an advertisement for noble parameters of excellence. The pastiched superiority of a gentleman's minor bloodline constantly fortified the institutionalized superiority of the major bloodlines above him and even offered the glittering promise of integration into the primary eugeneic base. Eighteenth-century pedigrees of genteel families (see Figure 6 in Chapter 3) prominently displayed any noble titles in their family tree, because their own claims to genealogical excellence were contingent on the affirmation of excellence in the dominant eugeneic group. By existing as a second-tier elite based on shared *nobilitas* and lesser *eugeneia*, that is to say, the gentry automatically validated and disseminated the hegemonic value of eugeneic excellence, while reinforcing the exclusivity of the first-tier elite whom they were required to recognize as better born than themselves.

What we describe as 'nobility' in European historiography can therefore be understood as a collection of the most successful and resilient sociopolitical strategies employed to fortify the process of seizing and maintaining power within lineal families. The myth of an open aristocracy could be seen as one more weapon in this arsenal. In fact, the apologist argument that anybody with sufficient virtue can be noble is as old as nobility itself (the catch is that one first has to attain noble status, as discussed later in this chapter). For anxious British loyalists at the end of the eighteenth century, stressing the unique accessibility of their nobility was an obvious recourse in the face of rising criticism. After all, international commentators had long remarked on the unusual structure of Britain's peerage, which restricted official titles to top-tier families and which had severely curbed tax exemptions for peers since the Restoration. Voltaire marvelled at the system in his *Letters Concerning the English Nation* of 1733, recording with astonishment that some titled peers even engaged in commercial trade (1733: 66–71). It is easy to see why such an idea should have remained so persistent and for so long. Both before and after the French Revolution, British nobles were perennially burdened with the weight of their own anachronisms. Though the institutions of peerage had been successfully reinvented after the Revolution of 1688, the continued dominance of this exclusive, unelected coterie of inter-related landowners required constant justification. Loud and unwavering assertions that Britain's noble institutions *worked* – that they were, in fact, a fundamental guarantor of Britain/England's special brand of 'freedom' – were not merely a way to show nobility in a positive light, but they were essential to its very survival. Accordingly, the myth of an open aristocracy marched confidently into the nineteenth century, with the French diplomat and political philosopher Alexis de Tocqueville opining in 1866 that English peers were more 'prudent', more 'skilled' and more 'open' than any other hereditary elite, and the Irish historian William Hartpole Lecky announcing in 1878 that the 'eminently popular character of the English aristocracy . . . has probably done more than any other single cause to determine the type and ensure the permanence of English freedom' (Tocqueville 1856: 108; Lecky 1878: 170). In reality, this myth only served to reinforce the underlying structure of the noble paradigm: it associated nobility with natural excellence; it highlighted the active performance of this excellence among contemporary nobles; and it maintained that this excellence, which supposedly provided evidence of systemic meritocracy, was nevertheless predominantly found in an exclusive club built on hereditary privilege.

To get a better understanding of noble power strategies in the eighteenth century, it is necessary to quickly dismantle this idea that nobility in Britain was in any way accessible to those outside of its immediate spheres. One thing to note about the 'open aristocracy' narrative is its often-striking ambiguity of terminology. 'Aristocracy', notes Amanda Goodrich, is a problematic word in the context of the eighteenth century; it often held derogatory connotations, and a full definition of the term was not featured in Johnson's dictionary until 1818, when it was described as a recent import from Revolutionary France (2005: 16; see Chapter 11). What is more, in modern historiography this and other terms can be used markedly differently by different historians. Perkin, for instance, mentioned at the start of this chapter, tends to confound nobility, gentry and lesser gentry when he speaks of 'aristocracy'. Lawrence and Jeanne Fawtier Stone, meanwhile, who were central to the academic backlash against the open aristocracy myth in the 1980s, defined a 'landed elite' according to the size and disposition of certain estates (1984: 8). Multifaceted or ambiguous terminology in this field, notes Michael W. McCahill, is confounded by the fact that Britain's gentry was delineated mainly by landownership rather than membership of a legally defined *petite noblesse* (1998: 601). Even if we accept the idea of the 'landed elite' in its loosest terms, however, one thing is certain: the idea that it was fuelled by social mobility is at best wishful thinking and at worst deliberately misleading. In 1984, Lawrence and Jeanne Fawtier Stone analysed an immense body of evidence from three English counties from 1540 to 1880 and concluded that social mobility into even the widest ranks of the landed elite remained negligible during that entire period (1984: 402). Voltaire's mention of peers involved in trade, they found, actually referenced two extremely unusual examples, both of which immediately triggered opposition from their families (Stone and Stone 1984: 236). When it came to younger sons, whom Perkin described as having 'to compete with those below them for positions in the professions and in trade and industry', the reality was something else entirely. The top tiers of the landed elite 'virtually never sent their sons into trade', the Stones found, and instead 'packed nearly all their younger sons off into the armed forces, with perhaps one in each generation going into the church' (1984: 236). While Perkin and like-minded historians politely balked at the Stones' ostensible irreverence in subsequent academic reviews (David and Eileen Spring, for instance, reprimanded the Stones the following year for having used *computers* in their data analysis), the raw numbers were hard to contest (Perkin 1985: 496–7; Spring and Spring 1985: 150–1).

Scholarship has since continued to steadily demolish the legend of Britain's good-old-boy elite. In 1985, J. C. D. Clark notoriously denounced the open aristocracy narrative as a typical 'Whig' history, arguing instead that the country continued to exist in a hegemonic *ancien régime* until the 1830s (1985: 2). 'England and France had more in common than either's patriotism was willing to concede.' Clark claims, 'both societies were dominated by a ruling group which justified its power by reference to similar patrician ideals' (1985: 95). David Cannadine, taking a different perspective, has warned against blindly accepting 'the aristocracy's own (and often deliberately misleading) self-image of antiquity and permanence', and to remember that towards the end of the century, especially, it was a locus of remarkable change and reinvention in both Britain and Ireland (1994: 10). Michael W. McCahill has pointed out that when comparing British and French landed elites in the eighteenth century, it becomes clear that both 'drew the bulk of their new members from groups that already enjoyed close ties to the established social and political orders' (1998: 603). While records do show a slightly higher number of 'new recruits' in Britain during this time, he notes, 'recruits to French nobility certainly were drawn from a wider and more varied social range than was the case in England' (McCahill 1998: 603). Others, like John Cannon, have noted that complaints that 'the peerage is not what it was' are as old as the peerage itself, upholding a narrative tradition that no doubt helped to bolster 'the impression that new men were continuously thrusting their way up into the ranks of the aristocracy' (1987: 15). Nicholas Hudson cautions that the myth of an open aristocracy has long been buttressed by the tropes of rank-inversion that abound in eighteenth-century literature, suggesting a certain obsession with 'the threat posed by interlopers penetrating the traditional social elite' (2005: 568). On closer inspection, however, those tropes usually criticize 'the appropriation of the visual symbols of rank and privilege among those who had no hereditary or even financial claim to them' rather than actual cases of social mobility (Hudson 2005: 568).

These tensions in the historiography of social elites are all the more important to keep in mind when we attempt to narrow down our selection of landed elites to a group that might be identified as nobility. To define nobility at this time, we must begin with the titled peerage, which was the only institution to be legally recognized as 'noble' in eighteenth-century Britain and Ireland. Nevertheless, this group alone is nowhere near sufficient when attempting to measure the actual reach of noble authority. In all, only 1,003 individuals held a peerage in Britain during the eighteenth century, and for most of that time only around 200 peers held a title at any one time (Wilson 2002: 159). Even in the self-contained Irish peerage – distinct from its British counterpart in myriad ways – a perceived explosion in elevations towards the end of the century only resulted in about 200 individuals holding a title, up from an average of 125 in the 1730s (James 1979: 55; Middleton 1985: 94). Despite a booming population, title distribution was tightly controlled through limited peerage creations and the fact that official honours were strictly primogeniturial (meaning that a peer's immediate family technically remained commoners). 'In England the word *noble* is of a narrower import than in other countries', reported the third edition of the *Encyclopaedia Britannica* (1788–97: entry 'noble', 8.90), 'being confined to persons above the degree of knights, whereas abroad it comprehends not only knights but what we simply call *gentlemen*'. Since the vast majority of peerage titles were created for men and were passed down to the eldest son and heir only, this figure of 1,003 is also disproportionately male. Certain peerages did contain a clause that allowed the title to be passed down to women, and a small number of titles were specially created for peeresses (often with the expectation that she would then pass the honour down to her son), but even at that John Cannon notes that only forty-nine peeresses held a title during the eighteenth century (1987: 11). Furthermore, many of the officially titled peers were effectively 'peers in name only', notes Cannon: the roughly sixty Catholic peers of eighteenth-century Britain 'lived almost as a group apart, excluded from public office, educating their children abroad, and marrying amongst themselves'; some titled peers had been declared lunatics; others could simply not afford to sustain a noble lifestyle; and a few unlucky inheritors had waited their entire lives for a title, only to die months or even days after their ennoblement (1987: 11–12).

The peerage, then, can only provide a starting point when identifying British nobility. Indeed, 'peerage' was not and (is not) directly synonymous with 'nobility'. While the former referred only to the titled heads of each noble family, the latter commonly made reference to the families as a whole, including wives, children, heirs and wider family members. Far from constituting an arena of rising talent, this network was markedly immobile – constituting a 'small and enclosed world of less than two hundred families' which dominated the House of Lords throughout the century (Hudson 2005: 570). This distinct rank has been described as the 'peerage class' by Richard G. Wilson (2002: 159), the 'magnate class' by Roy Porter (1982: 75), and, again highlighting the ambiguity of terminology in this field, as the 'British aristocracy' by Maura A. Henry (2002: 312–13). Even without precise legal definitions, they were manifestly set apart from the greater bulk of elite landowners in terms of wealth, status and connections.

Nobility also shared much in common with those in the greater gentry. It cannot be discounted, asserts Richard G. Wilson, that peerage families and wealthier gentry often shared a common education, including study of the classics, matriculation at Oxford or Cambridge and experience of the grand tour (2002: 163). Once their education was complete, the 'common pursuits of their class' from hunting and gambling to landscaping and estate management would have maintained a solid cultural coherence between them (Wilson 2002: 163–4). It is clear that the most 'substantial gentry', notes John Cannon, whose wealth could sometimes outshine that of poorer peers, 'would have been regarded as nobility by continental standards' (1987: 10). Yet, while this 'common bond of gentility' sometimes brought different ranks together, note the Stones, a subtle hierarchy of honour, respect and snobbery also broke those ranks down into highly nuanced degrees of precedence (1984: 424). Quite aside from questions of privilege and display, the top families of the British nobility usually occupied a very different rung on the ladder when it came to finances. By 1790 the incomes of 400 or so of the greatest landlords in England and Wales averaged at about £10,000, while among some of the most comfortable peerage families – such as the Dukes of Bedford, Bridgewater and Devonshire – incomes sometimes approached the astronomical figure of £50,000 (Mingay 1963: 19). Conversely, the wealthiest knights and baronets were only taking in an average of £3,000–4,000 at this time, while the lesser gentry might have expected between £1,000 and £3,000 per annum (Mingay 1963: 19–21). The vast economic clout of noble families constituted one of the most common justifications for their privileged access to political authority. If social mobility into the wider landed elite has been grossly overstated, then commercial entry into the spheres of noble influence was infinitesimal. As John Cannon notes, out of the 229 newly created peers between 1700 and 1800, a full 206 already boasted close connections to the peerage, with the vast majority being immediately related to an existing peer or holding previous peerages in Ireland or Scotland (1987: 24). The remaining twenty-three candidates invariably boasted a plethora of indirect connections to the peerage and were generally drawn from the very highest ranks of society (Cannon 1987: 25). The figures, Cannon asserts, especially in the context of a rapidly increasing population, suggest that far from being an 'open' institution, the structure of peerage in the eighteenth century fomented 'a considerable narrowing of the social heights' compared to the previous century (1987: 33).

The status and cultural authority of eighteenth-century peers and their families must also be understood through the prism of the institution's not-so-distant history. The term 'peerage' had first been used to describe England's hereditary elite as far back as the Rolls of Parliament of 1454, but its form and function had been profoundly reshaped by the upheavals of the seventeenth century. Since the beginning of the Stuart monarchy, English peers had become an object of widespread criticism. A relative glut of ennoblements under James I had left the institution bloated and ineffectual; only a few members had ever bothered to fulfil their parliamentary duties, and corruption and exploitation of noble privilege was rife. In fact, attendance at Westminster's House of Lords in the years leading up to the English Civil War was so poor that at certain points it was rare to have more than six peers in the chamber at any one time (Jones 1989: 1; Cannon 1982: 432–4; Swatland 1996: 9). Many had seen the war as an opportunity to dispose of the stagnant upper house completely, and this, as it turned out, is exactly what came to pass. In May 1649, only two days after the abolition of the office of king, the upper house was declared 'useless and dangerous', and the bill for its abolition was passed by forty-four votes to twenty-two ('An Act Abolishing the House of Lords' 1649: 297; Firth 1910: 213–15). '[N]o peer of this land', read the 'Act Abolishing the House of Lords', 'not being elected, qualified, and sitting in the parliament ... shall claim, have, or make use of any privilege of parliament, either in relation to his person, quality or estate' (1649: 297).

By its Restoration in 1660, the House of Lords was a decidedly changed institution, with its members relinquishing the great majority of privileges they had previously enjoyed. Only a few decades later, however, the peerage had already forged important new avenues of power in parliament. The practical reforms in the years following 1688 helped to rehabilitate the Lords' popularity, rebranding the upper house as an efficient tempering agent against monarchical despotism. 'A body of nobility is ... peculiarly necessary in our mixed and compounded constitution', remarked Justice William Blackstone in his celebrated *Commentaries on the Laws of England* (1765), 'in order to support the rights of both the crown and the people by forming a barrier to withstand the encroachments of both' (1765: 1.2.153). In addition, Westminster took far greater jurisdictional authority over the peerages of Scotland and Ireland, with the former being subsumed into the British peerage in 1707 and the latter being brought under intense new scrutiny (Brown 1991: 272; Paley et al. 2010: 219, 268). All of this, in the context of the newly established constitutional monarchy, paved the way for an unprecedentedly active role for the Lords in government. By the first decades of the eighteenth century, the House of Lords was already on its way to becoming a fully functional revising chamber with major influence over the form and content of the country's laws (McCahill 2009: 6–7). The Lords' own shared interest was a key factor in this rapid rehabilitation: like the Commons, they were primarily divided into Tories and Whigs; unlike the Commons, they also had full access to an exclusive, ironclad network of personal and familial connections. Members of the upper house were magnates and royal councillors, cousins and brothers-in-law; collectively, they all shared the memory of their institution's humiliating abolition, and collectively, they were all invested in its advancement (Paley et al. 2010: 195).

In addition to its political role, the peerage functioned to preserve the links between noble families and their ancestral claims to power. Every male peer had an automatic entitlement to a seat in the House of Lords, which in turn provided direct (or indirect) parliamentary representation for the country's most important land-owning families and their economic interests. The privileges of peerage and parliament, though much reduced after the Restoration, also helped to draw a dividing line between noble families and lesser landowners. Liberally interpreted (as they usually were), a peer's privileges could open up a wealth of advantages for his extended family. The right to freedom of speech in parliament, for instance, could be used as a protection against litigating debtors, while the parliamentary protection afforded to members' households, properties and lands could be used to protect servants and tenants from legal action (Paley et al. 2010: 185). Peers were also protected from arrest, except in the case of treason, felony or breach of peace; they could not be outlawed or legally tortured; and they were not obliged to testify under oath nor to sit on juries. They had special right of access to the monarch and held the right to be tried by a commission of fellow peers; they were protected against slander by a statute known as *Scandalum magnatum*, and their taxes were directly assessed by the Lord Chancellor and the Lord Treasurer. On a less official level, they were routinely offered the highest positions in the military and lieutenancies (Swatland 1996: 40; Stone 1965: 55).

Through the institution of peerage, Britain and Ireland's noble families were carefully arranged into a strictly ordered hierarchy, with each title reflecting a precise scale of precedence. This hierarchy had more or less taken shape by the end of Elizabeth I's reign and initially incorporated separate peerages for England, Ireland and Scotland, which were subsequently amalgamated following the Acts of Union first with Scotland (1707) and later with Ireland (1801). The accepted titles, in descending order of prestige, included the ranks of duke, marquess, earl, viscount and baron, as well as their female counterparts duchess, marchioness, countess, viscountess and baroness. At a glance, these titles appeared to tell a story of the bearer's ancestors; epithets such as the 3rd or 4th Earl of Shaftesbury ostensibly communicated generations of unbroken rank distinction. In practice, however, titles were a deceptively complicated matter: individual peers could don and shed several titles over their lifetime, with peerages not only being passed down through families but also being recycled for other families once they had disappeared from their original lines (McCahill 2009: x; Stone 1984: 421). Scottish and Irish peers, if elevated to the English peerage, were recognized in Westminster only by their highest English title, even if this situated them several degrees below their primary peerage. Thus, before the unions of 1707 and 1801, Scottish and Irish peers (respectively) could only sit in Westminster if they also possessed an English title (Paley et al. 2010: xx–xxi). It should be noted that those with lesser hereditary or life titles, such as knights or baronets, were not members of the peerage and their titles did not confer nobility. The peerage frequently incorporated the untitled sons of peers, however, who could be given the courtesy title 'Lord' and could be called to parliament with, or in place of, their fathers (Jones 1989: 3; Stone and Stone 1984: 229). Daughters of dukes, marquesses and earls could also be given the courtesy title 'Lady' (Stone and Stone 1984: 229).

While noble blood was an essential component of eugeneic authority, blood itself was not held to confer nobility per se. Rather, noble blood was traditionally imagined as a vector or a vehicle for the virtuous deeds of ancestral rulers, which could be transmitted from one generation to the next. That is to say, blood bestowed nobles with the *potential* for greatness, rather than greatness itself. This was, in fact, a core stratagem of the noble paradigm. Since antiquity, one of the most consistent criticisms levelled at nobility had been that its members were not as virtuous as they claimed to be. One might think of the Roman satirist Juvenal, who frequently mocked talentless *nobiles* who boasted of their illustrious genealogy ([c. 100 CE] 1745: 217–19), or of Sallust's *War against Jugurtha* ([41–40 BCE] 1756: 232), wherein the *novus homo* Marius says of the condescending Patricians that 'if on good ground they despise me, they do the same by their ancestors, whose nobility, like mine, took its rise from their noble behaviour [*ex virtute nobilitas coepit*]'. These criticisms are almost always countered with the same stock argument: that blood alone does not guarantee nobility and that each individual noble must actively embody the virtues of ancestors in every generation. This explanation deftly protects the noble paradigm from multiple angles at once: it associated the superiority of noble rank with active excellence rather than passive privilege; it provided an inbuilt excuse for the frequent absence of said active excellence while reinforcing that excellence as a marker of 'true nobility'; and, in a brilliant turn of doublespeak, it cast noble virtue as the product of individual merit while limiting that particular brand of merit to certain family lines. The sixteenth-century English diplomat Thomas Elyot illustrates this central paradox in his *Book of the Governor* (1531), which dutifully warns that 'nobility is not only in dignity or ancient lineage, nor great revenues, lands or possessions ... but [in] wisdom and virtue' (1531: 110). Yet, for Elyot, this same wisdom and virtue is essentially bound to genealogical credentials. '[I]n the beginning', Elyot explains, the people of the earth offered 'private possessions' and 'dignity' to those 'at whose virtue they marvelled ... and the persons were called Gentlemen' (1531: 108). These prodigious 'gentlemen', he continues, having been elevated by the community for their superior talents, then went on to intermarry over a long period of time. '[O]f those good men', he asserts,

> were engendered good children, who being brought up in virtue ... endeavoured themselves by imitation of virtue, to be equal to them in honour and authority ... and for the *goodness* that proceeded of such generation, the estate of them was called in Greek, *Eugenia*, which signifieth good kind or lineage; but in a more brief manner, it was afterwards called *nobility*, and the persons noble which signifieth excellent, and in the analogy or signification it is more ample than gentle. (Elyot 1531: 108–9)

Nobility, in other words, represented a distilled form of genteel virtue that could only be achieved through generations of controlled intermarriage. It did not negate the validity of non-noble virtue, nor did it pretend to exist in the absence of such, but its own brand of excellence was nonetheless inherently, inimitably, genealogical.

The assertion that nobility resided in virtue alone became particularly widespread in the decades after the Restoration, at a time when English peers faced harsh criticism for trying to reclaim their pre-war privileges. In 1718, the Suffolk squire Maurice Shelton explained in his *True Rise of Nobility* that nobility's critics had simply misunderstood the nature of noble blood. There was no mystical essence in the blood that rendered a peer noble, Shelton assured his readers; as everyone knew, nobility was contingent on virtue alone. Any attack on the established ranks of nobility, however (primarily distinguished, of course, by blood), would have such a destabilizing effect on the general distribution of virtue and wisdom that it would represent a threat to the very order of the universe. When people bemoan the 'corruption of [noble] blood', Shelton explains, it is because it is a corruption of the 'right of inheritance, which by the degrees of the communication of blood is directed' (Shelton 1718: 55). 'Distinction of rank', he continues,

> is highly necessary for the œconomy of the world, and was never called in question but by barbarians and enthusiasts. A just consideration for the several orders of men, as the orders of Providence have plac'd them above us, is useful not only to the correcting of our manners, and keeping our common conversation in the bounds of politeness and civility, but has even a better consequence, in disposing our minds to a religious humility; and in observing step by step

the several degrees of excellency above us, we arrive insensibly at last to the contemplation of the supreme perfection. (Shelton 1718: v)

Not all nobles, according to this stock argument, boasted the kind of true nobility that one might have liked, but nobility itself was nonetheless a repository of hereditary virtue. That virtue was not only enhanced by wealth, respect and privilege but also served to inspire similar virtues in society as a whole. In 1765, Justice William Blackstone voiced a similar sentiment, declaring that nobility 'creates and preserves that gradual scale of dignity, which proceeds from the peasant to the prince; rising like a pyramid from a broad foundation, and diminishing to a point as it rises' (1765: 1.2.153).

The legal or social *nobilitas* of peers and their immediate social circle was thus dependent on constant validation of their *eugeneia*. A peerage title meant nothing without the conviction that noble families were somehow distinct from other people and that this distinction justified an exalted role in government and society. This simple fact meant that rank exhibition was every bit as consequential to noble hegemony in eighteenth-century Britain and Ireland as were the political machinations of the Houses of Lords. Without the conviction that hereditary peers somehow *deserved* their right to a parliamentary seat, that they were more suitable for high office than, say, City merchants or colonial nabobs, the political authority wielded by peerage families was baseless. To consolidate their success in parliament, the eighteenth-century British nobility had to incessantly reaffirm the inimitability of their position at the top of the social hierarchy and thus made abundant use of one of the oldest strategies in noble tradition: spectacular, conspicuous display. Conspicuous consumption had the power to distinguish the upper orders by equipping them with a set of signifiers to which few others in society had access. The nobility's assertion of a natural and hereditary affinity with these same signifiers thereby characterized noble rank itself as beyond comparison (Veblen 1899: 25–6). The mere implication that opulent display was *not* a natural extension of noble rank could, at times, provoke outrage. When the private letters of Phillip Dormer Stanhope, 4th Earl of Chesterfield, were published in 1774, they immediately caused consternation by (among other things) frankly discussing 'true nobility' as something that could be learned. 'Attend carefully to the manner, the diction, the motions of people of the first fashion, and form your own upon them', Lord Chesterfield had advised his illegitimate son,

[t]he lowest peasant speaks, moves, dresses, eats and drinks as much as a man of the first fashion; but does them all quite differently; so that by doing and

saying most things in a manner opposite to that of the vulgar, you have a greater chance of doing and saying them right . . . the language, the airs, the dress, and manners of the court are the only true standard; *des manières nobles, et d'un honnête homme.* (Chesterfield 1774: 2.61)

Some commentators such as the Anglican minister Vicesimus Knox, notes Jenny Davidson, would later look back on such statements as a dangerous source of anti-noble radicalism in the 1790s (2004: 74). The *Letters*, wrote Knox in his *Personal Nobility* (1793: 319–20), had led the 'plebeian orders' to believe that 'what they have usually admired as all-accomplished, has been mere varnish'. Chesterfield's advice paints him as the very opposite of a true nobleman, who 'should from his heart abhor all simulation and dissimulation as the poor shifts of *ignoble* meanness and cowardice' (Knox 1793: 320). Alas, Knox lamented, by portraying nobility as a mere choreography of airs of graces, this man had taught common people 'to look unhurt, and with a naked eye, at that splendour, which formerly dazzled like the sun . . . Lord Chesterfield has let us all behind the scenes: he invites us to see the peer dress for public exhibition' (1793: 316).

It is certainly reasonable to say that the 'splendours' of the eighteenth-century British nobility had been dazzling to say the least. At court, a full calendar of birthdays, birth nights, grand balls, drawing rooms, anniversaries, funerals, weddings and coronations drew vast crowds of spectators – making for ideal occasions to display the graded ranks of ordered society to as wide an audience as possible. In London, this ceremonial exhibitionism was particularly pronounced. The British court, by consequence of the great fire which destroyed Whitehall in 1698, was not concentrated in one single complex. Instead, courtiers would constantly move between various palaces and royal buildings, thus rendering them and their entourages even more accessible to the public gaze. Certain sections of the court were technically open to everyone, so long as visitors presented themselves in suitably formal attire, and the provincial gentry considered attendance at one court ritual at least to be a rite of passage (Grieg 2013: 111). Court processions, meanwhile, were highly codified, with each member of each rank advancing according to precedence. Visual impact was key: teams of dressed horses in gilded headgear drew magnificent, crested carriages, each bearing the insignia of their proprietors, while the lesser invitees followed closely behind or alongside in a moving tide of sedan chairs. The press meticulously documented each arrival in due course, carefully describing the chosen attire of each guest. For Queen Charlotte's wedding in 1761, the *Gentleman's Magazine* went so far as to include a minutely detailed sketch of the procession, so readers could study who exactly held precedence over whom in the hierarchy of honour (1761: 418–19). Protocol was carefully monitored by courtiers and the Royal College of Arms – a body that demanded studious diligence in the representation of honorific shields and titles. In 1668, a painter-stainer named Parker had been imprisoned by the Garter Principal King of Arms for having displayed *eight* pearls rather than *six* at the funeral of the 4th Baron Gerard (Paley et al. 2010: 167). Over the course of the century, the streets around Westminster had come to promote the splendours of court through the medium of urban architecture. Modern residential developments such as those at Mayfair (designed for the Dukes of Westminster in the 1720s) or Bloomsbury (laid out by the Dukes of Bedford from 1730 onwards) sprung up around Westminster, with sumptuous squares built around, and named for, the urban palaces of Britain's peerage families.

In the countryside, landed estates communicated the authority of local potentates in their own way. The architecture of stately homes constituted paradoxes of exclusivity and exhibition, unreservedly proclaiming the symbolic remove of nobles and gentry from the rest of the community. Throughout the century, mansions were built further and further from the main road and from their local villages – shielded from the public eye with a 'cordon sanitaire' of high walls and thick woodland (Brown 1991: 272; Porter 1982: 60, 78; Henry 2002: 320). 'Where possible', notes Henry, 'houses were reoriented to sit in the centre of the park through the practice of engrossing and enclosure . . . [which] literally insulated the house and its occupants from the unwelcome noise from roads, markets and local villagers' (2002: 322). Sometimes, adjoining villages were entirely demolished and rebuilt elsewhere, as was the case with Houghton, Norfolk, in 1722 and Sledmere, Yorkshire, in the 1790s. Yet, the very raison d'être of these ostentatious mansions was for them to be looked at. Country houses, notes R. G. Wilson, were 'instantly recognized symbols of power and status', and the largest would have been 'on the route of every genteel tourist in Georgian Britain' (2002: 166). In older houses, the wings and turrets from previous phases of improvement told a story of permanence, corroborating the legitimacy of the family tree. In more modern structures, claims Jeremy Black, the conspicuous consumption of wholesale rebuilding constituted a status symbol in itself (2008: 96). Just as at the London court, the exclusivity of the landed estate was consolidated by offering limited access to the public: a number of great houses functioned as open galleries, where visitors could admire art collections or attend social events held in the stately rooms, all the while acknowledging the singular taste that could only accompany high breeding (Henry 2002: 322). The 'sheer grandeur and finery of the great house', notes Frank O'Gorman, with its extensive teams of servants and ubiquitous rituals of hierarchy and subordination, was itself a valuable tool for exercising power (2016: 114). Every aspect of the landed estate was designed to 'command respect', to inspire deference as an 'instrument of coercion' and to cultivate wherever possible 'an instinctive respect for and acceptance of authority' (O'Gorman 2016: 114).

At the centre of all this were the nobles themselves. The attendees at court events typically included titled peers, their family members, members of parliament and ladies and gentlemen in waiting (Grieg 2015: 12). Since the paradigmatic basis of nobility relied in part on a perceptible difference between nobles and other people, the presentation of the physical body at these and other public occasions was one of the most powerful means of rank distinction at a noble's disposal. 'The semiotics of court dress for the eighteenth-century British court', suggests Hannah Grieg, 'was arguably less about courtly rituals and court protocol, and more about the performances of power by the political elite' (2015: 12). Whether the greater public expressed admiration or ridicule at the sartorial spectacles of court and whether they celebrated its splendours or denounced its effeminate excess, there is no denying that noble self-presentation left a lasting impression. It is evident, notes Grieg, that newspapers and periodicals throughout the eighteenth century took a close interest in the outfits on display at court, with detailed descriptions of court fashion often appearing 'alongside politics, foreign affairs and social and moral comment' (2015: 4). For everyone involved, attendees' choice of clothing asserted a plethora of hierarchical, political and social distinctions, consolidating rank on several levels simultaneously. What one wore to a court occasion could, in fact, constitute a highly public political statement. As a rule, new (and often incredibly expensive) clothes were taken as a sign of support for the reigning monarch or whomever happened to be celebrated on the occasion. Re-used or 'old' clothes, on the other hand, could signify a pointed lack of respect (Grieg 2013: 119–22). Exactly how many 'new' clothes were presented at a certain event was therefore a frequent preoccupation of journalists and diarists in eighteenth-century London. In one letter addressed to the celebrated bluestocking Mary Delany in 1729, the correspondent mentions she had not even been to court that day but could still report that 'there was very little finery and many old clothes' (1729: 223).

While fashions among Britain's *beau monde* evolved over the course of the century, court protocol ensured that ceremonial attire remained relatively static. By the later eighteenth century, court costumes were still being deliberately tailored in an antiquated style, often built around silhouettes that had fallen out of general fashion more than half a century previously (Grieg 2015: 6). In place of the more modern frock coat, men at court typically donned the classical long coat, heavily embroidered with metal thread, and finished with lace jabots and a dress sword (Ribeiro 1984: 22–5). Women's fashions at European courts, notes Isabel Paresys, had essentially sustained the same basic silhouette since the Renaissance: a wide skirt topped with a tightly constrained bodice and low neckline (2018: 78). By the mid-eighteenth century, however, the dimensions of that silhouette had reached remarkable proportions. The visual and spatial impact of the enormous hoop structures worn at eighteenth-century courts can easily be underestimated: a mantua dress could be upheld by a whole system of quilted paniers, wicker trestles and whalebone supports and might incorporate over 7 metres of textiles – including a train, which was sometimes carried by servants (Paresys 2018: 71, 76). Some examples currently on display at the Victoria and Albert Museum measure some 2 metres across, while one hoop ordered by Lady Elizabeth Purefoy in 1741 specified a circumference of almost 3 metres (Vincent 2009: 73; see Figure 1). The impact of these garments was intensified by the effect they had on the movement and shape of the body. Panier structures, though sometimes collapsible, frequently had to be squashed or sidled through doorframes and into carriages, while high-heel shoes (no less than their modern equivalents) visibly affected posture and mobility (Paresys 2018: 76).

The heads of courtly men and women alike were adorned with extraordinary wigs of human hair, bleached with starch powder, sculpted with pomade and

Figure 1 Court dress, made in England *c.* 1750. Metropolitan Museum of Art, New York. Item no. C.I.65.13.1a–c. Public domain.

sometimes built around wire cages that could reach well over half a metre in height (Festa 2005: 54). These remarkable hairpieces were sometimes treated as wearable sculptures, harbouring jewels, ribbons, miniature models and fresh flowers complete with vases of water hidden inside the structure (Festa 2005: 54). No more than the cumbersome panier, contemporary satires suggest that wigs also presented grave challenges when negotiating doorways and carriages (Festa 2005: 54). Make-up, too, worn by both sexes, was applied in thick layers – often using the same basic materials as artists used on their canvases (Palmer 2008: 200). A white undercoat might be adorned with two bright spots of carmine rouge, sometimes made from red lead mixed with vermillion and complemented with carefully placed felt patches. Burnt Ivory was used as a kind of mascara, and eyebrows may have been plucked and replaced with false alternatives (Palmer 2008: 200; Ribeiro 1984: 109). Such cosmetic enhancements, like so much of the court's decorative repertoire, drew disdain and admiration in equal measure from the public. Some observers associated make-up with the stage and its attendant undertones of prostitution, while others linked it with the perceived sophistication of the French court, criticizing the 'slatternly' appearance of those who did not apply enough (Palmer 2008: 199, 203, 205). Regardless, the multitude of specialized handbooks offering advice and cosmetic techniques to women and men alike attests to the resolute popularity of the trend throughout the century (Palmer 2008: 203).

While the preposterous fashions at court attracted endless mockery from the press, Paresys notes that the very awkwardness of court attire was integral to noble rank performance. Under the weight of several kilos of fabric, hair and decorative adornments, the wearer was expected to gracefully execute the highest rituals of decorum, exhibiting 'the magnificence inherent in their social position' (Paresys 2018: 76). A courtier's aptitude for deportment, despite all these sartorial challenges, could thereby transform into a choreographed display of breeding and social education (Paresys 2018: 77). The exaggerated constrictions of court attire concordantly reflected contemporary ideas about how tight-fitting clothing influenced chastity, morality and the shape of the human body (Paresys 2018: 85; see Chapter 5). Clearly some did not approve: the Swedish natural historian Carolus Linnaeus demonstrated his distaste for constrictive stays by bestowing wearers with their own taxonomical category in his landmark taxonomy, the *Systema Naturae*: namely, the *Junceae puellae abdomine attenuato* (European girl with a long, rush-like waist), filed sardonically under the category *Homo monstrosus* (1758: 22). Physicians, too, had taken an increasing interest in the effects of constrictive clothes on the body, contributing

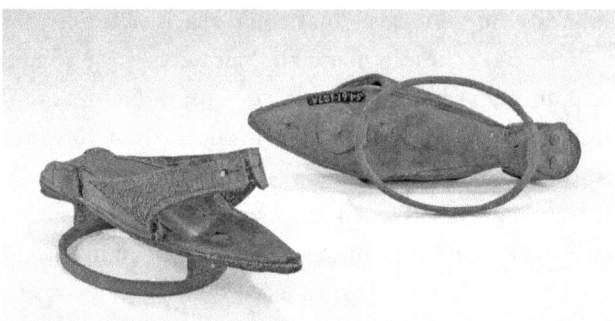

Figure 2 Outdoor pattens for high-heeled shoes. Unknown provenance, 1700–1800. Brooklyn Museum Costume Collection at the Metropolitan Museum of Art, New York. Accession number: 2009.300.1485a, b. Public domain.

to the gradual shift towards more comfortable muslins in the second half of the century (Paresys 2018: 83; see Chapter 6). For all this, it should also be appreciated that the extraordinary spectacle of the noble body was not always entirely artificial. While a courtier's height could be augmented several inches by way of raised patterns, high heels and a towering wig, the upper ranks would already have been among the tallest members of society, having benefitted from an incomparably richer diet than the bulk of the population (Porter 1982: 30; see Figure 2). They would probably have reached sexual maturity earlier than most other people, notes Roy Porter, and could have expected to live considerably longer too (1982: 30).

Virtue, that supposed arbiter of true nobility, was publicly displayed whenever possible. Alongside their physical appearance, nobles invested a significant degree of energy into exhibiting their nobility of mind. One of the few but highly valued privileges maintained by the peers (commonly claimed by their entire household) was the right to trial by fellow peers, something which the House of Lords had convinced the Commons to sign into a clause of the 'Bill for Safety and Preservation for the King' on their return to power in 1661 (Swatland 1996: 41). This particular privilege, only abolished in 1948, not only safeguarded peers from malicious litigation but actually provided some of the greatest opportunities for noble self-aggrandizement throughout the seventeenth and eighteenth centuries (Swatland 1996: 41; Krischer 2011: 67). Trial by peers was rare – in fact, there were only forty-four cases in England between 1500 and 1935 – but when they did occur, they constituted a 'spectacle of justice' and a priceless opportunity 'to stage noble distinctiveness by the performance of notable aloofness, resolution and civility' (Krischer 2011: 68, 89). In many ways, notes Frank O'Gorman, court ritual and legal ritual were natural bedfellows, making use of 'robes and wigs', 'fine and archaic language' and theatrical gestures of 'mercy and clemency' to 'elicit consent' from the greater public to institutional authority (2016: 114). An audience of over 4,000 people could be expected at an eighteenth-century London peer trial, with details of the defendant's conduct inevitably flooding into the press in the intervening weeks and months (Krischer 2011: 80). The pomp and ceremony of the legal process on these occasions was 'usually carried to extremes'; nobles literally paraded into the courtroom accompanied by their full retinue, all exhibiting symbols of their rank and title (Krischer 2011: 71). The spectacle, notes André Krischer, was largely based around the idea that the peer would accept his adversity with honour and dignity. It was prescribed, for instance, that he be first offered and then refuse assistance from a defence council, relying instead on his own inherent skill for rhetoric. It was ritual, too, that a guilty verdict be received with good grace and even thanks to the judges (Krischer 2011: 77–8).

It is vital to remember that this continuous exhibition of moral, corporeal and spiritual superiority existed alongside contemporary colonial discourses of the racialized human body. Britain's court buildings, note David Bindman and Henry Louis Gates Jr, just like those all over Europe, abounded in art and sculpture depicting Black Africans in particular – typically following in the allegorical tradition of representing the African continent (2011: 3). This artistic tradition must also have reverberated with echoes of the 'Royal Slave', a popular trope in plays, poetry and prose fiction throughout the century, which was centred on heroic, noble-born Africans sold into captivity (see Chapter 10). By the eighteenth century, representations of the exoticized Black body had become so pervasive that they had achieved 'a certain familiarity among the wealthy classes of Europe in the form of decorative and household objects' (Bindman and Gates 2011: 3). Luxury baubles and artworks representing colonial subjects satisfied the growing hunger for what Catherine Molineux calls a 'conspicuous form of involvement with the fashions and fashioning of empire' among the upper orders (2012: 23). One striking example can be found in a 1767 porcelain figure group produced in the Derby Porcelain Factory, depicting William Pitt, 1st Earl of Chatham (and prime minister 1766–8) positioned beside a kneeling Black supplicant (see Figure 3). The piece probably references Pitt's conciliatory declarations towards the American colonies, with the 'Black' female figure dressed in the conventional feathered headdress representing the American continent. While it was not unusual at this time for the Black body to be substituted for representations of other racialized groups (here, Native

Figure 3 Nineteenth-century engraving of the Viscount Pitt porcelain figure group, which was made in Derby Porcelain Factory c. 1767. From Arthur Herbert Church (1886), *English Porcelain*, London: Chapman and Hall, p. 24. Courtesy of Alamy.

Americans), the figure's colouring may also make for an implicit reference to slavery. The piece, indeed, constitutes a striking juxtaposition: the tall, poised and brilliant-white figure of the earl represents an inheritable status of political and social privilege; the jet-black hue of the kneeling figure, meanwhile, references the inheritable status of a racialized and commodified slave. In both cases, the subjects' rank and position in the universe is unmistakably manifest in their physical bodies. The fact that Pitt himself had only been elevated to the peerage in 1766 – before which he had been known colloquially as the 'Great Commoner', owing to the fact that his family's landed estate was founded on colonial wealth – only renders this representation more conspicuous. What his ancestry lacked in terms of noble race, it might be inferred, was more than compensated by his natural excellence as a white European.

It was not only in art that the inheritable status of nobility came face to face with the inheritable status of slavery. At court, note Bindman and Gates Jr, Black servants were commonly deployed as 'bandsmen or attendants in processions; actors and actresses in court theatricals; major-domos ushering in guests; personal servants to court officials, women and children; horse grooms; more menial servants; and very occasionally high officials' (2011: 17). Black servants were also commonplace in the homes of the nobility, where as highly fashionable additions to a household staff they would usually hold the most visible positions – footmen, servers or drivers (Chater 2009: 26). Frequently these servants were 'involuntary', having been imported from the colonies in order to be trained in European manners. Even when this was not the case, notes Molineux, there was a certain 'fuzziness' in British perceptions of their freedom, with the words 'servant' and 'slave' being deployed more or less interchangeably even in the later part of the century (2012: 8; for more on Black servants in elite British households, see Chapter 10). At the very same time, the racialized body could be employed by court society as a correlative for nobility itself, particularly in the form of exotic visitors such as the putative Tahitian prince Omai (discussed in Chapter 9) or African royalty such as William Sessarakoo (discussed in Chapter 10). In contrast to contemporary 'noble savage' tropes, these diplomatic visitors were patronized as exemplary specimens of civil nobility, unencumbered by the excessive materialism adopted by the domestic elite. That is, such visitors reinforced the paradigm of natural excellence and inborn nobility as an element of universal order, while their exoticization ensured that they did not threaten the implicit supremacy of their white counterparts.

Representations of the white noble body were elemental tools of authority in themselves. Eighteenth-century images of nobility ranged from the extreme reverence to vicious caricature. Where it could be controlled, however, it is interesting to see how the body formed part of strategic rank symbolism. This is exemplified in the collections of herald Francis Nichols, whose catalogues of nobility the *British Compendium* and the *Irish Compendium* were reprinted under various titles between the 1720s and the 1760s. Each volume exhaustively records the insignia and crests of each peerage title, starting with the monarch and working its way down the noble hierarchy to the lowest rank of baron. The action of moving through these pages functions, in itself, as an expositor of the noble hierarchies within: the number of crests on each page, for instance, increases exponentially as one moves down the social ladder, steadily ordering the train of distinctions into a conceptual pyramid of exclusivity. Most interesting, however, is the portrait that accompanies each degree of nobility (see Figure 4). The dukes, marquesses, earls, viscounts and barons of each peerage are represented with an indicative portrait, invariably depicting an

Figure 4 *A Marquis in His Parliament Robes*, from Francis Nichols (1729), the *British Compendium*, London: R. Nutt, p. 13. Courtesy of Alamy.

upright, stately man who displays the full ceremonial regalia of his order. Just as the parliamentary robes of each portrait are individualized according to his rank, the wearer himself is portrayed individually in every picture, donning a different periwig or assuming a different posture. The wearers' robes are different precisely because they represent a different 'type' of nobleman, and the individualized bodies only reinforce this idea. For, while these individuals are not representations of any specific individual, each represents a set of very real families: they are a personification of what this set of families have in common – their 'dukeness' or their 'earlness', and this embodiment of heraldic symbolism is as naturally aligned to each order as the king's recognizable portrait is aligned with his own crest. These human portraits seem inseparable from the myriad other status symbols that saturate these images. Bars of ermine on parliamentary robes, for instance, indicate the rank of the wearer (three for an earl, three and a half for a marquess and four for a duke), while black sable spots on coronation robes serve the same function. The human being inside, differentiated along with his robes, seems little more than another exhibition of rank – another element of noble 'intensification'. Certainly, the King and the Prince of Wales, whose stock portraits stand as unambiguous symbols of royalty, perfectly complete this rising system of hierarchical symbolism. Their coats of arms each swell to encompass an entire page, and the backgrounds to their portraits, just like their crests, are embellished with all the rich details of a royal household.

* * *

Nobility in eighteenth-century Britain and Ireland managed to be multiple things at once. On the one hand, the peerage and its wider rank of noble families represented an idea of practical governance: they were substantial landholders, with a vested economic interest in the running of the state; they were among the most educated individuals of their generation, more highly qualified than almost anyone else to tackle the complicated legal business of parliament; and they were heirs to a long line of ostensibly successful rulers, having been raised from birth to take the reins of power, and deeply invested in upholding the reputation of their forbears. On the other hand, however, British nobles represented something quasi-mystical: they were differentiated from their contemporaries on account of an inherent distinction of a family line, the part-symbolic-part-literal vector for the great deeds of their ancestors; they lived and functioned in a realm of ritualistic hierarchical symbolism, participating in a whole language of rank distinction upon which their very privilege was built; and, above all, their 'race' conferred upon them a superlative place in the natural order, above the masses not just in terms of wealth and power, nor just in terms of political influence but also in terms of moral necessity. The idea of untainted genealogy at the heart of noble tradition was in every way a product of the noble paradigm – far from being arbitrary or a vestige of harmless traditions, it was carefully designed to ensure continued dominance of one particular social group.

3

The race myth in retrospect

The noble paradigm illustrates how power strategies can shape the development of hierarchies. Far from constituting a cultural idiosyncrasy, the hierarchical standards of nobility reflected fundamental notions of what constituted superiority and inferiority, and indeed who got to decide as much. While blood-based privilege persisted as an integral part of British governance, however, natural historians, philosophers and slaveholders were developing racialized hierarchies based on a strikingly similar template. The concept of human race, which emerged towards the end of the eighteenth century, represented a marked departure from the centuries of human-variety theory that preceded it. This new race model, like nobility, was deemed to be quintessentially inheritable, inherent and inimitable. Just like nobility, it found its basis in an idea of untainted lineal family, whereby individuals or groups could be thought of as being contaminated, as it were, with the blood of inferior racial units. Like nobility, too, race was understood to have a corporeal expression, but the exact dimensions of the racialized body were often ambiguous and highly reliant on context and authority. Race, like nobility, also had to be constantly performed in order to exist, with the occasional lack of performance only serving to highlight common expectations of racialized identity. We can, in fact, see late eighteenth-century race theory as a grim pastiche of the noble paradigm, based on the understanding that:

1. White Europeans are naturally excellent.
2. This excellence can be transmitted genealogically.
3. This excellence naturally gives rise to cultural and economic dominance.
4. Whiteness must be re-performed in each generation.
5. The white body is both an expression and a tool of inherited excellence.
6. Integrity of genealogical, cultural, economic, performative and corporeal whiteness is essential for the continuance of inherited excellence in future generations.

The structural similarities between the paradigms of nobility and race should not even be surprising to us. The original construct of race, as will be seen in this chapter, was closely associated with nobility. It was only during the latter half of the eighteenth century that this genealogical template began to be projected onto the global population. The emerging concept of race was therefore both old and new: it involved a complete revision of the established taxonomical framework of human variety based on climatic influence but also a return to a profoundly familiar set of power dynamics, which had already shaped ideas of natural human hierarchy for millennia. This chapter breaks down the modern concept of race, beginning with the collapse of established race theory during the middle of the twentieth century, and tracing back the incoherencies that had always characterized its pseudo-scientific framework. It then examines the concept of race as it existed before the inception of 'major human races' when it predominantly existed as a discourse to express the blood dynamics of noble pedigree.

* * *

In July 1950, the British-American anthropologist Ashley Montagu spearheaded one of the most significant anthropological documents of modern times: UNESCO's *Statement on Race*. Drawn up by an international committee of anthropologists, sociologists and psychologists, and following in the footsteps of *the Universal Declaration of Human Rights* (1948) and the *Genocide Convention* (1948), the *Statement on Race* sought to overhaul the racist doctrines which had, a few years earlier, underpinned the human extermination projects of the Second World War. Yet, even for theorists of Montagu's generation, the exact nature of the concept they were undermining was not entirely clear. Never once, in fact, had there been a unanimous consensus among scientists about what exactly race *was*.

'Race theory' as we know it today has been attributed to a number of taxonomies published in the later decades of the eighteenth century, with one of the most commonly cited being *De generis humani varietate nativa* ('On the Natural Variety of Mankind') published by the German physician Johann Friedrich Blumenbach in 1795. *De generis*, considerably influenced by the earlier work of Immanuel Kant, had established some of the key elements of what was to become racial pseudoscience, dividing the world into five major subgroups – namely Caucasian, Mongolian, Ethiopian, American and Malay (see Chapter 7). Even over the course of its short life, however, so-called race theory had always faltered. For much of the nineteenth century, Blumenbach's model of 'major races' was forced to vie for attention against older, more traditional notions like climate theory and the ever-rancorous debate about whether all humans were descended from Adam. The successive shockwaves generated by Charles Darwin's *Origin of the Species* (1859) destabilized the original race concept still more in the second half of the nineteenth century. In Britain, arguments about the exact nature of racial classification were so controversial that they caused a rift in London's Ethnological Society, leading to the foundation of the Royal Anthropological Society in 1863 for those who preferred the theory of multiple origin over evolution. By the beginning of the twentieth century, the pseudoscience of eugenics, popularized by Frances Galton's *Inquiries into the Human Faculty* (1883), had splintered the idea of race still further. Though such theories leant heavily on the concept of identifiable human subgroups, eugenicists like Harvard University's William Z. Ripley and Franco-Russian anthropologist Joseph Deniker sometimes ended up mapping such absurdly complex catalogues of human types and subtypes that it quickly became difficult to distinguish between supposed races, families and individuals.

It was actually during the decades before the Second World War that some of the most powerful waves of condemnation against racial science within Western anthropology would emerge. In 1912, the American anthropologist Franz Boas struck a resolute blow to the field when he undermined the validity of the cephalic index (i.e. the practice of measuring skulls as a means of racial differentiation, fundamental to Blumenbach's race model). The children of immigrants born in America, he discovered, invariably demonstrated different skull shapes from their parents – showing that cranial dimension was dependent largely on nutrition and environment, not inherent type (1912: 530). Boas subsequently published a series of works over the following decades arguing that culture, rather than biology, was the main criterion of human physical diversity. 'All the evidence available', he wrote, 'argues against the theory that a people must conduct itself in a certain way merely because of its physique' (1937: 91). In 1933, the German political philosopher Eric Voegelin, soon to be exiled to the United States, similarly denounced the methodology of race theory as absurd. Racial scientists, he pointed out, were effectively using the methods of the humanities to support their doctrines, and collectively turning a blind eye to discipline's embarrassing dearth of empirical evidence (Voegelin 1933: 12). Five years later in 1938, the Franco-American historian Jacques Barzun asserted that 'in its mazes, race-thinking is its own best refutation. If sense and logic can lead to truth, not a single system of race-classification can be true' (1938: 11). Even among anthropologists convinced by racial theory, taxonomic consistency was always difficult to ascertain. The precise boundaries of racial type could vary wildly from one theorist to another and from one generation to the next. For all the ostensible precision of cranial measurements and anthropometric indices, no real evidence had ever been produced to support the idea that certain deviations in bone structure or skin colour or hair consistency signified the crossing over into a different *type* of human being. There was no evidence, in fact, that racial boundaries existed at all – that a supposedly 'mixed race' individual was somehow perched on a liminal frontier between two 'pure' identities while eschewing any unitary biological identity of her own. On the contrary, the reasoning of biological race continued to depend on constant recourse to cultural prejudice.

Why, then, had this idea proved so resilient? In 1950, UNESCO warned that it was not so much racial pseudoscience that posed a problem, as the engrained cultural myth that it helped to support. '[T]o most people', it reads, 'a race is any group of people whom they choose to describe as a race' (UNESCO 1950: 31). The very assumption that biological race was an established scientific fact allowed for a kind of mass confirmation bias: the hierarchies, animosities and alliances of any given society could, through this discourse, be interpreted as an element of nature. For many, race theory made perfect sense because it could almost always be adapted to reflect their own particular prejudice. Much of the public already assumed that scientists had established race as a scientific fact, Montagu explained in 1942, and 'scientists do little to discourage this view. . . . It is not difficult to see, therefore, why most of us continue to believe that "race" really corresponds to something which exists' (1942: 22). The UNESCO committee's conclusions, subsequently published in newspapers and academic journals across post-war Europe and America, were unambiguous. The previous century of racial science, it openly declared, had been baseless. More or less everything the general public thought they knew about race was untrue. The biological and physiological variations customarily attributed to race, the *Statement* explained, were dynamic rather than static: human genetic patterns and clusters were in a constant state of flux, appearing and disappearing all the time, rather than representing permanent subgroups (UNESCO 1950: 30–1). If race could be said to exist at all, in other words, then it was only as a transient wave of genetic tendencies – not as a set of concrete divisions within the human species. The popular myth of race, in turn, was to be actively discouraged. While the *Statement* did not go as far as to actually deny the existence of race, it did strive to separate the concept from its various social or ethical interpretations (Reardon 2005: 31). Controversially at the time, the document recommended that the very word 'race' should be proscribed, so as to dissociate it from the doctrines of pre-war pseudoscience (UNESCO 1950: 31, 33).

Though initially met with strong resistance, UNESCO's *Statement* was borne out over the following decades by advances in the field of molecular genetics. From this point of view, the case was cut and closed: genetically speaking, there is no such thing as racial purity. Quite the contrary, in fact – the reality of gene patterns frequently means that groups commonly identified as a single race are more genetically diverse within themselves than when compared to a putatively separate racial group. 'Comparing Europeans, Asians, and Africans' then, suggests Jonathan Marks, 'is thus something like comparing dogs, cows and mammals. Such a comparison is meaningless, because the third category incorporates the first two' (2002: 83–4). More than this, from a genetic standpoint the attributes traditionally used to identify race (such as stature, skin colour and hair type) are 'mathematically trivial' and are not significantly indicative of larger genetic make-up (Marks 2002: 82). If a race is defined by this arbitrary group of physical features, there is no reason why an alternative racial grouping should not be defined by an entirely different set of characteristics – hand size, say, or voice pitch. Further advances in molecular genetics heralded a steady decline in mainstream scientific support for traditional race groupings over the second half of the twentieth century. In 1950, the *Encyclopaedia Britannica*'s definition of race had remained almost identical to that of 1929, defining each group by its cephalic criteria of anatomical and cranial measurements (1929: 18.865). By the 1968 edition, race was redefined in the *Encyclopaedia* as 'a population or a group of populations distinct by virtue of a genetic isolation', which is 'neither an artificial construct [nor] a collection of individuals arbitrarily selected from a population' (1968: 18.985). In 1989, the fifteenth edition continued to list the racial subgroups of 'Caucasoid', 'Australoid', 'Mongoloid', 'Capoid' and 'Congoid', while cautioning that 'all racial groups currently existing are thoroughly mixed' (*Encyclopaedia Britannica* 1989: 9.876). By 2007, a revised entry finally announced that race was 'a cultural construct based on the popular but mistaken notion that humans can be divided into biologically distinct categories by means of particular physical features' (*Encyclopaedia Britannica* 2007: 9.876). Meanwhile, in 1998, the American Anthropological Association published a major new statement on race explaining that 'from its inception, this modern concept of "race" was modelled after an ancient theorem of the Great Chain of Being, which posited natural categories on a hierarchy established by God or nature' and which 'fused behaviour and physical features together in the public mind' (1998: 569–70). When genetic evidence is taken into account, the statement continues, it becomes clear that these myths and their resulting sociopolitical biases are all that are left to uphold the field of racial science. 'Scientists today', it declares, 'find that reliance on such folk beliefs about human differences in research has led to countless errors' (American Anthropological Association 1998: 569–70). The 1998 AAA statement largely marked the end of the road for Blumenbach's brand of race theory. This was not, however, because it succeeded in eliminating racial pseudoscience altogether. Lieberman et al. have studied the continued prevalence of race theory in institutions outside Western Europe and North America (2004: 910–11), while Ann Morning has noted elements of racial pseudoscience featuring in American high school textbooks used well into the 2000s (2011: 98). Rather, the statement's significance lies in its firm reiteration of criticisms dating back more than a hundred years: racial science has essentially constituted a succession of mutually incoherent studies in the pursuit of justifying a particular cultural narrative. The folk belief of race, rather than the pseudoscience itself, is the real engine of racialized thought. It thrives not on evidence but on ambiguity, existing in a realm of intimation, and always appealing to inferred cultural interpretations of what superiority and inferiority look like.

It is thus to the folk belief of race that we now turn. When racial theorists first applied the idea of race to their human varieties in the latter decades of the eighteenth century, they were making use of a concept that was already deeply familiar to most people in Europe and America. That was the concept of blood hierarchy, whereby human groups could be stratified and graded according to their genealogical credentials. 'Race' in this sense was a notion that had remained decidedly separate from the field of human taxonomy for most of the century. What is more, it represented a genealogical discourse that did not exactly correspond to what we might now understand as hereditary trait transmission. Traditionally, eighteenth-century historians have avoided talking about heredity at this time, since the biological concept (and indeed the discipline of biology itself) would not be fully defined until the early nineteenth century. As we will see in Chapter 6, this perspective tends to overlook the rapidly developing fields of enquiry into hereditary phenomena during this time, particularly in the realms of disease and animal husbandry. Nevertheless, it is important to remember that understandings of genealogy and unmixed lineage were built on very different premises than we might assume. In particular, the entire process of creating new human beings, right up until the later decades of the eighteenth century, almost always took into account the influence of the external environment. This was a time, notes the molecular biologist François Jacob, when human beings were not 'reproduced', they were 'generated'. 'Generation was always the result of a creation', he explains, 'which, at some stage or another required direct intervention by divine forces' (1993: 19). More than this, note Staffan Müller-Wille and Hans Jörg Rheinberger, trait transmission in the eighteenth century was inseparable from 'the contingencies of conception, pregnancy, embryonic development, parturition and lactation' (2007: 3). Thus, while parental traits were recognized as contributing factors to the traits of the offspring, so too was divine providence, which invoked in its turn a range of external forces such as upbringing, diet, climate, morality, religion, nationality and, somewhat notoriously, the mother's imagination during pregnancy.

It is amid these external and internal processes of 'generation' that we can find the curious discourse of race. The eighteenth-century race concept was decidedly different from what we would understand by the term today. In 1755, Samuel Johnson's *Dictionary* provided ten telling definitions for the English word 'race': (1) 'A family ascending', (2) 'a family descending', (3) 'a generation; collective family', (4) 'a particular breed', (5) 'a race [i.e. a root] of ginger' and (6) 'a particular . . . taste of wine', while the remaining definitions pertain to 'contest[s] in running' (1755: n.p., entry 'race'). Ideas of skin colour, anatomy or even human variety, it might be noticed, are entirely absent from Johnson's understanding of the word. In their place, however, is an intimate associative relationship between 'family ascending' (lineal descent) and a 'particular breed', referring here to the art of animal husbandry. Eighteenth-century race, claims Claude-Olivier Doron, can be understood as a 'genealogical style of reasoning', an entire mode of thought based on 'lineages and kinships', which were primarily related to 'nobiliary discourses', 'breeding practices' and 'spiritual status' (2012: 78–9).

Race, therefore, often made for a stark contrast with contemporary natural histories, which generally paid relatively little attention to familial ties and tended to focus instead on classification according to observable characteristics (Doron 2012: 82). As will be seen in Chapter 5, the human *varietates* of early eighteenth-century taxonomies might seem strikingly similar to later race categories, but they were more a catalogue of human bodily potential than a declaration of immutable subtypes. Let us take, for example, the landmark binomial naming system laid out by Carolus Linnaeus in his *Systema Naturae* (1735). This system, still used in modern biology, identified groups by reducing them to two or more observable features, becoming steadily more specific through *classes*, *ordines*, *genera* and *species*. At no point, however, is it implied that those categories are grouped together because they are somehow blood related. While Linnaeus's landmark genus *Homo*, for instance, contained four varieties of mankind (red, white, brown and Black), successive versions of the *Systema* ordered these alongside a whole catalogue of 'monstrous' human physiques ranging from European women, whose waists had been elongated through the wearing of stays, to Native Americans who had purportedly flattened their skulls through artificial manipulation, and even to mysterious cave-dwelling men with tails and red eyes (1758: 22–3). The 1735 taxon *Anthropomorpha* had ranged the genus *Homo* alongside apes (*Simia*) but also sloths (*Bradypus*) (1735: n.p. [10]). 'Race' discourse, on the other hand, essentially provided a way to understand nation, society and rank through the prism of lineal family. 'Race' was as applicable to entire populations as it was to individual families; it was as useful in understanding plants and animals as it was for humans, and it could take on a whole host of sometimes surprising secondary meanings. As a mode of understanding 'the lineage or continuity in families, especially royal or noble families', the word 'race' had been in use since the later Middle Ages and was already 'monnaie courante' by the sixteenth century (Hannaford 1996: 5; de Miramon and Lugt 2008: 10–11). In his 1611 Italian-English dictionary *Queen Anna's New World of Words*, the English-born linguist John Florio offered a definition of 'race' which more or less approximated that of Samuel Johnson's in 1755, though with even more emphasis on rank distinction. The Italian word *razza*, he explained, signified a 'race, kind, breed, lineage, [or] pedigree' (Florio 1611: 424; Hannaford 1996: 172). The French theologian Pierre Charron had used the French term *race* in his *De la Sagesse* (1601) to express the idea that noble action was nobler still when performed through successive generations – and, when the English genealogist Samson Lennard translated the work in 1612, the English word 'race' maintained this same sense. 'Nobility is a quality everywhere not common', he transcribes,

> It is a qualitie of race or stock. . . . There must . . . be two things in true and perfect nobilitie, profession of [militarie] virtue . . . and the race as subject and matter, that is to say a long continuance of this qualitie by many degrees and races. . . . For he is truly and entirely noble, who maketh a single profession of publick virtue, serving his prince and country, and being descended of parents and ancestors that have done the same. (Charron 1612: 197–8)

The early modern concept of race, then, had developed the body itself as a discourse of identity and distinction. Race could be conceptualized as a visible, outward identity or an invisible, almost figurative sense of difference, manifested through the mysterious, hidden qualities of blood.

In a colonial context, notes Kathleen Wilson, '"race" as a line of descent' was useful in order to identify groups by 'religion, custom, language, climate, aesthetics and historical time as much as physiognomy and skin colour' (2003: 11). In this way, race could easily blur with the idea of nation, since 'a racialized version of Britishness', equally identifiable in the metropole and the colonies, was explicitly contrasted with indigenous cultures. 'Both cultural ideas about race and racialized notions of nation', Wilson notes, 'identified a juncture where rationality, nationality and physical difference become intertwined, and where acquired characteristics are transformed into innate ones, the intangible inheritance of blood' (2003: 12). Conversely, Nicholas Hudson suggests that race was increasingly used throughout the century to erase nationhood from colonial subjects. 'Race', he points out, 'became the major term of ethnographic scholarship, while "nation" was reserved to describe the political and social divisions of Europe' (Hudson 1996: 248). Moreover, the sheer breadth of the term meant that it could be used to dehumanize other human varieties while lionizing natural European excellence. 'As previously used, "race" denoted the bloodlines of animals', Hudson notes, 'yet race also commonly denoted a "noble race" or upper social caste.... There was no dishonour or inconsistency in calling Europeans a superior "race"' (1996: 253–4). The very development of heredity as a unified concept, suggest Müller-Wille and Rheinberger, could be seen as the development of a 'knowledge regime' of biological identity, which grew up in tandem with advances in global colonization (2012: 3). The intertwined discourses of race and nation also underpinned traditions of biblical succession. As Ivan Hannaford (1996: 187) and Colin Kidd (2004: 264) have both noted, the evolving concept of race in the early modern period cannot be separated from theological developments – particularly the Protestant Reformation which introduced new motivations to ascertain the providential ordering of mankind.

Race became, in many ways, a discourse which could both challenge and consolidate traditional scriptural histories, depending on how it was employed. The myth of the Curse of Ham, for instance, demonstrates how seamlessly these older ideas of race as divinely sanctioned genealogical succession could feed into later ideas of the racialized human body. The Curse of Ham stood as an invaluable line of defence for slavery apologists in the eighteenth century, not least because its associations with lineal race were already centuries old. The story, David Goldenberg (2003: 142) notes, would have been accepted as biblical 'fact' by most people in eighteenth-century Europe, and usually went like this: shortly after the great flood, a sleeping Noah was found in a state of undress by his three sons; the first two, Japheth and Shem, averted their gaze and were thus rewarded by their father with rich lands and inheritance; the third son, Ham, mocked his father's nudity and was consequently punished with blackened skin, eternal servitude and the exile of his descendants into Africa. As the *Universal Magazine* recorded in 1749, this story was complemented with a host of other popular legends about the 'blackening' of Ham and his African progeny (1749: 244–6). One such legend recounted that Ham had refused to relinquish his wife on Noah's orders, 'which want of compliance marked all his black posterity, and the frightful complexion of the inhabitants of the torrid zone is the punishment of the profane ardour of their father' (*Universal Magazine* 1749: 245).

Even the *Universal Magazine* had to admit that few of these stories held up to scrutiny – first of all because 'the variety of complexions in the world may be accounted for, another way', and more pertinently because the details were simply absent from scripture (1749: 246). In Genesis 9, Noah curses his grandson *Canaan* with eternal servitude but never places a curse on his son Ham. There is no mention of either being burdened with black skin or exile into Africa. While another of Ham's sons, Cush, does travel to Africa, the cursed son Canaan migrates north to modern-day Lebanon. In fact, it was not until the fifteenth century that popular renditions of the story began to depict Ham as a Black African, with this new detail being embroidered into the legend through the writings of Portuguese and English slave traders. The biblical text does, however, recount a related story of lineal race. Genesis 9, which is chiefly concerned with genealogical succession, originated the popular legend that Japhet, Shem and Ham had each repopulated different parts of the earth after the flood. By the early Middle Ages, the Japhites were commonly held to have populated Europe, the Semites Asia and the Hamites Africa. In some renditions of this legend, each brother was aligned with a different feudal estate. The twelfth-century French theologian Honorius Augustodunensis recorded in his encyclopaedia of cosmology, *De imagine mundi*, that the world was divided: *in liberos, in milites, in servos. Liberi de Sem, milites de Iaphet, servi de Cham* (1110–39: 172.166). While Ham was later held up as the originator of Black African slaves, the story of his brother Shem was also adapted to reinforce ontological divides between Christians and Jews. In 1748, the Royal Society fellow John Peter Stehelin published a translation of the notoriously anti-Semitic writings of the German Hebraist Johann Andreas Eisenmenger, intimating that it was Shem and his Jewish descendants, rather than Ham, who suffered the Curse of Noah. Referencing another common legend, whereby Ham was said to be cursed on account of sexual misconduct aboard the ark, Stehelin states instead that 'Shem was punish'd on his skin, for from him was sprung the black Cus[h]'

(1748: 1.106; Braude 1997: 120). Some decades later in his *Self-Interpreting Bible* (1778), the Scottish theologian John Brown of Haddington explained that the descendants of Japhet, in the form of Greeks, Romans and Ottomans, had repopulated the former territories of Shem long before the birth of Christ – and that their descendants became Christians while 'very few of the descendants of Shem or Ham have so much as pretended it' (1778: 15).

There is still more to examine, however, within the eighteenth-century Curse of Ham tradition. Noah's third son, Japhet, was not only aligned with Europe and Christianity but also provided a traditional origin story for nobility. In his *True Rise of Nobility* (1718), the Suffolk squire Maurice Shelton recounted the legend that Japhet had bestowed his line with the 'native nobility' of Adam, adding that his descendants had passed it down ever since through primogeniture (1718: 6). It had been God's plan, Shelton explained, to cultivate a division between the few patriarchal leaders and the many followers, a pattern which 'other families afterwards following, constantly observed' and which continued to be observed in the noble dynasties of Britain and Ireland (1718: 6–7). The herald Francis Nichols, too, introduced the 1726 edition of his *British Compendium* by reasserting the medieval legend of Obilion, Japhet's great-grandson, who extolled his line's noble blood by assuming the world's first honorific title (1726: iii). According to the legend, Obilion learns of his 'native' nobility in part through realizing the innate superiority of the Japhetic line and in part through understanding the providential subordination of the Hamites. The order of nature is explained to him through a vision, in which he sees a three-cornered Olive tree; the branches representing Japhet and Shem reach upwards to the sky, while the branch representing Ham is thrust firmly into the ground. It was by this, Nichols explains, that Obilion understood 'he was chief of the blood of the three sons of Noah. And thus began Nobility, of which, Aristotle, in his *Politicks*, mentions four kinds' (1726: iii).

It is little wonder that the traditions of noble genealogy and biblical genealogy should so seamlessly overlap. The depiction of Noah's family tree provided in the *Universal Magazine* in 1749 (see Figure 5), for instance, works on the very same logic as contemporary heraldries, exemplified in the vast catalogues of bloodline compiled by English genealogists Joseph Edmundson and William Segar, the *Baronagium genealogicum: or the pedigrees of the English peers* (1764–84). Noble genealogies, like their biblical counterparts, also alimented wider spirals of hereditary identity, as can be seen in pedigree charts such as that of the Wingfield family (see Figure 6). In pedigrees like these, noble titles ultimately serve the same function as biblical figures do in national origin stories, bestowing a sense

Figure 5 *The Manner how the Whole Earth was Peopled by Noah and his Descendants after the Flood*, from the *Universal Magazine* (1749), vol. 4, London: J. Hinton, p. 240. Courtesy of Alamy.

of 'race' to the wider group, attesting to ancestral excellence (or lack thereof) and aligning their descendants with a certain rank in the order of creation.

The early modern idea of *noble* race, claims Arlette Jouanna, communicated a certain unchangeability of natural order (1981: 24). Natural states, according to its principle, can be temporarily improved but not transformed, precisely because their original state is constantly revived through blood. Race thus asserts that human beings are naturally unequal but also that the inherited social order reflects this natural hierarchy (Jouanna 1981: 24). For nobles, notes Jean Feerick, this idea of race was particularly valuable in that provided 'a way of "speaking the body" . . . it defined the body primarily through the qualities of its blood. That is, it propounded distinctions of rank above all else' (2010: 9). A distinction of blood, Feerick suggests, offered a sort of 'metaphysical separation from one's social inferiors' while reinforcing groups along the lines of family and kindred (2010: 9). Blood, in this sense, also acted as a unifying agent for Britain and Ireland's dispersed loci of socio-economic power – the genealogical model of a 'family tree' linked certain families with their illustrious ancestors but also connected them with other elite families as brethren in blood. 'Each seemingly separate tree was but a branch of a unitary tree . . .', notes Feerick, 'if there is a

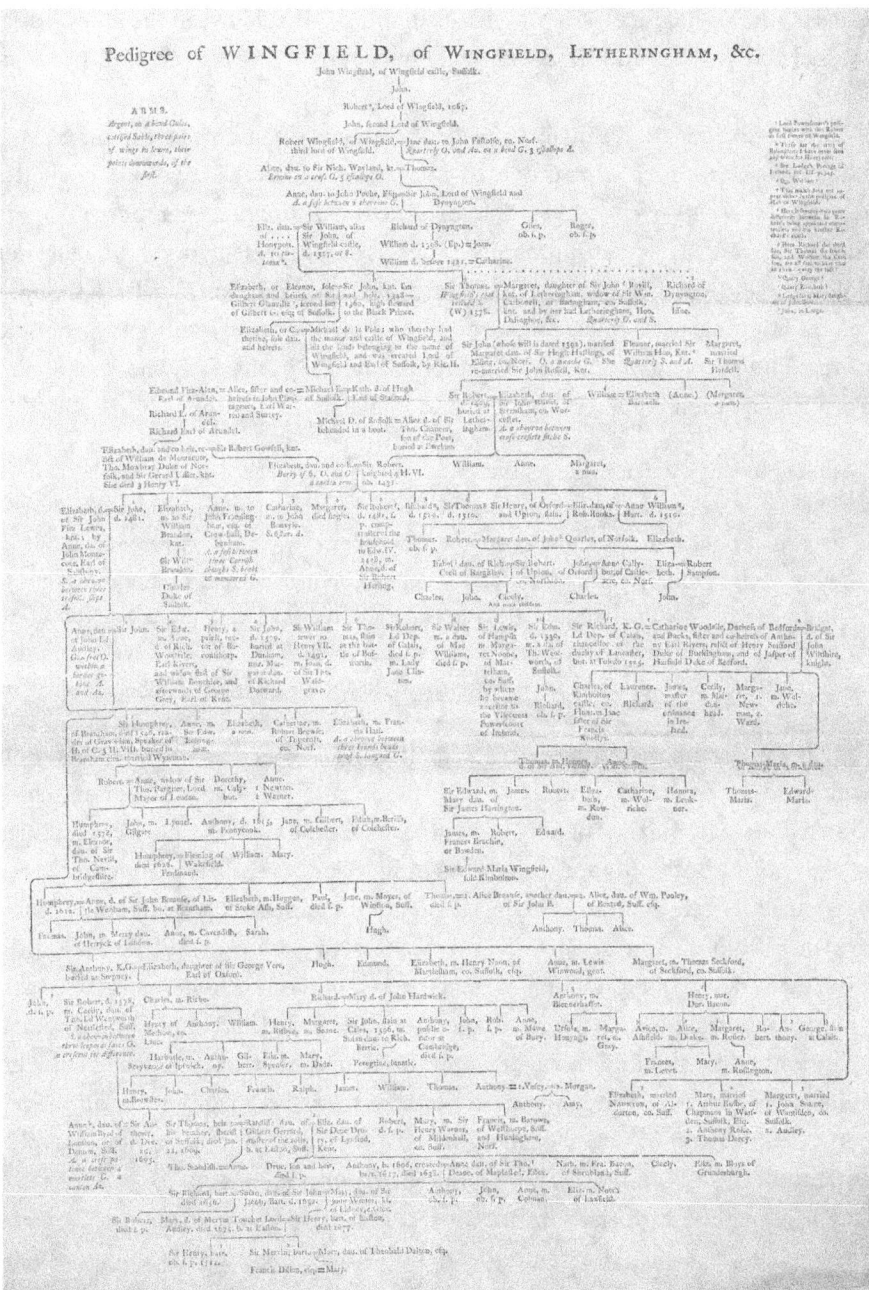

Figure 6 'Pedigree of Wingfield, of Wingfield, Letheringham, &c' (*c.* 1712–99). Wellcome Collection. Public domain.

crucial border that race-as-blood insists upon, it is that between the elite body – unified across space and time – and the mass body – dispersed and disordered' (2010: 14).

Étienne Balibar and Immanuel Wallerstein suggest that this idea of hereditary nobility as a *race supérieure* provided a necessary foil to the construct of chattel slaves as a *race inférieure* (1991: 207–9). The opposition between noble (super-humanity) and slave (sub-humanity), they assert, represented the attributes of bloodline and skin colour respectively, not only underpinning racialized thought but functioning as a vehicle for European national identity. Taking the example of the *limpieza de sangre* – statutes of blood purity in the early modern Spain, Portugal and their colonies – Balibar and Wallerstein explain:

> [T]he hereditary definition of the *raza* . . . serves in effect both to isolate an internal aristocracy and to confer on the whole of the 'Spanish people' a fictive nobility, to make it a 'people of masters' at a point when, by terror, genocide, slavery and enforced Christianisation, it was conquering and dominating the largest of the colonial empires . . . Aristocratic racism [was] the prototype of what analysts today call self-referential racism, which begins by elevating the group which controls the discourse to the status of a 'race'. (1991: 208)

In many ways, the tradition of hereditary privilege bears even more in common with modern concepts of race through the formation of arbitrary hierarchies than it does in its maxims of pure bloodline. Using the body as a physical signifier of superiority, both old race (family ascending) and the various pre-emptors of new race (discrete anatomical type) depend on their capacity to liberally pluck evidence from different domains in order to support a pre-existing prejudice. Both race and nobility function as imaginary subdivisions of humanity that can only become real through a vast discourse of intertwined and often contradictory assertions. Like nobility, race can only be deployed 'within particular belief systems . . . it is used metonymically to stand for and magnify the difference between slave and owner, the colonized and the colonizer, indigenous peoples and invaders, serfs and lords, poor and rich' (Hunt 1993: 340).

Earlier natural historians in Britain and Ireland did sometimes use the term 'race' to describe their human *varietates*, but they were mostly doing so as a conveniently vague synonym for type, family or nation. 'Race' – just as with the modern English word 'family' – held broad potential for figurative application. The term was often used, for example, to describe jobs or activities that might be associated with particular social groups, familial or otherwise. In 1712, the *Spectator* wrote of a 'race of coxcombs'; in 1720, the *Independent Whig* referred to a 'race of bishops . . . popes . . . and priests'; and as late as 1791, C. H. Elliot's *Republican Refuted* featured a 'race or generation of . . . legislators' (*OED*: entry 'race, n.6'). Bartholomew Stibbs's 1738 travel account, *The Journal of a Voyage up the Gambia*, notes Roxann Wheeler, offers a prime example of how malleable racialized identity could be at this time (Wheeler 2000: 4). The *Journal*'s English narrator describes the preparation for a canoe voyage up the river:

> On the 11th we met in council, and settled the number of whites and blacks that were to go on the expedition; *viz* 19 white men, including our linguister, who is as black as coal; though here, thro' custom, (being Christians) they account themselves white men. (Stibbs 1738: 243)

In this passage, it is Christianity and not skin colour which functions as the primary 'racialized' identity; furthermore, the white English narrator seems unperturbed by the suggestion that a Black African has, through his religion, become white in every way barring the incidental colour of his skin.

Skin colour, in fact, did not begin to commonly figure as a 'primary signifier of human difference' until the 1770s (Wheeler 2000: 7; Wahrman 2004: 86–8). This is largely because the vast majority of eighteenth-century natural historians approached skin colour as an expression of bodily adaptation, typically in reaction to climate, nutrition or exposure to European standards of civility. Paradoxically, these assumptions forged an intimate link between skin colour and the concept of race for entirely different (even contrary) reasons to those that typically characterize more recent discourses of racism. Diverse skin colours seemed to prove that the human species was constantly undergoing physical adaptation – that perceived varieties were not permanent subgroups but rather examples of every individual's bodily potential. Crucially then, while race-as-lineage and human-variety theory were decidedly separate ideas in the eighteenth century, they both relied on the same preconceptions of how the human body could change. 'True nobles', like human *varietates*, were not simply products of their lineage but of the environmental cultivation of that lineage over time. This, in turn, required a long-term process of change and adaptation, which even boasted its very own racialized discourse: 'breeding'.

The eighteenth-century idea of 'breeding', notes Jenny Davidson, provided a common language for two conflicting accounts of human nature: a 'hereditarian model in which birth determines one's character and one's place in the world' and 'a model that emphasises the power of education and other environmental influences to shape essentially malleable human beings into whatever form is deemed best' (2009: 1). In many ways 'breeding' worked similarly to race, being passed down from parents to offspring, and subsequently according with spiritual and worldly status. Yet, within this already-racialized discourse, breeding emphasized the notion of improvement or even perfection of inherent characteristics. Since the sixteenth century, the term 'breeding' had been synonymous with education and refinement among the upper orders while also implying the literal sexual generation of genteel or noble human beings within the confines of lineal families (*OED*: entry 'breeding' n. 3). Breeding, therefore, could be used to justify all the exclusive attributes of noble or genteel family that blood could not; blood, conversely, could be used to signify nobility or gentility when other elements of breeding were lacking. It followed that the discourse of breeding was entirely compatible with a racialized sense of human anatomy. In 1709, notes Davidson (2009: 4), Joseph Addison's literary journal the *Tatler* blamed lack of 'breeding' in genteel families not only for uncouthness in some of their children but also for those children's undesirable physical characteristics. 'One might wear any passion out of a family by culture', pronounced the journal's editorial persona, Isaac Bickerstaff,

> as skilful gardiners blot a colour out of a tulip . . . it is for want of care in the disposing of our children, with regard to their bodies and minds, that we go into an house and see such different complexions and humours in the same race and family. (Addison 1709: 8)

* * *

If anything held together the broad and often fragmented concept of eighteenth-century race, it was the idea that parentage and lineal family substantially determined identity and status. The early race construct is also notable for its immense adaptability – a quality that was essential for both the noble paradigm and the emerging construct of race theory. Most importantly, through this 'folk-belief' arbitrary hierarchies could be efficiently and convincingly reframed as a simple reflection of the natural order of things.

4

Human hierarchy and the Great Chain of Being

Race, like nobility, is contingent on the idea that its hierarchy reflects the order of nature. This premise allows both concepts to sustain the multitudes of internal contradictions that are essential to their survival. Throughout the eighteenth century, the vision of universal order that has been called the 'Great Chain of Being' framed each and every entity of God's creation as part of an interconnected fabric, making it possible to reconcile immensely different ideas of hierarchy with one another while vindicating arbitrary sociopolitical values as a reflection of nature itself. In order to understand how nobility influenced the development of emerging race theory, then, it is crucial to examine how both concepts interacted with these ubiquitous framings of natural order. The Chain of Being is central to this study because it represents a common construct of lineal ordering that ultimately underpinned both racialized difference and noble rank. That is, the very ideas of 'superiority' and 'inferiority' were intrinsically linked with a certain spiritual quality, a reflection of proximity to the divine, and, above all, a means of understanding human hierarchy. This chapter breaks down the power dynamics of the Great Chain of Being world view and shows how emerging race theory came to deploy the very same self-referential authority as nobility, effectively exalting the powerful on the basis of their power.

* * *

In 1933, when the American philosopher and historian Arthur Onken Lovejoy first delivered his lectures on the 'Great Chain of Being', the main auditorium of Harvard's Emerson Hall was, reportedly, only half full (Feuer 1977: 361). The idea he expounded, however – later concretized in his landmark study *The Great Chain of Being: The Study of the History of an Idea* (1936) – would go on to become one of the most influential notions in the study of the history of ideas. Lovejoy had put a name to a philosophical conceit that would have seemed perfectly obvious to scholars and philosophers in eighteenth-century

Britain and Ireland and whose roots could be traced right back to Greek and Roman antiquity. This was not a single philosophical movement, however. Rather, what Lovejoy described was a general current of thought that appeared with pronounced consistency in early modern discourses of science, philosophy and social organization (Formigari 1968: 1.325). The 'Great Chain of Being' refers to an overarching world view of the universe as an interdependent chain of individual entities – 'a hierarchical continuum that spans, without really including, the two endpoints of nonexistence and God' (Burns 2001: 122). Right up until the end of the eighteenth century, noted Lovejoy,

> most men of science, and, indeed, most educated men, were to accept without question . . . the conception of the universe as a 'Great Chain of Being' . . . ranging in hierarchical order from the meagerest kind of existents . . . every one of them differing from that immediately above and immediately below it by the 'least possible' degree of difference. (1936: 59)

In many ways, the Great Chain of Being expresses one of the structural necessities of the Western hierarchical tradition: namely, the recognition of a lineal scale of precedence whose very existence requires the implicit participation of everyone (and everything). The development of the Chain motif as a theological framework, however, meant that it could function as a transcendental super-hierarchy against which all other hierarchies could be vindicated. Disparate notions of social, spiritual and scientific precedence could, by this conceptual mechanism, be considered in direct relation to one another as equal constituents in the greater scale of creation, sharing the same subordination to a divine ladder of precedence.

The Chain model of creation reached a zenith of sorts in the eighteenth century, largely due to the international success of Alexander Pope's *Essay on Man* (1733–4), discussed later in this chapter. The three major principles of Western philosophy upon which it was built, however, all find their roots in Platonic and Aristotelian philosophy. *Plenitude*, the first of these principles, can mainly be traced to Plato's *Republic* ([*c.* 380 BCE] 1908: 509b), wherein the 'Idea of the Good' – as the 'summit' of knowable things – 'provides the logical basis of a world of *sensibilia* conceived as graded with respect to perfection' (Formigari 1968: 1.325). Essentially, if the universe reflects its maker and if the maker is perfect, then the universe must also be perfect – and thus must be complete in every way. The attendant ideas of *gradation* and *continuity* stem from Aristotle's various writings on creation as a *Scala naturae* such as *De Anima* (Aristotle [*c.* 335–323 BCE] 1931: 414a–415a; Lovejoy 1936: 59). The principle of gradation holds that nature constitutes a ladder-like scale of existence, with each progressive degree of complexity being built upon the rung immediately below it. The principle of continuity, on the other hand, recognizes that these relationships are overlapping and not necessarily linear. To use Aristotle's own analogy, the various relationships of the universe rather resemble an ostensibly chaotic household, wherein each individual element quietly plays its own part in the greater order of things ([c. 335–323 BCE] 1928: 1075a).

It was the Christian interpretation of the *Scala naturae* in late antiquity and the Middle Ages which most powerfully established these principles as part of an enduring model of creation. In the fourth and fifth centuries, writings such as St. Augustine's *City of God* (c. 412–26 CE) helped to disseminate the idea of a divinely sanctioned *ordo* throughout the Christian world. The concept was initially quite useful as a tool for rationalizing Roman-style social hierarchy within a Christian framework. No matter who ascended to political power, Augustine asserted, be they Plebeian or Patrician, Christian or non-Christian, it was ultimately an expression of divine will, for 'he who gave power to Marius, gave it also to Caius Caesar. . . . He who gave it to Christian Constantine gave it also to the apostate Julian' (1871: 1.219). The Augustinian interpretation of *ordo* was later adapted by medieval philosophers such as Thomas Aquinas in the thirteenth century, who vaunted the idea of continuous, graded universal hierarchy in his *Summa Contra Gentiles* (c. 1264). 'The better a thing is, the higher place does it hold in the intention of the agent who produces it', declared Aquinas, '[b]ut the best thing in creation is the perfection of the universe, which consists in the orderly variety of things' (1905: 107). Aquinas also promoted what was to become one of the more persistent tropes of the Chain tradition: that mankind forms a 'mid-point' on the Chain, since humans were composed of both earthly and spiritual matter. The human constitution of *aequaliter complexionatum* (equal temperament), he claims, is situated at the very bottom of the 'intellectual' Chain, as well as standing at the very top of the 'earthly' Chain, rendering the human soul the 'horizon and boundary line of things corporeal and incorporeal' (Aquinas [c. 1264] 1905: 133; Lovejoy 1936: 79).

By the seventeenth century, the Chain model had been adopted in a rather different way by rationalist and empiricist philosophers, including, most notably, the German mathematician Gottfried Wilhelm Leibniz, who asserted that the 'fullness' of the universal Chain was evident in mathematics, not favouring one number over another but instead constituting an ostensibly infinite chain of interdependent alterity (Lovejoy 1936: 147; Leibniz 1714: 132–4). Others, such as Robert Fludd, a physician and alchemist at the court of James I, saw the Great Chain of Being as delineating an 'unfinished map' of the universe, wherein the unknown realms of creation could be theoretically charted according to their observable hierarchical course (Godwin 1991: 5; Formigari 1968: 1.327). Fludd's depiction of the *Integrae naturae speculum artisque imago* ('the mirror of the whole of nature and the image of art'), which appeared in his great opus the *Utriusque cosmi maioris scilicet et minoris metaphysica, physica, atque technica historia* (1617), depicts the universe itself as a diagram of knowledge and discovery (1617: n.p. [1.v]; see Figure 7).

The image is a starburst of circular gradations, radiating outward from the basic earthly elements of land and water and ascending through minerals, vegetables, animals and heavenly bodies. In the outer circles, angels revolve around the universe in a series of flaming rings, marking the limits of the knowable world from the infinite perfection of higher divinity. Dominating the scene is the figure of nature, who stands with her feet in the inner circles; her hand is animated by the hand of the maker (shackled, literally, by a chain), while

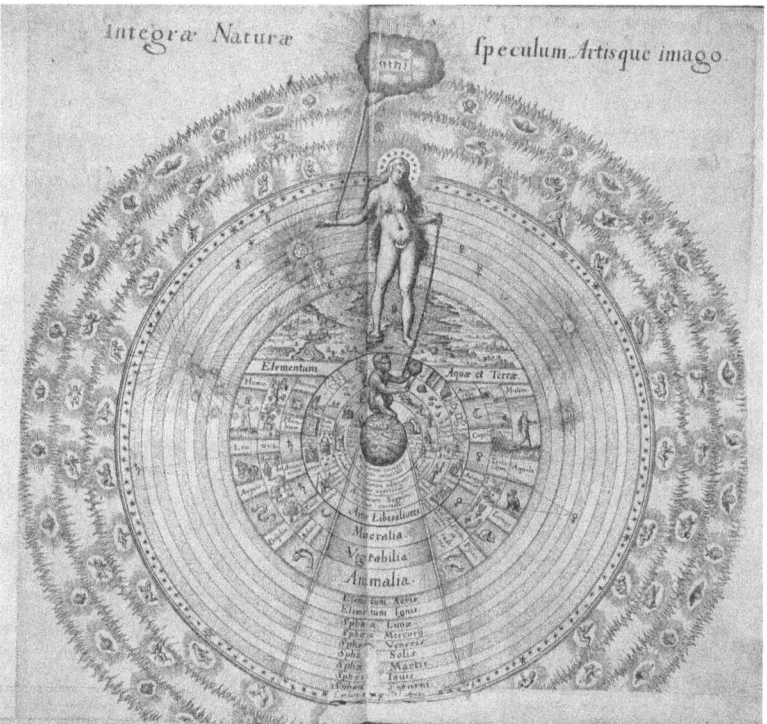

Figure 7 *Integrae Naturae* from Robert Fludd (1617), *Utriusque cosmi maioris scilicet et minoris metaphysica*, Oppenheim: J. T. de Bry. Wellcome Collection. Public domain.

she, in turn, controls the hand of an ape (representing human artifice 'aping' nature). The central spheres of the diagram depict a graded scale of human activity: closest to the earth are the arts of distillation and mineral purification; next in line is arable cultivation and horticulture; then come the arts of livestock cultivation, including bee-keeping and medicinal extraction; and finally the liberal arts, among which are counted engineering, painting, arithmetic and music (Godwin 1991: 22). The *Integrae Naturae* is remarkable in many respects: first, it envisions the Chain as the universe in all of its multiplicity, assimilating alchemy, astrology, astronomy, theology, society and indeed humanism into one great plan. Second, it presents the figure of nature (and her mimic artifice) as a kind of medium by which all these aspects can be understood together: her haloed head remains in the domain of the angels, her feet are firmly planted on earth and her hand moves only by the will of God. Third, it presents the Chain of being as a readable, decipherable diagram of universal relationships: Man, for instance, is aligned with the sun and a vineyard, while Woman is depicted beside the moon and a field of wheat; both hold a position at the top of the Chain of animals, representing the summit of living beings on earth. The Chain of Being, here, is not only asserted as a great pattern into which all of Creation ultimately falls, it is also imagined as a systematic method of understanding the complexities of that Creation.

The English divine Thomas Sprat's 'encyclopaedic' programme for the Royal Society in the seventeenth century, notes Lia Formigari, was 'witness to this symbiosis of the techniques of experimental research and the idea of a full and hierarchical universe' (1968: 1.327). The task of natural philosophy, according to Sprat's model, was to retrace each and every element of the universal Chain. All new experiments into all known things, he proclaimed in 1667, will always be useful, perhaps not immediately, but for future generations – for all things are necessarily implicated in the greater scheme of creation, and so even the most obscure entity can shine new light on the workings of nature.

> [T]his is the highest pitch of human reason; to follow all the links of this chain, till all their secrets are open to our minds ... to rank all the varieties and degrees of things, so orderly one upon another, that standing on the top of them, we may perfectly behold all that are below. (Sprat 1667: 110)

The idea of the universe as a Great Chain of Being not only delineated a cosmic hierarchy to which all things belonged, but also functioned as a theoretical schema of the unknown: a construct by which philosophers could continue ranking things, indefinitely, in recognition of universal interdependence and ultimate unity.

Practically speaking, however, the Chain model of creation was far from the coherent scheme of interdependent relationships Fludd or Sprat might have liked it to be. In fact, the most intriguing aspect of the Great Chain of Being – and perhaps the real reason for its long-term resilience – was its apparently limitless tolerance for inconsistency. At the end of the day, the idea of universal order served to bolster an arbitrary scheme of established hierarchy, be it ecclesiastical, political, social or even an element of natural history. That is, the Chain did not exist in isolation; it was informed by its hierarchical context in every age and in every discourse wherein it was invoked. Philosophers discussed the Chain in terms of metaphysical abstraction, and their teachings were disseminated through the structures of church, state and academy – yet those philosophers themselves were informed by the hierarchal hegemony around them. While hierarchies (real and imagined) could be related to the Chain, the Chain itself was always and by its very nature arbitrated by who controlled the hierarchical discourse. By and of itself, the Chain of Being was therefore a profoundly political construct – acting as a vast mechanism of power and subordination that permeated science, society and spirituality. In the very act of implicating society in the 'natural' course of the universe, the Chain of Being validated a certain vision of that society and signalled the dangers inherent in its transgression.

Just as the Great Chain of Being functioned as an unfinished map of the natural world, it could also be invoked as an unfinished map of human society – a correlative and indicative hierarchy for the disparate and ostensibly unrelated elements of humanity. In this way, the Chain could vindicate any given political reality, so long as it was sufficiently favoured by the established authority. The witchcraft debates of the seventeenth and eighteenth centuries offer a case in point. To abolish the crime of witchcraft, argued the English polymath Sir Thomas Browne in his *Religio Medici* (1643), would, in effect, be to deny the existence of one the ranks of earthly creation. This would not only destabilize the order of the universe but would potentially constitute an act of atheism. To deny one part of the Chain, Browne's argument went, was to deny its veracity as a whole and thus to deny the existence of God. It was a mystery, he declared, how 'so many learned heads should so farre forget their Metaphysicks, and destroy the Ladder and scale of creatures, as to question the existence of Spirits' (1643: 30.254). This sentiment was echoed some decades later in a posthumous publication of Joseph Glanvill's famous work of demonology, the *Sadducismus Triumphatus* (1681). '[H]e that believes there is no witch, believes a devil *gratis*', Glanvill declares, '[all] things hang together in a chain of connexion . . . and 'tis but an happy chance if he, that hath lost one link, holds another' (1681: 3). In their respective use of the Chain of Being to defend society as they knew it, both Browne and Glanvill showcase a crucial facet of this tradition: its function as a tool of social conservatism, justifying the maintenance of a certain type of social order by linking it with the will of God. Paradoxically, this defensive invocation of the unchanging Chain also reveals quite how malleable the Chain of being idea could be. For, despite Browne's and Glanvill's portentous misgivings, English witchcraft legislation was indeed repealed in 1735 (alleged witches were instead penalized for malicious pretence), and not only did the Chain model of creation survive unscathed, the construct's popularity continued to climb to new heights (Kreuger 2010: 26). After all, the repeal of the witchcraft laws was also an act of authority – which, like the accused witches themselves, was also rooted in hierarchy and which, like the crime of witchcraft, could also be justified by the divine Chain. In short, just as the Chain could be invoked to defend the retention of witchcraft legislation, it implicitly underlay the authority of those who decided to remove it.

This was, in essence, the very same dynamic which underpinned claims and contestations of hereditary power in eighteenth-century Britain and Ireland. No more than accused witches, the British peers relied on the concept of the Chain of Being in order to ensure their conceptual existence. Their rank, too, had been briefly 'removed' from the Chain during the abolition of the House of Lords, and their apologists too argued that the maintenance of a special, superior rank of human being ('true nobles') was essential for the functioning of an ordered universe. Humanity itself, as seen within the Chain model, was largely based on a synergetic relationship between authority and hierarchy – a relationship which disguised the arbitrary and changeable nature of each. Through the Chain philosophy, any established authority could validate any given hierarchy through law and custom (deciding, for instance, whether witches did or did not exist), while the accepted hierarchy thus became the basis upon which that authority claimed dominion. Put another way, the Chain model offered those in power a way in which to promote hierarchies that justified their own power – an action that continually served to reinforce both the hierarchy and the power at its apex. Furthermore, the Chain motif meant that it did not matter what *kind* of hierarchy was favoured by the powerful or what *kind* of claims lay behind their power, since everything, in one way or another, could be related back to the divine pattern of the universe. A noble by blood, a noble by merit, a noble by conquest or a noble by royal decree were all equally noble as long as their 'nobility' was validated by the dominant authority; concordantly, the means of acquiring their nobility – blood, merit, conquest or decree – were implicitly reinforced as structural elements of the Chain, by evidence of having attended the attainment of noble rank. It is worth looking once again at Maurice Shelton's *True Rise of Nobility* (1718), quoted previously in Chapter 2: 'Distinction of rank is highly necessary for the œconomy of the world . . . [as] in observing step by step the several degrees of excellency above us, we arrive insensibly at last to the contemplation of the supreme perfection' (1718: v). Here, the high breeding of nobility, having been cultivated within exclusive family lines across generations immemorial, serves as an implicit organizer of human society. It 'corrects' the manners of the lower ranks and maintains 'our common conversation in the bounds of politeness and civility' (v). Nobility, through its own performance, both reinforces the structure of the Chain and reminds the rest of society of its greater purpose. The highest ranks of society have, in a word, become waymarks to the divine by practising the rituals of high civility.

All this considered, it is fitting that the most enduring symbol of the Chain of Being in eighteenth-century Britain was not created by a philosopher, an alchemist or a mathematician but by a poet. Alexander Pope's *Essay on Man* (1733–4), was probably the most influential champion of the Chain tradition throughout the entire century. In succinct heroic couplets, the poem took the views of universal order expressed by Plato, Locke, Leibniz, Spinoza and King and reduced them to a single, easily comprehensible text. For many, it constituted an unacceptable simplification of lofty philosophies: Samuel Johnson dismissed Pope as being 'in haste to teach us what he had not learned' (1779: 130), while even the poem's dedicatee Henry St. John Bolingbroke was said to have mocked the *Essay* in private at any chance he could get (Warburton 1756: 327). Yet, none of the Pope's critics, no matter how virulent, could argue with the poem's astronomical success. The *Essay* presented philosophy in a form that was at once digestible and entertaining for the reading public, and Pope soon became a household name throughout Europe. During the hundred years following its publication, notes Ian Campbell Ross, the *Essay* was translated into every major language on the continent, with no fewer than twenty-four editions in German alone, eighteen in Italian, sixteen in French, six in Dutch, five each in Polish and Latin, four in Swedish, as well as various others in 'Czech, Danish, Hungarian, Icelandic, Portuguese, Romanian, Russian, Spanish, Turkish and Welsh' (1985: 77). The central message of the poem is a warning against aspirations of social mobility. Its first epistle famously vindicates 'the ways of God to Man' with the concise assertion: 'whatever is, is right' (1734: epistle 1, lines 16 and 286). No individual can be happy in isolation, asserts Pope, and none can achieve happiness by taking the place of his superior, because true satisfaction depends on fulfilling one's unique role in the cosmic system. Trying to 'improve' this role, therefore, is inherently contradictory, since every entity is already a reflection of perfect Creation. Accepting the social order as God has made it is thus not only necessary in order to honour the work of creation but also required in order to find spiritual fulfilment:

> Order is Heav'n's first law; and this confest,
> Some are, and must be, greater than the rest,
> More rich, more wise; but who infers from hence
> That such are happier, shocks all common sense.
> ...
> Condition, circumstance is not the thing;
> Bliss is the same in subject or in king. (1734: epistle 4, lines 47–50 and 55–56)

To imagine that certain people might be better suited to different social roles from their own, notes Pope in the fourth epistle, is to approach the whole concept of divine order from the wrong perspective. Yes, bad people were sometimes born into high positions, while the virtuous were sometimes born into subordination, but it would be criticism of God's Creation to suggest that this was a mistake. Rather, claims Pope, if it appears that 'virtue starves while vice is fed', it is because some people have failed to truly embrace the cosmic role that they have been assigned (1734: epistle 4, line 147). Likewise, the talented, virtuous subject born into a low station, but who believes herself better suited to a higher rank, is missing the point of divine creation – virtue does not necessarily mean aspiration, instead it comes from embodying one's God-given place in the world. 'Act well your part', the *Essay* implores, 'there all the honour lies' (Pope 1734: epistle 4, line 184). Wealth and privilege may create material differences between the ranks, but the underlying order they represent is what really matters:

> Fortune in Men has some small diff'rence made,
> One flaunts in rags, one flutters in brocade,
> The cobler apron'd, and the parson gown'd,
> The friar hooded, and the monarch crown'd,
> 'What differ more (you cry) than crown and cowl?'
> I'll tell you, friend! a Wise man and a Fool. (Pope 1734: epistle 4, lines 185–290)

By laying out the Great Chain of Being philosophy in such simple terms, the *Essay on Man* also highlights the more sinister conclusions that necessarily follow from this narrative of universal order. Pope's 'natural', ordered sense of inequality also extends to the colonial sphere – not only implying that slavery and the subordination of native peoples reflected the rungs of God's divine ladder but that such conditions were naturally aligned with certain peoples. In this regard, suggests Helena Woodard, Pope's construction of a 'universal, unbiased ranking of humanity advocates a concept that has far reaching racial implications' (1999: xv). Consider, for instance, the poem's first epistle, wherein Pope speaks of a 'poor Indian' whose ignorance of Christian faith and civility has, ironically, led him to embrace his place in the Christian universe more happily than many a cynical and aspirational European:

> Lo the poor Indian! Whose untutor'd mind
> Sees God in clouds, or hears him in the wind;
> His soul proud science never taught to stray,
> Far as the solar walk, or milky way;
> Yet simple nature to his hope has giv'n,
> Behind the cloud-topt hill, an humbler heav'n
> ...
> He asks no Angel's wings, no Seraph's fire;
> But thinks, admitted to that equal sky,
> His faithful dog shall bear him company. (Pope 1734: epistle 1, lines 95–100 and 106–8)

Here, the ignorance of the 'poor Indian' is identified as part of his natural state and his resignation to a condition of relative inferiority is the key to his spiritual integrity. In this way, suggests Woodard, while the *Essay* does not explicitly advocate racialized subordination, 'the pernicious manner in which [Pope's] doctrine can serve the interests of the powerful at the expense of the dispossessed is keenly apparent' (1999: 8). In other words, Pope had created an accessible Chain model, which, among other things, lent itself extremely well to racialized hierarchies. To conceive of a 'human variety' in terms of God-given rank was, in effect, to impose a certain level of inferiority on that variety. What is more, asserts Woodard, 'when a hierarchical theory of humanity accompanies the identification of a specific indigenous racial group (deemed repugnant), it requires only a small nudge to shift discussion from an abstract idea to specific theories about racial hierarchies' (1999: 15).

In fact, Pope's doctrine considerably facilitated the development of a socio-racialized discourse in the eighteenth century, providing an accessible language of divine hierarchy. Both Woodard (1999: 7) and Lovejoy (1936: 207) note a striking instance of this confluence in Samuel Richardson's enormously popular novel *Pamela* (1740), wherein the eponymous heroine recalls the verses of Pope by reciting her own heroic couplets on the subject of the Chain of Being:

> The meanest slaves, or those who hedge and ditch,
> Are useful by their sweat to feed the rich.
> The rich, in due return, impart their store;
> Which comfortably feeds the lab'ring poor.
> Nor let the rich the lowest slave disdain:
> He's equally a link in nature's chain;
> Labours to the same end, joins in one view;
> And both alike the will divine pursue:
> And at last, are levell'd, king and slave,
> Without distinction in the silent grave. (Richardson 1740: 2.55–6)

Here, Pamela is dutifully rehearsing the tenets of Pope's fourth epistle – there is a place for the rich and a place for the poor; they function together within the greater construct of society, and this, as God has intended, is good. There is no place, however, for the rich to thus think themselves better than the poor; on the contrary, in their very act of despising their inferiors they are debasing themselves below the rank of the virtuous poor, who have at least recognized the cosmic importance of their own humble position. Performing one's moral role, be it that of a servant or a noble, is, in the words of Pope, where 'honour lies' – and this, notoriously, is Pamela's forte (1734: epistle 4, line 184). Reacting to the incivilities of her high-born persecutor, the treacherous Lady Davers, Pamela uses her own 'pure' blood to justify her spiritual superiority:

> [M]any of these gentry, that brag of their antient blood, would be glad to have it as wholesome, and as really untainted, as ours! . . . These reflections occurred [from] this proud letter, of the lowly Lady Davers, against the high-minded Pamela. Lowly, I say, because she could stoop to such vain pride; and high-minded I, because I hope I am too proud ever to do the like! . . . [P]ray I, to be kept from the sinful pride of a high estate. (Richardson 1740: 2.54–55)

Pamela's assertion of her 'untainted' peasant blood deliberately inverts the traditional language of *eugeneia* while casting aspersions of 'mongrel' ancestry on the upper orders. Yet, in its spiritual dimensions, it also constitutes a very real criticism: Pamela's physical condition, that is to say, her 'untainted' peasant lineage which expresses itself in her good looks and rustic naiveté, bespeaks generations of ancestors who have embraced their natural, cosmic role (rather than usurping and aspiring like some of the upper orders) and who are infinitely more virtuous for it. This aspect of Pamela's body and blood are themselves constituent parts of her idealized rank performance – they identify the validity of her peasant rank in the very same way as bloodlines identify the upper orders, while she, unlike the degenerate elites in the novel, has the virtue to follow through with an appropriate social display of this rank. When Pamela does finally marry into the gentry, her rank performance follows suit immediately, transforming her on her wedding day into a paragon of quality.

As such, claims Woodard, it is notable that Pamela's poem links the relationship between inferior and superior ranks to '[t]he meanest slaves, or those who hedge and ditch, [who] are useful by their sweat to feed the rich'. Pamela is speaking as a European servant, notes Woodard, for whom this role within the universal order applies to her rank – and yet the poem that she uses to illustrate her point 'hearkens to a brutal chattel slavocracy that is more consistent with Euro-African trade than with Pamela's indentured servant status' (1999: 7). The mere mention of slavery in the context of Pamela's Chain of Being polemic necessarily introduces a racialized aspect to her argument of natural order. Slaves too, following her (and Pope's) reasoning, play a role in the universal order which, in its perceived interdependence with the higher orders of society, is comparable to the lower social orders of free white labourers. It must likewise be inferred that the bodies and blood of non-white slaves can be taken as a premise for their rank on the Chain, just as Pamela's undiluted peasant blood has unambiguously identified the rank within which she has been born to excel.

The idea that the physical body presupposed a certain spiritual rank in the Chain of Being was, in fact, a frequent conceit in the discourses of natural history during the eighteenth century. In his *View of the Earth* (1771), for instance, the Oxford geographer Richard Turner footnoted his description of populations in Africa with this remark:

> Some writers have supposed these people to be descendants of Cain [i.e., Ham];[1] who for his cruelty to his brother, has that mark set upon him. – Others have esteemed them to be a different species of being, and therefore ranked them a link lower than us in the chain of existence: – whilst many have attributed that dusky hue to the nature of their diet, and intense heat of the country. (Turner 1779: 17)

Here, the Chain of Being acts as a syntactical link between two opposing notions of racialized humanity. It allows the author to assert both the traditional narrative of a biblical curse and the contemporary geographical discourse of climate theory, by relating both to the natural scheme of divine order. Meanwhile, the Chain is invoked to identify a group of people defined by their physical features

---

1 The stories of Cain and Ham (also spelled Cham) were commonly confused, probably owing to the similarity of their names in printed texts and the characters' relatively similar stories.

as an inferior species, using the very same reasoning of natural rank that had been evoked in *Pamela*. A similar sentiment was advanced at the end of the century by the English physician Charles White in his *Account of the Regular Gradations in Man* (1799), which used the idea that 'nature exhibits to our view an immense chain of beings' in an attempt to prove that Black Africans were closer to great apes on that chain than they were to white Europeans (1799: 39–42). In his *Considerations on the Negro Cause* of 1773, the English parliamentarian and West Indian planter Samuel Estwick directly quoted Pope's defence of social ranks in the *Essay* in order to suggest that Africans constituted a separate and inferior species. No amount of instruction or time could ever amend the immorality, cruelty and violence of the tribes of Africa, he proclaimed, 'for the Ethiopian cannot change his skin, nor the leopard his spots' (1773: 81).[2] Yet, were it otherwise, he suggests, it would perhaps be unnatural – since the barbarity of the African is as much an element of the Great of Chain of Being as is the civility of the European:

> I infer that the measure of these beings may be as compleat, as that of any other race of mortals; filling up that space of life beyond the bounds of which they are not capable of passing; differing from other men, not in kind, but in species, and verifying that unerring truth of Mr. Pope, that
>
> Order is Heaven's first law; and this confest,
> Some are and must be greater than the rest. (Estwick 1773: 82)

Estwick even manages to interpret the tenet of plenitude as evidence of racialized determinism: the 'space' on the Chain that Africans occupy, their unique facet of universal being, is here expressed in terms of their corporeal limitations – the 'bounds' beyond which they 'are not capable of passing'. He goes on to cite these 'corporeal and intellectual differences of Negroes from other people' as well as 'the irreclaimable savageness of their manners' as evidence not only that they are an inferior 'race of people' but also that 'they should be considered and distinguished (as they are) as articles of [legal] trade and commerce only' (Estwick 1773: 82).

* * *

Besides the fact that the Chain model of creation underpinned an entire discourse of order and hierarchy in eighteenth-century Britain and Ireland, the

---

2 Estwick here references Jeremiah 13.23 (KJV), '[c]an the Ethiopian change his skin, or the leopard his spots? Then may ye also do good, that are accustomed to do evil'.

idea of the Great Chain of Being is central to this study for one main reason: it illustrates how the eighteenth-century understandings of universal order did not make any particular distinction between gradations of 'natural' hierarchies and societal ones. The model of a great cosmic Chain meant that all hierarchies, living or otherwise, earthly or divine, even those that overlapped or contradicted each other, could be thought of in relation to a vast supra-hierarchy. The great Chain ran from barren soil, through sea life, through various breeds of animals, through different social ranks of mankind, through different 'national types', through to demons, witches, angels and astrological bodies. It not only united each being with its ostensible inferior and superior but also bound together multiple modes of hierarchy – no matter how diverse – by relating each one back to the greater divine plan. Thus, the duke and the earl, as portrayed in Francis Nichols's *British Compendium*, with their slightly differing ermines and crowns, occupied different ranks of the Great Chain in just the same way as did a frog and a cat. A father and a daughter occupied different places, as did a king and a beggar, a butcher and a baker, a butterfly and a bird, a lion and a tiger – all these differences in grade and importance, from all these different perspectives, formed part of the same *Scala naturae*.

5

Civilized anatomies in eighteenth-century human-variety theory

Nobility and human-variety theory in eighteenth-century Britain and Ireland were both upheld by the same matrix of 'civility'. As we have seen thus far, the noble paradigm allowed hereditary elites to invoke aspects of civility as needed to justify arbitrary inequalities through the association of different groups with different grades in the order of the universe. Just as noble rank was called into being through a language of codified performance and choreographed social protocol, the very essence of an inferior human variety lay in a perceived or projected absence of civilized conduct. Likewise, just as nobility could be simultaneously lauded as both the origin and the outcome of civility, a lack thereof could be cited both as the cause and the consequence of inferior varietal status. More than this, eighteenth-century natural histories firmly situated this matrix of civility in a discourse of human anatomy. Civilized behaviour, across the spectrum of human-variety theory, was consistently placed on the same sliding scale as physical deformity or indeed monstrosity. This chapter reviews the major currents of climate theory that dominated the field of human-variety theory throughout the eighteenth century. In particular, it looks at how exposure to high civility was understood as an agent of anatomical transformation and a fundamental element of human-variety categories.

* * *

Climate theory tells the story of a battle between the temperate and the extreme, of the normal and the abnormal and of the perfect and the degenerate human body. For eighteenth-century physicians and natural historians, the ancient teachings of Hippocrates in his *Air, Water and Places* (300–200 BCE) had remained an integral reference on this point, with a new English translation released by the Royal Society's Francis Clifton in 1734. Hippocrates' hypothesis rested on the bodily impact of dryness, wetness, heat and cold, which were accordingly associated with the four seasons. To this he added the ostensible influence of geographical position, access to clean water and mode of life, including 'drinking', 'feasting', 'idleness', 'exercise' and 'labour' (Hippocrates 1734: 1–12, 2). Furthermore, these elements appeared to be interdependent on one another. As the 1734 translation puts it, 'you will generally find the complexions and manners of people to correspond to the nature of their country' (Hippocrates 1734: 35). Hippocrates theorized that temperate environments would engender beautiful human anatomies, while extreme environments would give rise to physical monstrosities and aberrations (1734: 20–4). The Phasians (an ancient people associated with the river Phasis), who he claimed to live in marshy and torrid surroundings, were thereby rendered 'large and thick' with skin of 'pale yellow, like that in a jaundice', while the climate had also generated 'cowardice' and 'effeminacy' in the peoples of Asia (Hippocrates 1734: 24). Environmental influences, in turn, could be passed down through families. It was not improbable, Hippocrates theorized, that 'the affair of generation is influenc'd by [the environment]' and that the observable diversity of human anatomies 'shou'd thus happen in the formation or mixture of the seed . . . for which reason I think the Europeans differ more than the Asiaticks in appearance' (1734: 32). Eighteenth-century commentators often interpreted these highly tenacious ideas in 'mechanical' terms, speculating that Hippocrates may have been observing how temperature and geography exercised a constrictive or a relaxing effect on the smallest fibres of the human body (Miller 1962: 135). In his *Esprit des lois* (1748), for instance, the French philosopher Montesquieu explained that Central Europe's geography and climate soothed nerve fibres in the human body and had thereby fostered coherent and steady governments; the harsh climes of Asia, on the other hand, inflamed nerve fibres and had subsequently endowed the inhabitants with an 'extreme' constitution, whereby brave, active warriors lived cheek by jowl with effeminate, weak civilians (1748: 14.2, 146–7; 17.3, 222–3). At the same time, climate theory was amenable to what Andrew Wells has called 'the twin supports of Renaissance-learned culture – scripture and antiquity' (2015: 435). That is to say that the conviction that human anatomy tended to change allowed observers to reconcile dispersed global populations with biblical history. Early studies of human variety, such as the seminal *Dissertation on the Origin of the Native Races of America* (1642) by the Dutch theologian Hugo Grotius, had constituted grand hypotheses of human migration, fuelling the popularity of theories that linked New World societies with biblical tribes (1642: 8–18). The supposed effects of climate, in this context, were in many ways essential in order to account for anatomical diversity while respecting the scriptural dictum of universal descent from Adam.

Climate theory, however, is in many ways a misleading term: first, it did not only concern the climate per se but rather the overall influence of the external environment on the human body and mind as well as the providential design involved in placing people in that environment. Nor was it a unified theory unto itself: there was little doubt in eighteenth-century Britain and Ireland that factors such as sunlight or nourishment could alter the human body, but different theorists came to their own conclusions about the potential extent of these effects, whether they could be held responsible for significant anatomical diversity and the degree to which such diversity might be transmissible between generations. Climate theory also overlapped with some other major and sometimes contradictory theories of human development in the eighteenth century. 'Stadial theory', for instance, as advanced by commentators such as Adam Smith, Adam Ferguson and John Millar, suggested that humans in different parts of the world were at different stages of societal progress. In his *Origin of the Distinction of Ranks in Society* (1771), Millar pointed out that climate did not appear to account for the ostensible differences between the Irish, Scottish and English, nor did it explain why Italy's climate had produced, at different times, the Ancient Romans and the modern Italians (1771: 11). The ancient precepts of humoural theory also played an elemental role in understanding climatic influence. Heat, cold, wind and altitude could all influence the inner workings of the body, resulting in 'cool' or 'hot' blood, or imbalanced bile. While eighteenth-century climate theory marked a certain departure from 'the ancient correspondences between the outer and inner complexion', notes Mary Floyd-Wilson, the power of geohumouralism nonetheless remained a significant factor in ideas of human diversity. In fact, she suggests, humoural discourse could be seen as a kind of 'ethnology' in itself, surviving into eighteenth-century taxonomies such as those of Carolus Linnaeus (Floyd-Wilson 2003: 77, 86). Roxann Wheeler points out that, whatever form it took, 'climate or humoural theory . . . provided the most important rubric for thinking about human difference' in the eighteenth century; it was simply 'the common sense of the day, and a magnet for contradictory beliefs. To be sure, it was probed and prodded, partially refuted by a few, but it was also easily adapted to new conditions' (2000: 21, 24).

There was, however, something else underlying the discourse of eighteenth-century human-variety theory: anxieties about the precise parameters of humanity itself. From the mid-seventeenth century onwards, natural historians in Europe had gained unprecedented access to the bodies of great apes. Until this time, primate anatomy had largely been shrouded in mystery, but for the first time gorilla, bonobo and chimpanzee specimens were arriving on British and Irish shores on a regular basis. Since it was often difficult to tell whether these specimens represented multiple species or simply different sexes or stages of growth within a single species, a range of great apes were commonly conflated under the catch-all term 'orang-outang' – a moniker popularized in the previous century by the Dutch physician Jacobus Bontius in his *Historiae naturalis et medicae Indiae orientalis* (1631: 84). In this work, Bontius had described a mysterious ape who walked erect and demonstrated uncannily human behaviour, supplementing his description with an unnervingly humanoid sketch of the creature (1631: 84). The 'orang-outang' had long since become established in the literature of natural history as a semi-imaginary compound, embroidered all at once with ancient monster-myth, genuine research on primate anatomy and growing speculation about the potential existence of human–animal hybrids. 'European folklore was filled with ape men, were-animals and the monstrous products of every kind of bestiality', notes David Brion Davis, and various mythologies 'had always acknowledged an uneasy awareness of kinship with the lower animals' (1966: 453–4). This ingrained cultural tradition also meant that new specimens of great apes were very often approached as degenerate humans rather than humanoid animals. When the Royal Society's Edward Tyson undertook a dissection of what was 'reputed to be the first hominid ape to reach England alive', one of his missions was to prove that his subject was *not* a human being (Brown 2010: 30). Tyson's 1699 publication, *Orang-outang, sive Homo sylvestris: or, the Anatomy of a Pygmie*, constituted an exhaustive anatomical description of a chimpanzee cadaver, not only rendering it the 'first scientific study of the measurements of an anthropoid ape ever made, but also the first devoted to a systematic comparison of animals and human anatomy' (Meijer 1999: 42). This 'point-by-point comparison', notes Silvia Sebastiani, reverberated throughout the eighteenth century, leading subsequent anatomists to more closely investigate the possibility of 'continuity between the animal and the human world' (2015: 106).

Tyson's motivations reflected the potent influence of monster-myth in the realm of human-variety theory as well as the degree to which climate theory and other doctrines implied connections between the 'exotic' human body and diminished humanity. Since antiquity, the so-called monstrous races had been a stock feature of travel narratives and the othering of unfamiliar populations. Pliny's vast *Natural History* (77–9 CE), whose catalogue of human societies included dog-headed Cynocephali, headless Blemmyae and cannibal

Anthropophagi, remained a primary reference point for early modern natural historians, with a new English translation appearing at the beginning of the seventeenth century (1601: 5.8; 6.30). Importantly, centuries of monster tradition had consolidated the notion that 'extreme' human anatomies were a product of environmental influence. Aside from noting the physical effects of climate, Hippocrates had asserted that consistent external influences on the body were responsible for peoples like the Macrocepheli, or 'long-heads', whose supposed practice of binding infant skulls into a conical shape had settled into an inherent characteristic (1734: 22–3). Medieval and Renaissance *mappae mundi*, such as the 'Hereford map' of 1300, divided the world into central temperate zones and peripheral torrid zones, complete with a catalogue of monstrous races and their habitats (Van Duzer 2012: 390–1). The European appetite for these 'monstrous races' remained as insatiable as ever, with hydras, unicorns, dwarves, 'wild men' and Patagonian giants continuing to feature in taxonomies throughout the eighteenth century. Even Blumenbach, in the 1795 edition of his *De generis*, referenced persistent reports of far-off nations of men with tails (1795a: 258–9). For most eighteenth-century climate theorists, monstrosity and human variety merely represented different degrees of the same phenomenon – a view that all the time bolstered the conviction that any *deviation* from 'temperate' norms represented *degeneration*.

One of the longest-standing catalogues of 'monstrous races', the Italian philosopher Fortuno Liceti's *De Monstrorum causis, natura et differentiis libri duo* (1616), perfectly illustrates the part-empirical–part-mythological discourse that could inform investigations into the extreme human body. A number of Liceti's monstrous specimens appear to manifest genuine birth defects, with sketches of pituitary dwarves, conjoined twins and babies born without limbs printed side by side with images of grape vines with human hair and men with eyes on their shoulder blades (1634: 25, 67, 71, 80, 131). This curious juxtaposition of the real and the fabricated is an important reminder of the extent to which studies of the human body relied on second-hand reports. It also highlights the monstrous resonance of any anatomical deviation from a given 'temperate' anatomy. In this sense, the exotic human body too fell within the spectrum of the monstrous, having been conceptually dehumanized by reason of its perceived anatomical deviance. Distinctions between the 'exotic' and the 'monstrous' in eighteenth-century Britain and Ireland could certainly be extremely blurred. The public and the academy alike flocked to see John Coan, the so-called Norfolk Pygmy, who was weighed and measured by William Arderon of the Royal Society in 1750 (Fox 1995: 7). Later they marvelled at Charles Byrne, known as the 'Irish Giant', who was exhibited in London for an entry price of half a crown in 1782 (Fox 1995: 8). This same public was paying to gape at Cherokee chiefs transported to London in 1762 and exhibited in a pub (Fox 1995: 9), or perhaps most famously, Saartjie Baartman the 'Hottentot Venus' who was exhibited at fairs and galleries across Britain and Ireland and whose dissected genitalia were put on display in Paris's *Musée de l'Homme* until the late twentieth century (Schiebinger 2004: 27–9).

In many ways, the emerging field of human-variety theory began to construct its own monsters in the eighteenth century. The ever-maligned figure of the Hottentot, although loosely based on the South African Khoekhoe peoples, was so invested with European anxieties about sexuality, bestiality and civility that it could arguably be considered an imaginary entity. The unabashedly hateful descriptions of the Hottentots that invariably accompanied eighteenth-century descriptions of African populations certainly bordered on the fantastical at times, suggesting that the Hottentots' rhetorical dehumanization by way of contrast to European norms was far more important to some observers than actual descriptions. 'They are the very reverse of human kind', declared the English curate John Ovington in his *Voyage to Suratt* (1689),

> if there's any medium between a rational animal and a beast, the Hotantot lays the fairest claim to that species... [they] are as squalid in their bodies as they are mean and degenerate in their understandings... stinking grease is their sweet oil, and the dust of the streets the powder of their hair. They anoint their bodies to render their nerves supple and active... they dispatch the supernumeraries [unwanted children] to the Other World without remorse for the horrid crime, or consciousness of the e[xe]crable sin of murther. (1696: 489–96)

These are a people, Ovington explains, who ornament their legs with twisted sheep guts, which, once 'made more savoury by the dirt', they later use as food (1696: 490). They remove one testicle from their men, he adds, amputate one little finger from their women and are above all incurably lazy – with only a few souls capable of such toil that they might make useful slaves for the Dutch (Ovington 1696: 497).

The sexual characteristics of Hottentot women were of singular interest to observers, who commonly linked the reportedly rapacious sexuality of female 'savages' with physical degeneration. Ovington was just one of many explorers who manifested a voyeuristic fascination with the 'Hottentot apron' (also referred to as the *sinus pudoris*), referring to an elongation of the *labia minora* that was possibly induced through artificial means (interest in the *sinus pudoris*, it might be noted, was the reason why Saartjie Baartman's dissected genitals were publicly exhibited). These elongated labia, Ovington hypothesized, might be considered proof of hermaphroditism in Hottentots – even though two of his 'gentlemen' acquaintances assured him that this was not, in fact, the case (1696: 498). Robert Gordon, the Dutch-born son of a Scottish general, mentioned genital examinations of Hottentot women four times in his travel journals, while Captain James Cook noted that the Hottentot apron was a commonly referenced puzzle among natural historians (Huigen 2007: 8; Cook 1821: 2.362). In the 1810 edition of his *Essay on the Causes of Variety of Complexion and Figure in the Human Species* (originally published in 1787), the president of the College of New Jersey Samuel Stanhope Smith recounted hyperbolic travel accounts of 'protracted and pendulous breasts' among Hottentot women, which were rumoured to have been sold as tobacco pouches in the Cape of Good Hope (1810: 133). Significantly, the same trope of distended breasts as a sign of monstrous incivility had previously been posited by multiple writers in the early seventeenth century – not in relation to the Hottentots but to the Irish. In 1617, the English travel writer Fynes Moryson claimed that Irish women, who did not wear corsets, had 'very great duggs, some so big as they give their children suck over their shoulders' (1617: 315). In 1632, the Scottish commentator William Lithgow suggested in his *Rare Adventures and Painefull Pereginations* that the pendulous breasts of the Irish might be recycled into pouches, recounting:

> I saw in Ireland's north parts . . . [women] laying the dugges over their shoulders, would give sucke to the babes behinde their backes . . . such kind of breasts, me thinketh, were very fit, to be made money bags for East or West Indian merchants, being more than half a yard long, and as well wrought as any tanner . . . could ever mollifie such leather. (1632: 433)

While reprimanding such fabrications, Stanhope Smith nonetheless goes on to explain that the origin of these legends (in the case of both Hottentot and Irish) most likely lay in the effects that poverty, hardship and toil naturally have 'not only on savages, but on poor women in the lowest classes of civilized society, to render their breasts, in time, flaccid and thin' (1810: 133). Blumenbach attributes these reports of distended breasts in the Irish and the Africans alike to the rumoured custom of breastfeeding infants over the shoulder. He also notes, however, that a similar phenomenon had been noted 'amongst the immature and girlish prostitutes who flock to London' owing to their 'precocious venery' (Blumenbach 1795a: 248). The Hottentot women had likewise been charged with darkening the skin of their offspring artificially: 'Their children . . .', recounted William Dampier and William Funnell in their *Voyage Round the World* (1707), 'are sometimes inclining to be white' and were it 'not for their nasty way of greazing them [i.e., body-painting]' they would have remained that way (1707: 290). The celebrated French natural historian Buffon quite agreed, asserting in 1749 that Hottentots were 'not true negroes, but blacks beginning to approach towards whiteness', and would be much lighter-skinned if it were not for their habit of body-painting with black pigments (Buffon 1780–5: 3.156, 3.154; 1749–88: 3.470, 3.473).[1] The Dutch, Buffon relates, were reported to have 'carried off a Hottentot girl a few days after her birth, brought her up amongst themselves, and soon she became white as any European' (Buffon 1780–5: 3.158; 1749–88: 3.476). Even as late as 1775, the Royal Society's John Hunter could still write with confidence in his *Disputatio inauguralis* that 'all blacks are born white' (1775: 372–7).

Running parallel to this insidious discourse of monstrosity was the emergence of standardized human taxonomy, which set about classifying different varieties of human beings in relation to one another. In his *Nouvelle Division de la Terre* (1684), the French physician François Bernier compiled one of the first empirical lists of humanity's 'races'. In some ways, this is less significant than it might at first appear: the terms *race* and *espèce* as used by Bernier are highly ambiguous descriptors, essentially synonymous with 'kind' or 'type', and not indicative of the immutable subgroups that would come to characterize human taxonomies a century later (Bernasconi 2001: vii). Nevertheless, it is notable that Bernier divides the global population into a relatively small number of categories, defined primarily by their physical features (1684: 133–4). Bernier effectively groups together the peoples he considers to be physiologically comparable: the populations of Western Europe, the Middle East, India and North Africa form one type; sub-Saharan Africans form another; East Asians form a third; and the Sami people (described as 'vilains animaux') are assigned a type all to themselves (1684: 134–6). Thus, Bernier's human types are distinguished almost entirely on account of their bodily description, rather than their strict geographical location. This represents a significant departure from earlier empirical investigations into population diversity, such as that of Grotius, which was primarily concerned with migratory patterns rather than physiology. In Bernier's *Nouvelle Division*, classification is determined by a people's bodily description, regardless of familial, cultural or geographical connections. It follows that if Amerindians are considered

---

1 The foregoing translation and subsequent translations of Buffon in this study are taken from William Smellie's 1780-5 English translation of Buffon's *Histoire Naturelle*, the *Natural History, General and Particular*. Like most contemporary translations of Buffon, Smellie's edition liberally rearranges and sometimes omits much of the original French text, which will therefore be referenced alongside it.

to sufficiently resemble Europeans, then they can be theoretically ranked within the same human category, despite their cultural and geographic disparities; likewise, if Hottentots are judged to look sufficiently different from other peoples in their close proximity, then they must be considered a group apart.

In 1735, however, one major innovation in empirical categorization would irrevocably transform the very basis of human taxonomy. The Swedish botanist Carolus Linnaeus's *Systema naturae sive regna tria naturae* (1735) presented a revolutionary new formula of taxonomical classification which included a human genus named *Homo*, later to be refined in 1758 as the species *Homo sapiens*. At first glance, Linnaeus's genus *Homo* occupies an unprepossessing corner of the *Systema*'s *Regnum Animale*, ranged in the class of *Quadrupedia* (a pre-emptor of *Mammalia*) alongside *Simia* and *Bradypus* (sloths and anteaters) (1735: n.p. [10]). Yet, this subtle presentation actually plays out an act of incredible scientific audacity: herein, humanity is represented in a language of pure natural history; the genus *Homo* is not justified by God or scripture, by moral duty or by celestial providence but is instead exclusively delineated by the observational gaze of other human beings. *Homo sapiens*' name (knowing man) is its description, and its description is its definition, all reflected in its cursory subtitle, which tells the 'knowing man' reader to *nosce te ipsum* (know thyself). Within twenty years of the *Systema*'s first edition, Linnaeus's new taxonomy had gained him international recognition as a revolutionary natural historian (Koerner 1999: 26). Albrecht von Haller, a Swiss-born contemporary at Göttingen University, declared in 1746 that Linnaeus seemed to think himself a 'second Adam' – and this, remarkably, was exactly how Linnaeus was depicted on the frontispiece of one German edition of the *Systema* in 1760, portrayed in the role of Adam naming the animals of Paradise (Koerner 1999: 24).

It is through the act of naming that Linnaeus set out his new parameters for humanity. The original genus *Homo* was divided into four distinct *varietates* (Linnaeus 1735: n.p. [10]), defined by skin colour and geographical origin. These were, in Linnaeus's order:

Homo europeanus albescens (white European Man),
Homo americanus rubescens (red American Man),
Homo asiaticus fuscus ('sooty'[2] Asian Man),
and *Homo africanus niger* (black African Man).

---

2 The foregoing list uses vocabulary from William Turton's seminal 1806 translation of the *Systema*, but it might be noted that the original Latin edition of 1758 swaps the term *fuscus* (dark, swarthy) for *luridus* (sallow).

Despite their initial appearance, these varieties were fundamentally distinct from later human 'races'. For one thing, the *varietates* were not represented as familial units. Instead, their anatomies were linked to various influences of climate, geography, civility and humoural disposition and were understood chiefly in terms of changeability. That is to say, the *varietates*, in line with most human-variety discourses of the time, are not intended to delineate discrete subspecies of human beings but rather to demonstrate the potential for human anatomy to transform. Nonetheless, the influence of Linnaeus's *varietates* on later templates of human variety cannot be underestimated. Not least, defining the human being as an observable species brought the limits of *in*humanity into much sharper focus.

By the *Systema*'s 1758 edition, the genus *Homo* had been divided into two species: *Homo sapiens* (knowing man) and *Homo troglodytes* (cave-dwelling man). The first of these, *Homo sapiens*, now included two additional varieties: *Homo sapiens ferus* and *Homo sapiens monstrosus*. 'Feral Man' is described as 'four-footed', 'mute' and 'hairy' and is supplemented with a list of recently documented cases of feral children, including the *Juvenis ursinus lithuanus* (Lithuanian 'bear-boys' discovered in 1664), the *Pueri pyrenaici* (the wild children of the Pyrenees, reported in 1719) and *Juvenis Hanoveranus* (best known as Peter the wild boy, who possibly suffered from Pitt-Hopkins Syndrome) (Linnaeus 1758: 20). 'Monstrous Man', meanwhile, represents a fascinating taxon of real, semi-mythological and entirely fictional beings, including mountain dwarves, who are 'small, agile and timid' (probably referring to the Sami people); Patagonian giants, who are 'large and indolent'; the one-testicled *Hottentotti*; the Chinese *Macrocepheli*, who have 'conical heads'; Canadian *Plagiocepheli*, who have 'flattened heads'; and, as previously mentioned, the *Junceae puellae, abdomine attenuato*, referring to 'rush-like' European girls whose waists have become distended from the use of spiral-laced stays (Linnaeus 1758: 22). The 1758 edition's second species, *Homo troglodytes*, represents one of the most puzzling taxa of the entire Linnaean tradition. *Troglodytes* subsumes humanoid creatures that Linnaeus had previously relegated to the monstrous taxon of *Paradoxa*, notably in the *Satyrus*, which had represented a tailed, bearded wild man as widely reported by travellers (1735: 10). In its new iteration, the *Troglodytes* comprised qualities that were at once too animalistic to be human and too human-like to be animal. It simultaneously existed within the sphere of humanity (in the genus *Homo*) and outside it (not being a *sapiens*). That is to say, the taxon approximates the human *varietates* while remaining firmly at a remove from human*ness*. Though Linnaeus directly identifies *Homo troglodytes* with the orang-outang as described by Jacobus Bontius, he also describes his new creature as a *Homo nocturnus* (as opposed to *Homo sapiens*, who is a *Homo diurnus*), characterized by white hair, albino skin and beady, iridescent eyes, dwelling underground in the caves of Ethiopia and the island of Java (1758: 21).

In many ways, then, Linnaeus's *varietates* of *Homo sapiens* are based on the very same sense of anatomical deviance as the monstrous races. Moreover, the respective anatomies are explicitly related to their environment and behaviour, each of which ostensibly acts as an influence on the other. The 1758 edition of the *Systema* introduces the four original *varietates* with a standard set of physical and cultural attributes: each is linked with a humoural disposition while also being aligned with a certain style of clothing, a personal character and a political inclination. The *Homo europeanus*, claims Linnaeus (1758: 21), is characterized by his flowing yellow hair and blue eyes; he is sanguine, acute and inventive; wears 'close vestments'; and is regulated by laws. The *Homo americanus* typically has black hair, a harsh face and a scanty beard; he is choleric, merry, and free, he paints himself with fine red lines and he is governed by customs. The *Homo asiaticus* has dark eyes, black hair and sallow skin; he is melancholic, haughty and avaricious; dresses in loose garments and is governed by his opinions. The most detailed description of all is reserved for the *Homo africanus* – who is described as having black, 'frizzle'd' hair, silky skin, a flat nose, thick lips and a relaxed demeanour; he 'anoints' himself with grease; is phlegmatic, indolent and negligent; and is ruled by 'caprice'. The implicit hierarchical framing of the *varietates* is not difficult to identify. The list spans from light to dark, from rational to irrational and from civilized to barbarous – ending, tellingly, with the entry's only reference to human women. The *Homo africanus niger* is the sole category that includes the sub-category *feminis*, under which Linnaeus notes the *sinus pudoris* (Hottentot apron) and *mammae*, under which he records the attribute of *lactantes prolixae* or prolonged lactation (Linnaeus 1758: 22). Interestingly, this last detail seems to have gone a step too far for the translator William Turton, whose 1806 English edition of the *Systema* omits this mention of African women, despite its appearance in the original Latin tenth and thirteenth editions (Linnaeus 1758: 22; 1788: 1.23; 1806: 1.9).

As far as Linnaeus's reputation extended, for much of the eighteenth century his theories competed with those of the esteemed intendant at Paris's *Jardin du Roi*, Georges Louis Leclerc, Comte de Buffon. An arch-critic of Linnaean taxonomy, Buffon dismissed as patently absurd his contemporary's attempts to order the natural world according to strict categories. In Buffon's mind, Linnaeus privileged logical, rational classifications over the concrete truths of nature, to which classificatory systems rarely if ever aligned. To talk of a 'species', Buffon claimed, was to talk of the perfect specimen, the 'common origin' of that one life form. If nature was properly observed, it would appear obvious to anyone that each individual entity actually represented a slight degeneration from such an ideal, so as to form the infinite building blocks of the Great Chain of being (Sloan 1995: 139). In his *Variétés dans l'espèce humaine* (1749), Buffon proposed that human population diversity, far from constituting a set of distinct *varietates*, should instead be interpreted as individual 'shading', with local skin tones generally moving from light to dark as one approached the equator (with variations depending on altitude and temperature) and back to light again as one continued towards the poles (1749–88: 3.526–30).

Buffon's version of climate theory invoked three main influences. The first was the direct influence of heat, cold, sun, wind and air on the body, which ensured that a people's appearance accorded with their exact latitudinal degree from the equator. The swarthy features of the Spanish, he notes, began to become more perceptible on passing south of Bayonne, while the dark hair and eyes of Latin Europe noticeably declined as one reached England, almost disappearing entirely on arriving in Scandinavia (1749–88: 3.442–3). Human variety, then, was a process that was necessarily 're-enacted' with each generation. In Spain, he remarks, '[t]heir children are born fair and beautiful; but as they grow up, their colour changes in a surprising manner: the operation of the air and of the sun soon renders them so tawny that a Spaniard is easily distinguished from a native of any other country in Europe' (Buffon 1780–5: 3.127; 1749–88: 3.442). Contact with the air, Buffon continued, was a primordial element of this colour change: African children, he notes, were reportedly born with reddish-white skin and remained that way for several days until contact with the outside air (1749–88: 3.522). This indicated that a hereditary process was acting alongside the climate, rendering the effects of the sun and air more extreme. 'It is certain that the rudiments of blackness are communicated to [children] by their parents', Buffon surmises, 'this fact, however, implies not that the colour will remain the same after successive generations' (1780–5: 3.201; 1749–88: 3.523). It might take ten or twelve generations, claimed Buffon, but it seemed likely that the blackest skin could eventually turn white and vice versa (1749–88: 3.524, 3.528, 3.530). Anatomical variations within the same climate were largely attributed to geography. In France, Buffon claims, people who live in elevated terrains are invariably 'more active, nimble, handsome, ingenious and beautiful than those who live on the plains', where the peasants are crude, cumbersome, ill-formed and stupid, along with their women who are almost universally ugly (1780–5:

3.206; 1749–88: 3.529).³ When Spanish or Barbary horses are introduced to such a place, he continues, they will begin to degenerate from the first generation, lest their stock be continually revived by outbreeding with new stallions (Buffon 1749–88: 3.529). The effects of climate were further conditioned through Buffon's second main principle of population diversity, which focused on the effects of nutrition. It was clear to see, he proclaims, that people who lived in the towns and cities were better formed and more beautiful than those in the countryside:

> Coarse, unwholesome and ill-prepared food makes the human species degenerate. All those people who live miserably [i.e., in destitution], are ugly and ill-made. Even in France, the country people are not so beautiful as those who live in towns; and I have often remarked that in those villages where the people are richer and better fed ... the men are likewise more handsome and have better countenances. (Buffon 1780–5: 3.205–6; 1749–88: 3.528)

Buffon's third major influence is inseparable from the first two – reintroducing an old and familiar trope of human physiological difference, namely, the corporeal effect of civility:

> A polished people, who are accustomed to an easy, regular and tranquil mode of life ... will for these reasons alone be more strong, vigorous and handsome, than the savage and lawless nations. ... Supposing two nations, thus differently circumstanced, to live under the same climate, it is reasonable to think that the more savage people would be more ugly, more tawny, more diminutive and more wrinkled than the nation that enjoyed the advantages of society and civilization. (Buffon 1780–5: 3.130–1; 1749–88: 3.446–7)

This effect of civility also seems to have a hereditary component, much like the impact of air upon the skin. Using the word 'race' in its loose and primarily familial capacity, Buffon notes that in Calicut, 'the *naires* or nobles ... seem to be a different race from the burgesses, for the latter, both males and females, are of a smaller stature, and are worse shaped, and more ugly' (Buffon 1780–5: 3.99; 1749–88: 3.414). Only when the degrees of climate, nutrition and civility have reached a certain coalescence, Buffon claims, can the most beautiful variety of human be achieved – which, for him, is obviously and unquestionably the white, metropolitan European. Moreover, if we are to accept this variety as the most beautiful, he suggests, it follows that we should consider it the 'true' human form, against which all other forms should be judged as degenerative (1749–88: 3.530).

---

3 Much of this passage is abridged in Smellie's English edition and subsequent major translations.

Buffon's theories also incorporated some curious and often contradictory ideas about the parameters of humanity. Men in a pure state of nature, he claimed in a 1766 entry in the *Histoire Naturelle* titled the *Nomenclature des singes*, had probably been physically indistinguishable from the higher apes – something which was no longer observable only because the human physique had since been so refined by civil society (1749–88: 14.30). The only difference between the lowest possible humans and the highest possible animals, he concludes, is that the former is possessed of a soul, which is in turn expressed through thoughts, and, consequently, speech (1749–88: 14.30). This idea of speech as a defining boundary between the animal and human world was already a common trope – notably aligning with John Locke's theory of abstraction and speech as a frontier between humanity and beasts (Locke 1690: 2.11.11). Decades previously, Jacobus Bontius had already asserted in his *Historiae naturalis et medicae Indiae orientalis* of 1631 that the orang-outang of Java was so similar in every way to a human being, 'ut nihil ei humani deesse diceres praeter loquelam' ('so that you would say it lacks nothing human except speech') (1631: 85). The question was still featuring regularly in natural history into the late eighteenth century, including fresh dissection reports from the Dutch physician Petrus Camper (1779: 139). Buffon, however, undermines his own theoretical standpoint by referencing reported interbreeding between orang-outangs and the humans who shared their habitat. Describing the Hottentot body as a template for how 'natural' humans may once have looked, he cites the possibility of 'voluntary or forced intermixture of the negresses with the apes; the produce of which has entered into both species' (Buffon 1780–5: 8.66; 1749–88: 14.31). In the context of his comparative anatomy, notes Silvia Sebastiani, this mention of interbreeding between Africans and orang-outangs makes it all the more 'possible to move easily from the savage to the Black, to the orang-utan' (2015: 114). In fact, Buffon was here drawing on widely circulated reports about orang-outang–human interbreeding. Like 'Wild Men' and Satyrs, notes Raymond Corbey, orang-outangs were 'believed to regularly capture women and rape them', a tradition that was frequently used to explain their humanoid appearance (2005: 16). 'The "fact" that Negroes and apes sometimes had "a beastly copulation or conjecture"', claims Winthrop Jordan, was reinforced by the observation that these mysterious great apes were largely found in Africa (1968: 229). Jacobus Bontius had disseminated the same idea a century previously, reporting that the people of Java considered the orang-outang a product of lust between local women and apes (Bontius 1631: 85; Meijer 1999: 125). Even Edward Tyson admitted that the creature's notorious 'venery' often extended beyond their species to 'fair *women*', recounting a story he had heard of 'an ape, which grew so amorous of . . . a celebrated beauty, that no chains could keep him within bounds', and another of a 'woman who had two children by an *ape*' (1699: 42–3).

Such ideas about human–ape hybrids further reveal the discursive overlap between civility as an agent of anatomical change and developing notions of heredity and its role in physical variety. Membership of the human species was effectively gauged on the weight of two criteria: the fecundity principle (the ability to successfully procreate with a human) and certain markers of human civility (such as the faculty of speech, in the case of Buffon and others). If orang-outangs could achieve both, even theoretically, this not only made a case for their humanity but brought the humanity of other human varieties into question. That was certainly the argument put forth by the British colonial administrator Edward Long, whose infamous *History of Jamaica* (1774) already stood out as one of the most extreme works of pro-slavery racialism of the entire century. Orang-outangs, Long reports, were known to use knives and forks, to live in huts, to have recognized the benefits of bleeding to relieve illness and indeed to have endeavoured 'to surprize and carry off negroe women into their woody retreats' (1774: 2.360). If animals were capable of such human-like behaviour, he proposed, were the uncivilized mores of Africans really enough to qualify them as human? The denizens of 'Negro-land', Long declared, were 'void of genius, and seem almost incapable of making any progress in civility or science'; such beings could thus boast little pretention to humanity apart from 'what arises from their exterior form' (1774: 2.353). If the orang-outang was recognized as an 'inferior species' of mankind, one would also have to admit that the African too was a species apart. 'I do not think that an oran-outang husband would be any dishonour to an Hottentot female', Long concludes, 'for what are these Hottentots? . . . in many respects they are more like beasts than men . . . that the oran-outang and some races of black men are very nearly allied is, I think, more than probable' (1774: 2.364–5).

The mere suggestion that orang-outangs were somehow human – whether on account of interspecies copulation, on account of their capacity for human civility or both – held implications for the whole spectrum of human hierarchy. This is particularly apparent in the work of James Burnett, Lord Monboddo. A Scottish judge and notorious eccentric, Monboddo's forays into natural history were pointedly ridiculed by his contemporaries, including Blumenbach who, in 1806, dismissed him as a 'downright caprice-monger' (Blumenbach 1806a: 296). In retrospect, however, Monboddo's theories about human variety were no more fantastical than the more widely accepted doctrines of his time. In fact, his most scorned theory – the suggestion that great apes may have potentially *transformed* into human beings over many generations – would in later decades be celebrated by evolutionists as evidence he was a visionary before his time (see, e.g., Knight 1900: 20). Monboddo's *Origin and Progress of Language* (1774) takes a Rousseauian perspective on the ourang-outang question, drawing significantly from the French philosopher's *Discours sur l'origine et les fondements de l'inégalité parmi les hommes* (1755). Rousseau had referenced the Dutch Physician Olfert Dapper's reports that orang-outangs might represent human–ape hybrids, and he speculated that certain hominids apes might be a lost tribe of *hommes sauvages*, having wandered the woods in a primitive state since ancient times (1755: 222, 225). Like Rousseau, Monboddo dismissed the received notion that mute creatures could not form ideas, believing instead that speech was an acquired trait (1774: 191). This one attribute left aside, he contended, the creatures were 'exactly of the human form . . . it is impossible we can refuse them the appellation of men' (Monboddo 1774: 186, 188).

Both Monboddo and Rousseau, notes Dror Wahrman, envisioned humanity as existing in a state of progress, 'turning ape into human through cultural tutelage' (2004: 133). Monboddo, however, pushes this argument even further. If apes could transform into men through self-improvement, he ponders, could men transform into even more sophisticated beings? 'By education and culture continued for many years', he theorizes in the *Origins*, mankind could 'be transformed almost into an animal of another species' (1774: 23). If they continued to cultivate their minds, 'human nature may, by such culture, be so exalted, as to . . . possess the rank of such as are immediately above us in the chain of being' (1774: 23). Some years later, Monboddo noted in his *Ancient Metaphysics* (1779–99) that those endowed with the highest levels of civility historically tended to intermarry among themselves – and it might thus be questioned whether anatomical differences observed within the same climate should be attributable to 'race; or, in other words, whether the distinction of birth and family, of which we hear so much, be not merely a political distinction, without any foundation in nature' (1779–99: 3.235, 3.233). After all, he argues, it was quite natural at the dawn of civilization for the 'excellency of the species' to form distinct family lines, which instinctively remained separate from their inferiors over time (1779–99: 4.178). It had been reported, he claims, that the princes of India were 'handsomer, of larger size, and more dignified appearance, than the rest of the people', while the Brahmins, 'being the best race of men in India . . . are easily distinguished from the rest of the people by their look, their figure and their appearance' (1779–99: 4.206–7). To this evidence he adds recent reports from the South Seas, wherein Louis Antoine de Bougainville had judged that 'the nobles of Otaheite are so much distinguished [in size and figure] from the Tootoos, or lower sort of people, that he is inclined to believe them to be of a different nation' (1779–99: 4.207; see Chapter 9). The same, Monboddo concludes, must once have been the case for Britain's own nobles – before their bloodlines were so recently diluted by mercantile upstarts. 'I am persuaded', he pronounces, 'that, in Britain, and in every other part of Europe, a man of rank and family was, some hundred years ago, as readily known at first sight as a horse of blood is now' (1779–99: 4.207).

Civility and heredity became increasingly intertwined with natural history over the second half of the eighteenth century. The same year as Monboddo's *Origins* and Long's *History of Jamaica* were published, the Anglo-Irish physician and playwright Oliver Goldsmith released an amateur work of natural history that would have surprisingly resonant consequences for the framework of human-variety theory in Britain and Ireland. In his own day, Goldsmith's *History of the Earth and Animated Nature* (1774) was snubbed as a piece of ill-informed hackwork and it has largely been neglected, if not dismissed, by historians until relatively recently. Yet, Goldsmith's work was actually pivotal to the history of race in Britain and Ireland – not because it was original or innovative (on the contrary, the *History* contains so much material directly translated from Buffon that one 1810 edition printed by the Apollo Press described its authorship as 'from M. de Buffon, Goldsmith and others'), but because it was so accessible. Much as Alexander Pope had done for the philosophical principle of universal plenitude, Goldsmith presented human-variety theory in a relatively digestible format and his text ultimately endured as a primary English-language reference for European natural history for over half a century (Lytton Sells 1977: 178). In essence, Goldsmith's work re-presented the ideas of various major theorists, often erroneously, as if they formed one comprehensive doctrine. By consequence, he inadvertently highlights the common bedrock of human hierarchy that underpinned them all. He was also moved to create his very own model of major human varieties, which would, somewhat haphazardly, go on to exert an astonishing degree of influence on the formation of modern race theory.

Goldsmith based his schema of human variety first on Linnaeus's original four *varietates* of Man, before embellishing this list with two additional 'varieties' he gleaned from Buffon's extensive catalogue of human anatomical diversity. From studying Linnaeus and Buffon together, in other words, Goldsmith concluded that there were not four but six principal varieties of human being: the Laplanders (including the Arctic peoples of the New World), the Tartars or Chinese (East Asians), the Asiatics (South Asians), the Africans, the Americans and the

Figure 8 *The Laplander*, from Oliver Goldsmith (1774), *A History of the Earth and Animated Nature*, London: J. Nourse, p. 2.213. Courtesy of Alamy.

Europeans (Goldsmith 1774: 2.12–230; see Figure 8). Furthermore, Goldsmith's 'hybrid' system of human variety integrates both the Linnaean notion of fixed human types and the Buffonian notion of skin-colour gradation by climate, nutrition and civility. That is to say, while Goldsmith's system distinguishes defined varietal boundaries within the human species, the influence of climate can lead to movement between his varieties. Most importantly, he distils the ostensible differences between his six varieties by defining them above all by skin colour. Different skin colours, Goldsmith asserts, 'are actual marks of degeneracy of the human form; and we may consider the European figure and colour as standards to which to refer all other varieties, and with which to compare them' (1774: 2.239). In this, notes Wheeler, Goldsmith became 'the first [natural historian] to single out [skin colour] above all other characteristics by which humans were distinguished', while his *History* stood out as 'one of the only natural histories in the eighteenth century to have illustrations of varieties of men' (2000: 180, 243).

Goldsmith's interpretation of Linnaeus and Buffon, confused as it was, rippled persistently through subsequent works of natural history in Europe. Most notably, it would appear that Johann Friedrich Blumenbach studied Buffonian principles of human variety at least partly through a reading of Goldsmith. In the 1795 edition of Blumenbach's *De generis humani varietate nativa*, one of the landmark texts of modern race theory (which will be explored more closely in subsequent chapters), he attributes 'six varieties of Man' to Buffon. Buffon, of course, had never compiled a list of human types at all. Instead, Blumenbach cites *Goldsmith's* categories of (1) Lapp or Polar, (2) Tartar (3) South Asian, (4) European, (5) Ethiopian and (6) American (1795a: 267). This would suggest that the theorist who largely established the modern vocabulary of race theory was sometimes more familiar with Goldsmith's flawed interpretation of Buffon than with the work of the French theorist himself. In fact, in the original 1775 edition of *De generis* Blumenbach references Goldsmith's six varieties without making any mention of Buffon at all (1775: 99). It therefore seems probable that Blumenbach accepted Goldsmith's compound interpretation of Linnaeus and Buffon as authentic Buffonian theory. The reverberations of Goldsmith's popular work did not end with Blumenbach. The success of Goldsmith's *History* in the English-speaking world meant that many of his errors (and this one in particular) became received wisdom for subsequent scholars. By 1810 Buffon's supposed 'six varieties' were already being referenced in *Encyclopaedia Britannica's* entry on 'Man' (1810: 544), and today they continue to resurface on a regular basis in the academic literature of race studies.

Another aspect of Goldsmith's work, which seems to have considerably influenced later theorists, was his rendition of the Buffonian principle that nourishment and civility worked in conjunction with climate to mould the human body. Goldsmith considers the states of barbarity and civility to be universal conditions, expressing themselves in the same way on every continent and in every culture (1774: 2.231). Even in the hottest of climates, Goldsmith proclaims, certain peoples will manifest lighter skin tones because of their different levels of civility:

> [T]his [variation] ever proceeds from some accidental causes; either from the country lying higher and consequently the country being bolder ... or the natives bathing oftener and leading a more civilized life ... we find the peasants of every country, who are most exposed to the weather, a shade darker than the higher ranks of people. (Goldsmith 1774: 2.235–6)

Goldsmith's uncivilized peoples are invariably less sensitive, physically and mentally, than the more civilized Europeans – an idea, as will be seen in the next chapter, which already characterized medical interpretations of social rank. Some 'women of savage nations' he confidently affirms, just like 'the hard-working wives of the peasants amongst ourselves' experience the pains of childbirth 'with much less sensibility' (Goldsmith 1774: 2.224). Such pains, he adds, 'seem greatest in all countries where the women are most delicate, or the constitution enfeebled by luxury or indolence' (1774: 2.224). This was an inescapably loaded statement: the idea of savage women giving birth without pain carried with it a 'whiff of polygenism', notes Suman Seth, since the agonies of labour were associated with the punishment of Eve (Seth 2018: 181). By the early eighteenth century, the notion had already become 'a common axis on which to compare the various peoples of the world' (Seth 2018: 181). It would also become, as discussed in Chapter 6, a corporeal symbol of social rank.

The clothes of barbarous nations, claims Goldsmith, which are designed to accommodate the more 'sensual' pleasures of their inhabitants, reflected an attendant dearth of sensibility. The 'effeminate silk vestments' of the Asian peoples are, for Goldsmith, inextricable from the idea that Asians are 'satisfied with sensual happiness alone, they find no pleasure in thinking... [they are] too dull to find rapture in any pleasures, and too indolent to turn their gravity into wisdom' (1774: 2.225). A chronic lack of civilized behaviour, he explains, is also the reason why North Americans manifest a 'tawny' skin colour despite living at roughly the same distance from the equator as Europeans. Not only does their savage mode of life leave them at the mercy of the sun, but they actively contribute to the darkening of their skin by 'painting [it] with red ochre and anointing it with the fat of bears' (Goldsmith 1774: 2.236). The ostensibly civilized behaviour of Europeans, conversely, including the use of undergarments and tight-fitting clothes among wealthier ranks, can be seen as 'precautions to brighten their colour', which, if the Amerindians would take the pains to emulate, 'they would in time come to have similar complexions; and, perhaps; dispute the prize of beauty' (Goldsmith 1774: 2.236).

Blumenbach's *De generis*, originally published as an MD thesis one year after the publication of Goldsmith's *History*, also seems to have taken significant influence from Goldsmith's thoughts on civility and climate theory. 'It is scarce worthwhile', Blumenbach declares,

> to notice the well-known difference which occurs in the inhabitants of one in the same country, whose skin varies wonderfully in colour according to the kind of life they lead. The face of the working man or the artisan, exposed to the force of the sun and the weather, differs as much from the cheeks of a delicate female, as the man himself does from the dark American, and he again from the Ethiopian.

> Anatomists not unfrequently fall in with the corpses of the lowest sort of men, whose reticulum comes much nearer to the blackness of the Ethiopians, than to the brilliancy of the higher class of European. (Blumenbach 1775: 108)

This passage reinforces links between social rank and human-variety theory from multiple perspectives. First, the darker skin of the 'working man' – just like Goldsmith's darker-skinned peasants, or Buffon's ugly, physically deformed and mentally diminished rustics – is here understood as a widely acknowledged aspect of the lower orders. Second, the lower ranks, with their presumed darker skin, are rationally considered on the same scale as racialized varieties. Blumenbach posits a logical digression from European labourer to Amerindian and from Amerindian to Ethiopian. Third, the 'brilliancy of the higher class of European' here unambiguously identifies elite society with 'racial' (a term which, in Blumenbach, we can begin to understand in its modern sense) superiority; Blumenbach is at once asserting that social elites manifest brilliant whiteness – the 'whitest' of white peoples – and expressing this whiteness as part of a sequence of degeneration which first passes through the labouring poor before moving into the hierarchically organized colour variations of the human species.

By the later decades of the eighteenth century, assertions of civility as a marker of social rank and civility as an agent of varietal adaptation had become all but indistinguishable. 'Stereotypes of the lower classes and of non-Europeans came to be linked together', notes Silvia Sebastiani, through the central idea that exotic peoples and the lower orders both represented a degeneration from humanity's perfect form (2000: 224). The entry 'negro' in the third edition of the *Encyclopaedia Britannica* (1788–97), Sebastiani notes, agreed that the 'way of life that shaped the form and character of men' in far-off countries was also observable among the domestic poor (2000: 222). 'Besides the climate', the *Encyclopaedia* records, 'food and clothing and modes of life have prodigious effects on the human form and features. This is apparent even in polished societies, where the poor and labouring part of the community are much more coarse in their features' (1788–97: 12.795). One of the *Encyclopaedia*'s primary sources for this entry was the ardent monogenist Samuel Stanhope Smith, who had written extensively in his *Essay on the Causes and Variety of Complexion and Figure in the Human Species* (1787) about the effects of civility on the human anatomy. 'The poor and labouring part of the community', Stanhope Smith had observed,

> are usually more swarthy and squalid in their complexion, more hard in their features, and more coarse and ill-formed in their limbs, than persons of better

fortune, and more liberal means of subsistence. They want the delicate tints of colour, the pleasing regularity of feature, and the elegance and fine proportions of person. (Stanhope Smith 1787: 52)

This phenomenon, he continued, was visible throughout the ranks of white labourers in America, who were distinctly darker than their British counterparts. It was most marked of all in the poor and labouring ranks of Georgia and the Carolinas, who 'degenerate to a complexion that is but a few shades lighter than that of the Iroquois' (Stanhope Smith 1787: 22). The well-known effects of climate, Stanhope Smith contended, were 'augmented by a savage state, and corrected by a state of civilisation' (1787: 44). Some American labourers had thereby become so unrecognizable that 'the philosophers who espouse the hypothesis of different species of men would have produced them in proof' (Smith 1787: 23). A similar dynamic, he notes, could be observed among slaves. Field slaves, who 'retain many of the customs and manners of their African ancestors', were consequently 'slow in changing the aspect and figure of Africa' (Smith 1787: 58). Domestic slaves, on the other hand, quickly acquired 'agreeable and regular features, and the expressive countenance of civilized society':

> [they] are straight and well proportioned, their hair extended to three, four, and, sometimes even, to six or eight inches; the size and shape of the mouth handsome, their features regular, their capacity good, and their look animated. (Smith 1787: 58)

Meanwhile, Stanhope Smith echoed Monboddo in linking the anatomical effects of civility with the most 'civilized' members of society. Noble anatomies were distinct from those of the common people, he contended, because 'such distinctions become more considerable by time, after families have held for ages the same stations in society'. Having better choice when it came to matrimonial connections, 'the great and noble ... have generally distinguished their order, as much by elegant proportions of person, and beautiful features' (Stanhope Smith 1787: 74). The countries in which the physical difference between high and low was most conspicuous were therefore 'those countries in which the laws have made the most complete and permanent division of ranks' (Smith 1787: 53). Such effects were observable in Britain, he asserts – not so much in England, where the dependably indomitable spirit of liberty and meritocracy had dimmed such distinctions – but in Scotland, where the anatomy of clan chiefs was almost irreconcilable with that of their subjects:

> What an immense difference exists in Scotland between the chiefs and the commonality of the highland clans? If they had been separately found in different

countries, the philosophy of some writers would have ranged them in different species. A similar distinction takes place between the nobility and peasantry of France, of Spain, of Italy, of Germany. (Smith 1787: 53–4)

In fact, Stanhope Smith sees the same effects replicated in nobilities across the world. Again echoing Monboddo, he insists that the '*naires* or nobles of Calicut' have frequently been taken for 'a different race from the populace', so striking is that 'manly beauty and elevated stature so frequently found with the profession of arms, especially when united with nobility of descent'. The working people, meanwhile, are not only 'more deformed and diminutive in their persons' but – crucially – are 'more black' (1787: 54).

* * *

From tall tales of monstrous races, through the various human varieties of Linnaeus, Buffon and Goldsmith, and into Monboddo or Stanhope Smith's vision of anatomically superior nobles, the idea of civility and its influence on the human body remained a benchmark of human-variety theory throughout the eighteenth century. Linnaeus's delineation of human types as geographically, physiologically and culturally distinct was in many ways countered, but in many other ways enriched, by Buffon's theories of individual degeneration in extreme environments. Goldsmith's subsequent inference of six principal types allowed these theories to convey a certain hierarchical determinism while simultaneously assigning that determinism to various levels of degeneration. Meanwhile, Monboddo's Rousseauiean approach allowed him to draw direct links between the underlying implications of climate-based transformation and the developing ideas of anatomy as a reflection of pure, untainted genealogy. In short, climate theory was developing a framework of corporeal inequality; a catalogue of expressions of the human body in which each classification was one step further removed from the ideal shape, mind and sensibility of a perfect human being. Human-variety theory, it might be said, was taking on the same lineal and hierarchical shape as the societies which created it.

6

Superior blood

Horses, ethno-histories and hereditary disease

For most of the eighteenth century, what we would think of today as 'heredity' was splintered into multiple and often mutually incoherent ideas about intergenerational trait transmission. These notions, dispersed across various fields including medicine, philosophy, jurisprudence and animal breeding – not to mention the fields of human variety and genealogy – contained many of the seeds that would eventually grow into a unified biological concept of heredity in the following century (Poczai and Santiago-Blay 2021: 1). The fact that this stand-alone biological process would not be fully formulated until the nineteenth century, however, can sometimes obscure the intense scrutiny that physicians and natural historians applied to hereditary phenomena before this time. Scholars of heredity, notes Kevin Siena, have typically pinpointed the turn of the nineteenth century 'as a moment when ideas about heredity hardened', which can create some notable historiographical inconsistencies, particularly regarding eighteenth-century enquiries into hereditary disease (2019: 233). Franck Roumy, for instance, stresses that heredity in eighteenth-century France was a purely legal concept, distinct from bloodlines and the body, and derived from the ancient legislative codes of *hereditas* (2008: 41). Yet, this is just one dimension of a much broader concept. Denis Diderot and Jean le Rond d'Alembert's *Encyclopédie*, to take one example, does indeed define *hérédité* as a matter of succession and inheritance of office but goes on to explain that the adjective *héréditaire* also describes diseases that pass directly from parents to children (1765: 157). The Spanish Royal Academy's *Diccionario de la Lengua Castellana* (1726–39) likewise mentions that the 'legal' term *heredar* can sometimes refer to the 'power of the blood' to transmit good or bad qualities from father to son (1734: 141). The English vocabulary of heredity was equally capacious. In its adjectival form, notes Carlos López-Beltrán, the English word 'hereditary' forged an analogy between the juridical language of intergenerational property transfer and the transmission of traits from one human body to another (1994: 211). Even at that, the analogy was already self-referential: if we accept that hereditary trait transmission within lineal families functioned as a metaphor based on intergenerational property transfer, we must also accept that intergenerational property transfer was built around the institution of lineal family and its descending bloodlines. The disparate notions of trait transmission that existed in the eighteenth century thus offer an invaluable insight in so far as they represent a kind of deconstructed heredity – highlighting the desires, motivations and power dynamics that underpinned hereditarian thinking in the first place. The centrality of hereditary trait transmission to the skin-colour caste systems of Atlantic slave societies (see Chapter 7) is a case in point, attesting to quite how consequential eighteenth-century understandings of hereditary phenomena could be. To explore the common hereditarian framework with which both nobility and race engaged, this chapter examines three ostensibly different models of blood-based trait transmission in eighteenth-century Britain: the culture of elite horse breeding, the discourse of ethno-history and, perhaps most importantly, the realm of hereditary disease. Each, it will be seen, found recourse in the paradigmatic codes of nobility as a template for temporalized and bodily human hierarchy.

* * *

The early eighteenth-century craze for elite horse breeding in England was largely inspired by the physical magnificence of so-called Arab stallions. Since the seventeenth century, in particular, lighter and more agile horses had been regularly imported from North Africa and the Middle East in order to bolster the more cumbersome and diminutive native stock (Nash 2005: 248). While many traditional chivalric pursuits had long since disappeared, these fine animals helped contribute to the contemporary fashion for equine dressage – a stylized pastiche of martial equestrianism popular among the upper orders (Nash 2005: 248). The most renowned of England's seventeenth-century horse breeders was William Cavendish, 1st Duke of Newcastle upon Tyne, who published one of the bestselling equine care manuals in early modern Europe. The volume was originally printed in French in 1658, but the two English translations appearing in 1667 (*A New Method and Extraordinary Invention of Dressing Horses*) and 1743 (*A General System of Horsemanship in All Its Branches*) attest to its continued popularity well after the author's death. Cavendish had been a Knight of the Bath, a resolute royalist and one of the wealthiest men in England. His work, which pioneered a peculiarly nationalistic equine training regime, was commonly presented as a Protestant, English counterpoint to French *haute école* tradition of dressage (Raber 2005: 233–4). When training a horse, Cavendish asserted, it was first necessary to appreciate their unique national character. Turkish horses, for instance, were 'swift, strong, and good winded', while Barbary horses 'always retain their original natural strength and vigour' (1743: 1.21). No more than in human *varietates*, a horse's exposure to civility was impossible to separate from its blood. Each country's traditional mode of horse breeding was understood to have moulded that horse's physical and mental attributes. The natural grandeur of Middle Eastern stallions was commonly attributed to their grooms having maintained them in a state of luxury while jealously guarding their precious bloodlines over the course of millennia. This was a belief that persisted until at least the end of the century. 'The Arabs take every precaution to keep [their horses] pure and unmixed', declared the natural historian Thomas Bewick in 1790, 'they preserve with the greatest care, and for an amazing length of time, the genealogies of their horses – those of the first kind are called nobles, being "of a pure and ancient race, purer than milk"' (1790: 5).

Successive editions of Cavendish's *New Method* accordingly illustrate the unique qualities of different horse breeds in a series of plates, wherein each equine variety is depicted alongside a dark-skinned groom, ostensibly representing its nation of origin. The grooms, in fact, are arguably the most important elements of these images. They communicate Cavendish's dictum that a horse's character is moulded by its environment, with the complexion of the groom denoting the specific environment and brand of civility that had engendered the horse alongside him. The models for these images, note Susanne Seymour and Sheryllynne Haggerty, were possibly servants in Cavendish's own household or might have lived in Antwerp where the original paintings had been commissioned (2010: 38–41). At the same time, notes Karen Raber, by depicting his exotic horses and grooms in the bucolic landscape of his own English estate, Cavendish depicts both as harnessed by a firm English hand (2005: 238–40). In one illustration, Cavendish is depicted triumphant on the battlefield, rearing aloft a Barbary stallion while his page boy looks on in admiration (see Figure 9). He has tamed the equine magnificence of the east, we may infer, appropriated its strengths and passions and rendered them still more glorious through the application of English virtue.

By the beginning of the eighteenth century, however, something else was happening in the world of English horse breeding. The traditional method of improving horse stocks had, until this point, mostly relied on the practice of outbreeding: that is, regularly hiring prized Arab stallions to replenish one's stock

Figure 9 *The Duke of Newcastle upon Tyne, with Page*. Engraving by Peeter Couwet after Abraham van Diepenbeeck (*c.* 1658), from William Cavendish (1743), *A General System of Horsemanship in All Its Branches*, London: J. Brindley. © National Portrait Gallery.

(Nash 2005: 262). From around the turn of the century English stud farmers increasingly sought to 'preserve the pedigree' of their best specimens by emulating Eastern breeders. The goal for many was to create their own, consummately English 'horses of blood', combining the agility of an Arab steed with the doughty strength of native varieties. From the 1680s onward, breeders began to track and document the exact degree of Middle Eastern or North African blood in each breeding pair. By the 1720s, particularly pure specimens were already being referred to as 'thoroughbreds', lending a new vocabulary to the idea of elite blood in horses. Certain blood credentials bestowed a higher value than others, particularly those linked to three celebrated foundation sires that were brought to England between 1680 and 1729: the Byerly Turk, the Darley Arabian and the Godolphin Arabian (Nash 2005: 250). This new and ostensibly English strain of horse was bestowed with its own nationalistic origin story. The Godolphin Arabian was commonly said to have been gifted to Louis XV in 1730, only to be neglected and later abandoned to pull carts through the streets of Paris. Only the discerning eye of a passing Englishman, Edward Coke, was able to recognize the innate nobility of this unassuming creature – whom, the story goes, he immediately transported by to London to beget the greatest race of horses ever to have lived (Nash 2005: 254).

There was one obvious reference point for a true horse of blood: nobility. Breeding methods promoted by equestrians such as William Osmer in the mid-eighteenth century, explicitly sought to establish and maintain a *nobility* of horses – mimicking the genealogical patterns of the upper orders in order to preserve the integrity of Eastern bloodlines. '[T]he thorough-bred horse', claimed Osmer in his *Treatise on the Diseases and Lameness of Horses* (1760), 'when properly chosen, is, for every purpose, far superior to him that is half-bred' (1760: 267). Horses, of course, were already considered particularly 'noble' animals. Expensive to acquire, even more expensive to maintain and requiring substantial tracts of land, they had stood as symbols of hereditary privilege since antiquity. As the fashion for dressage amply demonstrated, equestrianism also allowed the upper orders to style themselves after a more martial, chivalric past, wherein the physical resplendence of the equine body implicitly suggested the corporeal excellence of its master. Perhaps it was because of these ancient associations that thorough-breeders were so ready to disregard the established wisdom of animal husbandry when it came to their horses of blood. Their pursuit of ever-purer bloodlines did not resemble selective breeding as we know it today, nor did it align with the 'in-an-in' breeding methods, widely proliferated by Robert Bakewell later in the century. Privileging bloodline credentials above all else meant that the best sire was not always paired with the best mare. In fact, the growing preference for illustrious genealogies over physical robustness constituted a growing worry for some breeders, including Osmer who reminded readers in his *Dissertation on Horses* (1756) that, for all the importance of blood, they should not ignore anatomical form and function (1756: 9, 13). Those same readers might have been forgiven for following the advice of other stud farmers such as Richard Wall, who, in his *Dissertation on the Breeding of Horses upon Philosophical and Experimental Principles* (1758), announced that 'there is one fundamental maxim which will always hold good . . . PROPERTIES DESCEND' (1758: 56). A well-bred sire and dam, Wall declared, 'ought to be the first and principle care' in the mind of any breeder, who should 'be likewise partial to the merits of their ancestors through as many generations as possible!' (1756: 58).

The documentation for equine bloodlines would eventually be formalized in James Weatherby's *General Stud Book* of 1791, which purported to trace the lineage of all thoroughbred horses back to the late seventeenth century. The precise parentage and fraternity of every horse of blood is carefully documented in the *Stud Book*, usually accompanied by a breeder with comparable ancestral credentials. The horses' value, like that of their owner, effectively depended on the logic of *eugeneia*: inherent excellence was transmitted genealogically and would invariably blossom under appropriate cultivation. The very application of *eugeneia* reasoning to animals thereby created an interesting dynamic of its own. First, this was an idea of nobility conceived purely in terms of anatomical excellence and presumed to be comparable to a certain corporeal excellence among the upper orders; second, in seeking to emulate noble blood purity, thorough-breeders were in actual fact reproducing a *political* strategy inherent to the noble paradigm, which in turn relied on presenting itself as an inexorable element of natural order; and third, the transplantation of purity politics from the realm of nobility to that of animal husbandry created an arena in which *eugeneia* could be tested in an almost empirical manner.

Breeding animals according to noble genealogy came with obvious implications for nobles themselves. In fact, one of the most famous literary representations of horses in the early eighteenth century, Book IV of Jonathan Swift's *Gulliver's Travels* (1726) used the thoroughbred craze to satirize the empty ostentation of noble genealogies. Swift's Houyhnhnm land 'reflects ironically upon a nation obsessed with horses', notes Donna Landry, 'but also one in which that obsession was increasingly focused on matters of breeding, with its overtones of race' (2009: 145). The Houyhnhnms, a literal nobility of horses, are strictly stratified – physically, socially and politically – according to their bloodlines. As the Master Houyhnhnm explains to Gulliver:

> the *White*, the *Sorrel*, and the *Iron-Grey*, were not so exactly shaped as the *Bay*, the *Dapple-grey*, and the *Black*; not born with equal talents of mind, or a capacity to improve them; and therefore continued always in the condition of servants, without ever aspiring to match out of their own race. (1726: 2.95)

One of the main satirical elements of the Houyhnhnms is that these talking thoroughbreds can boast far greater genealogical integrity than the humans upon which they are implicitly modelled. It was not until the *Travels* were republished by George Faulkner in 1735 that the rest of the chapter would appear in something approximating its original, uncensored form (Karian 2002: 14). Gulliver explains to his Houyhnhnm host:

> *Nobility* among us [is] altogether a different thing. . . . Our young *noblemen* are bred from their childhood in idleness and luxury . . . when their fortunes are almost ruined, they marry some woman of mean birth . . . the productions of such marriages are generally scrophulous, rickety or deformed children; by which means the family seldom continues above three generations, unless the wife take care to provide a healthy farmer among her neighbours or domesticks, in order to improve and continue the breed . . . a weak diseased body, a meagre

countenance, and sallow complexion, are the true marks of *noble blood*; and a healthy robust appearance is so disgraceful in a man of quality, that the world concludes his real father to have been a groom or a coachman. (Swift 1735: 332)

The joke, here, pivots on Gulliver's naïve suggestion that noble families are driven to find recourse in the more traditional methods of 'outbreeding' to keep their stock healthy. 'Thoroughbred nobles' are indeed corporeally distinct from commoners, it is implied, but only because their breeding practices render them vulnerable to degeneration. The humour was certainly not lost on Swift's original publisher Benjamin Motte, whose adjustments to the 1726 edition speak for themselves: 'noble blood' was changed to 'a great man', 'domesticks' was changed to 'acquaintances' and 'groomsman or coachman' was changed to 'one of the inferiors of the family' (Swift 1726: 2.97). In any case, this is an interesting (and early) denigration of nobility as having become degenerate through inbreeding – a practice that, traditionally, was studiously avoided in animal husbandry. Swift's association of inbreeding with hereditary diseases, meanwhile, holds a significance of its own, which will be explored later in this chapter.

The very existence of thorough-breeding in the eighteenth century highlights a developing sense of corporeal heredity that was directly informed by the noble tradition of *eugeneia*. The hereditary dynamics of nobility were here being transposed in a practical manner onto a set of animals in the earnest pursuit of improving their physical stature over the course of multiple generations. Moreover, the role of strictly controlled genealogy in the anatomical superiority of thoroughbreds would eventually become a favourite analogy among those who wished to defend the importance of noble blood. It might be remembered that Lord Monboddo, when describing his physically superior 'governing man', drew comparisons with well-bred horses. 'Nobody will deny, who knows anything of horses', he declared in his *Ancient Metaphysics* (1779–99)

> that the spirit of a horse of blood is very different from that of a common horse . . . he has a gentleness of nature and a kindly disposition . . . which distinguishes him from a vulgar horse . . . I say that the character of a governing man is as easily to be discerned . . . as blood is in a horse, by his look, and movements. (Monboddo 1779–99: 3.237, 4.179)

Monboddo did not doubt reports that Arabian horses boasted genealogies dating back 2000 years, he adds in a note, since 'the genealogies of their horses are on record, as our lands are in Scotland, and the succession of heirs in them' (1779–99: 3.237). This resilience of the equine-noble comparison – with horses representing a readily observable case study of descent in action and nobility representing a touchstone of genealogical engineering – thus demonstrates quite how politically loaded notions of heredity could be. Like nobility, notes Richard Nash, thoroughbreds are neither entirely real nor entirely imaginary; 'they operate as "natural" living metaphors for a particular set of cultural values that they thereby reify as innate' (2005: 246).

* * *

Around the same time as the thorough-breeding craze was gaining momentum in England, certain commentators began to emphasize the historical role of genealogy over environment in the formation of national character. Some of the most interesting examples of such 'ethno-history' can be found in the work of the French nobleman Henri Bernard, Comte de Boulainvilliers (1658–1722). Said to have been France's first *anglomaniac*, Boulainvilliers' fondness for the English was amply returned by his admirers across the Channel (Ellis 1988: 166). When the first (and posthumous) edition of Boulainvilliers' *État de la France* was printed in London in 1727, its subscribers' list included forty-four of the most illustrious peers in Britain, the entire royal family, the Lord Lieutenant of Ireland and a host of international nobles. 'The subject [Boulainvilliers] treats of is so interesting to a free people' declared the volume's translator Charles Forman, 'and so demonstrably shews the superiority of your royal British progenitors over the generality of French kings . . . [that] he cannot possibly fail of meeting with a gracious reception from a Prince [of Wales], sprung from the loins of the protectors of liberty' (1739: v). Though Forman somewhat exaggerates Boulainvilliers' supplications, the Frenchman had certainly succeeded in flattering the English monarchy and peerage. Unlike the French *noblesse*, he claimed, who had been emasculated by Louis XIV's absolute rule, English peers had been wise enough to consolidate their incontrovertible claims to political power (1739: 129–30). Boulainvilliers' lavish praise for English nobility, however, also stemmed from a peculiar conviction. In his *Essais sur la Noblesse de France* (1732) he theorized that the English and French nobilities were in fact sprung from the same nation, distinct from the common people of both countries by way of their pure Germanic bloodlines.

The very idea of 'nation' is significant in the context of racialized thought and its development at this time. A nation did not delineate the kind of geopolitical territory that we might now understand as a nation state. Rather, it usually designated a group of people, often incorporating the received wisdom that those people's character, culture and appearance had been shaped by the land upon which they lived. Samuel Johnson's *Dictionary of the English Language* would define 'nation' in 1755 as 'a people distinguished from another people; generally by a language, original [i.e., origin], or government' (1755: entry 'nation'). The term's relative flexibility rendered it a useful mode of group distinction both within the metropoles of Europe and in the discourses of colonization and the classification of global populations. The idea that different nations manifested different mental and physical characteristics, asserts Kathleen Wilson, had arguably become the most widespread method of stratifying humanity by the eighteenth century, providing a map of 'human diversity, human nature, and the impact of climate, government, language, and laws on both' (2003: 6). As seen in the previous chapter, the political regime of a nation could mould its people's character, but the people thus moulded could in turn influence the polity of the nation. Nation, from this point of view, implies a certain degree of agency that is markedly absent from the idea of race. The gradual shift away from 'nation' as a form of varietal group distinction over the course of the eighteenth century, suggests Nicholas Hudson, could be seen to reflect a 'general influence of imperialism and slavery', which deliberately sought to deny 'nationhood' to whole swathes of the global population (1996: 251). By redefining colonized nations in terms of race, all distinctions of government and society are cast aside in favour of an essentialist discourse of unchangeable, inborn identity. This process also had racializing implications for European nations, by way of defining them against human varieties rather than against nations comparable to their own.

The work of Boulainvilliers falls right at the axis of this complex power relationship between government, nation and race. The nobilities of both England and France, he declared in his *Essais*, were descended from Frankish invaders who had ruled France since the sixth century – dividing the country into a caste of Frankish *seigneurs* and *maîtres* who ruled benevolently over 'all the vanquished and the Gaul, who themselves came to be like the people, the nation, in German *die Leute* [the people], *homine* [Man], *populus* [the people], *gens* [race or clan]' (Boulainvilliers 1732: *supplément*, 3).[1] That is to say, a conglomeration of noble races, conserving the traits of their original Germanic nation, had long ruled over the French, whose national identity was in turn partly formed by its subservience to this natural ruling caste. To a significant extent, Boulainvilliers' historical conceit formed part of a domestic political agenda: by identifying French nobility as representatives of a distinct ethnicity within

---

1 My translation: 'tous les vaincus & Gaulois, qui devinrent tous alors proprement comme le peuple, la nation, en allemend, die Leuthe, homine, populus, gens' (Boulainvilliers 1732: supplément, 3).

France, he not only aimed to undermine the 'new national idea' expounded by the French monarchy but also refuted the notion that nobility was born solely of monarchical authority (Arendt 1951: 163; Ellis 1988: 25–6, 108; Buranelli 1957: 477). Furthermore, Vincent Buranelli notes that the 'Germanist theory' of noble origin had been deployed in France as far back as the sixteenth century as a means to undercut the political authority of the Third Estate (1957: 483). Nevertheless, as André Devyver has asserted, it is Boulainvilliers' line of reasoning, and not the historical coherence of his claims, that makes him an important figure in the history of race (1973: 376). The *Essais*' attempt to vindicate pure-blood nobles on account of their historical ethnicity not only provides one of the earliest and most complete conceptions of ethno-racial hierarchy in the eighteenth century but is also a prime example of the ease with which noble discourses of blood purity and inherited virtue could be used to assert the superiority of entire peoples, cementing links between the providential dominance of their nation and the unmixed blood of their ancestors.

Violence and conquest had originally distinguished the upper ranks from their inferiors, Boulainvilliers explains in the opening pages of his *Essais*, but that divide had long since become a law of nature (1732: 1). All people were born equal in their possession of reason and humanity, but true nobles were uniquely identifiable by their inimitable virtue:

> [Virtue] is more common in good races than in others. We must also acknowledge that virtue requires the sparkle of fortune to make itself known, and normally it is birth which confers this fortune, or some other work of destiny which is not always attached to true merit. Noble birth is thus the most common means by which virtue is honoured and upheld. (Boulainvilliers 1732: 7–8)[2]

Noble virtue was particularly evident in the case of Romano-Gallic France, he claims, as by the sixth century the old Roman elite had become so diluted by social-climbing foreigners that its noble institutions were all but devoid of competent statesmen (Boulainvilliers 1732: 16–17). The invading Franks, on the other hand, stemmed from ancient Germanic stock, and thus carried the legacy of a people skilled in war and talented in the art of government. Their ancestors' women were modest and their men were faithful to their wives, Boulainvilliers

---

2 My translation: '[la vertu] est plus ordinaire dans les bonnes races que dans les autres. On doit aussi convenir que la vertu a besoin de l'éclat de la fortune pour se signaler, & cette fortune, c'est la naissance qui la donne ordinairement, ou certaine fatalité qui n'est pas toujours attachée au vrai mérite. Une naissance noble est donc la moïen le plus commun de faire valoir et de faire honorer la vertu' (Boulainvilliers 1732: 7–8).

explains, two attributes which favoured hardy and robust children (1732: 336). These *Germains* also boasted a striking physique:

> The *Germains* were all of about the same size and shape, providing proof that their blood had never been tainted by any foreign admixture. All of them were of great, vast corpulence, with white flesh, straight hair that was blond or red, green twinkling eyes, a proud, terrifying expression and a startling voice. (Boulainvilliers 1732: 337)[3]

With their wealth of social, moral and physical virtues, writes Boulainvilliers, the conquering Franks effortlessly took control of the noble institutions established by the degenerate Roman elite and returned them to their rightful function. Ever since, they had defended their bloodlines against successive generations of ambitious commoners and power-hungry monarchs, who tirelessly attempted to appropriate the offices of nobility for their own gain. For Boulainvilliers, only this race of Germanic nobles constituted true nobility: 'It is easy to show that, after the conquest of the Gaul, only those of Frankish origin were considered noble'; he assures his readers, 'that is to say, they were masters and lords, while the destiny of the Gaul was decided according to the will of the conqueror' (Boulainvilliers 1732: 40).[4]

Boulainvilliers' admiration for the English peerage was largely based on his perception of this rank as representative of the Germanic spirit. Unlike their repressed cousins in France, they had ardently maintained their noble privileges against both king and commoner. A powerful and influential House of Lords, he held, was the natural legacy of Germanic national assemblies and their tenets of freedom (Ellis 1988: 194; Boulainvilliers 1732: 44–7). 'Our neighbouring nations', he remarks, 'more attached than we are to the distinction of rank, have maintained the idea of superiority in their nobility as dependent on birth into the bloodline of the conquerors' (Boulainvilliers 1732: 44).[5] For Boulainvilliers, the 'blood of the conquerors' had become a permanent and inheritable genealogical essence, which could be altered and even suppressed, but was ultimately ineffaceable. His vision of the English and French nobility, claims

---

3 My translation: 'les Germains étoient tous à peu près de même taille, & habitude de corps, preuve que leur sang n'étoit point alteré par le mélange d'aucun sang étranger. Tous étoient d'une grande et vaste corpulence, la charnure blanche, les cheveux droits & blonds ou roux, les yeux verds et étincelans, le regard fier, terrible, la voix étonnante' (Boulainvilliers 1732: 337).
4 My translation: '[i]l est facile de faire voir qu'après la conquête des Gaules, les François originaires furent les seuls reconnus pour nobles ; c'est-à-dire pour maîtres et seigneurs, tandis que toute la fortune des Gaulois étoit bornée selon la volonté du vainqueur' (Boulainvilliers 1732: 40).
5 My translation: 'Les nations voisines de la nôtre, plus attachées que nous ne le sommes à la distinction des rangs, ont conservé à leur noblesse l'idée de la supériorité, comme dépendante de la naissance prise dans le sang des conquérans' (Boulainvilliers 1732: 44).

Devyver, is distinctly racialized not merely because of its identification of certain social groups with certain ethnicities but because to preserve these social groups in positions of inferiority and superiority one must forbid the *mixing of blood* between master and servant (1973: 372). This was, indeed, one of Boulainvilliers' main laments for the contemporary French nobility: decadence and ambition had contaminated their noble blood with that of impure aspirants (1728: 181).

Boulainvilliers' work helped to fuel an entire discourse of ethno-history in eighteenth-century Britain and Ireland, which both followed in the tradition of biblical succession and quite comfortably set the ethno-nation within a hierarchy of universal order. His ideas are echoed, for instance, in the work of his contemporary and friend Henry St. John, 1st Viscount Bolingbroke, who suggested in his *Remarks upon the History of England* (1730–1) that the conquering Normans had immediately found common ground with the Anglo-Saxons on account of shared Germanic blood. 'They came out of the same northern hive', Bolingbroke explained, and once the Normans set foot on Saxon soil 'the old spirit of liberty' was automatically rekindled in their hearts (1730–1: 2.48–9). His sentiments, in turn, echo those of the English statesman William Temple, who had written in his *Introduction to the History of England* (1695) that 'both nations [Saxon and Norman], deriving their original from those ancient Goths, agreed in several customs or institutions deduced from their common ancestors' (1695: 159). Even as late as the 1770s the entry on 'nobility' in *Encyclopaedia Britannica*'s third edition recounted that 'the origin of nobility in Europe is by some referred to the Goths; who, after they had seized a part of Europe, rewarded their captains with titles of honour to distinguish them from the common people' (1788–97: 8.89).

By the latter half of the century, however, ethno-historical narratives had garnered a new set of implications. For some, emphasizing specific lines of heredity in certain 'nations', and thereby prioritizing the effect of bloodline on a people's physical and mental condition, could constitute a direct challenge to prevailing climate theory. This was certainly the case for the Scottish poet James Macpherson, who used an ethno-historical narrative to rehabilitate the reputation of Scottish Highlanders, both in his infamous 'Ossian' poems (purported translations of ancient Highland verses, published between 1760 and 1765) and in his later historical work, the *Introduction to the History of Great Britain and Ireland* (1772). The Ossian poems were largely debunked as fraudulent in later years, apparently representing a mixture of his own material and appropriations of Irish mythology. Nevertheless, even as their authenticity was debated, the poems provided the Scottish Highlands with a canon of classical epics built on ideas of blood purity. True and ancient traditions, Macpherson explains in the foreword to his *Temora* (1763), are to be found only

> among a people, from all time, free of intermixture with foreigners.... Such are the inhabitants of Scotland. We, accordingly, find that they differ materially from those who possess the low and more fertile part of the kingdom. Their language is pure and original, and their manners are those of an antient and unmixed race of men ... [the Highlanders] are the genuine descendants of the antient Caledonians, and not a pretended colony of Scots [i.e., *Scoti*, meaning Irish]. (Macpherson 1763: ii, iv)

Macpherson reiterates this assertion in his *History*, vehemently rejecting the contemporary idea that Gaelic-speaking Highlanders were descendants of settlers from Ireland, and insisting that the learning and civility of true Caledonians stood as a testament to their unspoiled ancestry (1771: 71). There was a wider implication to such claims. At the time Macpherson was writing, human-variety theorists commonly referenced Scottish Highlanders as a stock example of 'mountain-dweller' deformity. For contemporaries like Oliver Goldsmith, it had already become a truism that, because of their harsh environment, 'the natives of the Highland of Scotland ... are short, broad and hardy', while 'those of the Lowlands are tall and shapely' (1774: 2.238). By writing Highlanders into an ethno-historical narrative, Macpherson could radically recast them in terms of untainted race. His Highlanders, carefully distinguished from Irish-descended Gaels and English-descended Lowlanders, were indeed a distinct human variety, *not* because of climatic influence but because of their untainted blood. Macpherson uses the term 'Celt' for his pure-blood Highlanders, which in this context can be understood as something similar to Boulainvilliers's *Germains* – a catch-all fantasy of Central-European ethnicity that could be deployed as a counterpoint to Mediterranean or Middle Eastern ancestry. Unlike other European peoples like the Tartars, Macpherson explains, who were 'low of stature, a squat swarthy race of men', the Celts 'under whatever climate they were placed' were

> tall, robust and lusty, of a ruddy complexion, with yellow hair and large blue eyes.... Of all the branches of the *Celtæ*, the ancient Britons, the Germans not even excepted, were the greatest in the height of their bodies. They generally exceeded by half a foot the tallest Romans. (1771: 203)

Linking pure blood with mental and anatomical excellence also favoured the construction of ethno-historical stories that could be constantly embroidered to further glorify a people's past. Macpherson's Celts not only recall the upright, blond and 'unmixed' nobility of his Ossian poems but are sometimes so idealized as to drift into almost novelistic rhetoric. Consider, for example, his 'historical' account of Celtic women:

> The women did not yield to the men in stature . . . [they] were fair, blooming and stately, just and full in the proportion of their limbs; active, high spirited and bold. Their long yellow hair flowed carelessly down their shoulders, and their large blue eyes animated their looks into a kind of ferocity less apt to kindle love than to command respect and awe. (Macpherson 1771: 206)

The uncorrupted chastity of Macpherson's Celtic women, as with Boulainvilliers' Gothic women, is earmarked as one of the reasons for the Celts' remarkable size, deliberately linking ideas of chastity and decorum with physical appearance. Likewise, Macpherson is careful to subvert earlier ethnic stereotypes by refuting the common notion that the Celts went unclothed, instead insisting that they wore close-fitting trousers and shirts, unlike the Persians who 'adopted the womanish stole of the east' (1771: 215–16). Considering the prominence of clothing in human-variety discourses such as that of Linnaeus's *Systema*, this insistence is notable. In addition, Macpherson adds, the Celts were the cleanest among all the ancient peoples: 'the cleanliness of modern nations proceeds from luxury', he states, but 'it was the result of nature among the *Celtæ*' (1771: 216).

Ethno-historical discourses like those of Boulainvilliers, Bolingbroke and Macpherson provide a crucial insight into the eighteenth-century concept of heredity for two main reasons: first, because they use genealogical reasoning to delineate ethnicized categories of the human physique (and, in the case of Macpherson, because they implicitly set this reasoning against the tenets of climate theory), and second, because within this narrative the superlatively pure bloodline of a nation's nobility practically becomes a metonym for the ethno-nation itself. The paradigmatic template of eugeneic race, in other words, is here deployed to mark out the anatomical parameters of a perceived ethnic group. This hints at a gradual shift in the 'common-sense' logic of race and lineage in eighteenth-century Britain and Ireland. The traditional conception of noble blood constituted an enigmatic combination of inherited experience and inherent predisposition: bloodline expressed the legacy of great deeds and virtues in former generations, as well as the expectation that this legacy be upheld; at the same time, it provided an exclusive foundation upon which this legacy could be borne out in subsequent generations. In ethno-historical discourse, however, that tradition is held up against a counter-narrative of climatic and environmental conditioning, wherein the discourse of blood purity is implicitly pitted against the environment in the battle for influence over the human body. Only the purest of blood (itself ultimately an expression of environmental influence), according to ethno-historical narratives, can withstand the constant pressures of climatic transformation.

* * *

Out of the three models of eighteenth-century heredity outlined in this chapter, none approaches the modern notion of heredity more closely than the field of hereditary disease.

As far back as 1619, the Irish physician Dermutio de Meara (Diarmuid Ó Méadhra) suggested in his *Pathologia Hereditaria Generalis* that some *haereditarii morbi*, having attached themselves to a parent, could be passed into the body of the offspring (de Meara 1619: 183). Such ideas, in fact, had formed an integral element of European medical discourse since antiquity and remained prominent throughout the eighteenth century. When it came to discussing disease, notes Carlos López-Beltrán, some eighteenth-century texts were already using the term 'hereditary' in something approximating its modern sense (1994: 222). Ephraim Chambers's *Cyclopedia* (1741), for example, first defines the word 'hereditary' in conventional terms, as 'something appropriated to a family or belonging thereto by right of succession, from heir to heir', but goes on to record that

> [h]ereditary is also applied figuratively to good or evil qualities, habitudes, etc., capable of being transmitted, by blood, from father to son. The gout, the king's evil, madness, etc. are hereditary diseases, *i.e.*, are transmitted from the parents in the stamen or first rudiments of the foetus. And such, probably is the origin of numerous other chronic diseases. (Cyclopedia 1741: n.p. vol. 1, entry 'Hereditary')

Haereditarii morbi, notes López-Beltrán, carefully distinguished 'inbuilt' hereditary diseases from other maladies that might be considered hereditary in the more widely understood sense – that is, stemming from familial character or habits that could affect the constitution of a child, even during pregnancy (1994: 222–3). Such ideas could easily transfer to a more 'hereditary' view of human variety, as in John Hunter's *Disputatio Inauguralis* (1775), which claimed that climate theory would be 'idle and futile' if it were not accepted that some acquired features were passed down from parent to child. 'Diseased conditions [which long infest the same family]', the Scottish physician proclaimed, must be looked on in the same light as other mutations of the corporeal condition.... Surely that change which is the origin of the production of black skin may just as easily be communicated by the parent to its offspring, and is no more difficult to explain, than that by which gout is handed down in the same way. (Hunter 1775: 386)

In a series of lectures between 1786 and 1787, Hunter concluded that a set of unchanging 'hereditary principles' always attended the process of trait transmission, exemplified in the very fact that animals reproduced their own species (1786–7: 140). These principles, he continued, not only proceeded regardless of the influences of climate but were independent of 'every external influence in nature' (Hunter 1786–7: 140).

At the beginning of the eighteenth century, the very significance of 'blood' as a metaphor for heredity had, somewhat ironically, been undercut by new understandings of blood as a tangible liquid. William Harvey's landmark study of blood circulation, the *Exercitatio anatomica de motu cordis et sanguinis in animalibus* (1628), had given way to a new generation of anatomists, who increasingly forwent traditional Galenic and Hippocratic humour theory in favour of a Cartesian view of the human body as a mechanical network of vessels and tubes. Some, like Thomas Willis (with his *Cerebri anatome* in 1664), had investigated the role of the brain in regulating human passions; others like Richard Lower (with his *Tractus de corde* in 1669) led pioneering explorations into the transformative capacities of the heart. Many more, however, went on to focus on the exact same phenomena as Boulainvilliers and Macpherson – only this time, from a medical perspective. What role, exactly, did genealogical purity play in the physical make-up of the human body? Could the effects of unmixed bloodline be measured in a quantifiable way? And in what exact manner could the effects of lifestyle, civility and virtue be inherited through the body itself?

Noble tradition, unsurprisingly, constituted an invaluable test case when it came to medical enquiries into trait inheritance. 'Sempiternal ideological views about the purity of blood' notes Beltrán, 'were always easily fuelled by any kind of consideration of transmissibility of ills through family lines' (1994: 229). Not only were nobles equipped with extensive genealogical documentation, they were often known for their propensity to hereditary diseases – particularly gout, scrofula, nervous disorders and madness. '[T]he apparently gouty and nervous aristocracy', notes Kevin Siena, were thus 'especially useful' to physicians who hoped to study the familial dynamics of these ailments (2019: 233). In eighteenth-century Britain and Ireland, the upper orders were commonly said to suffer from 'diseases of civilisation', which sprung from material luxury and rich diet and were held to render the sufferer more physically delicate, more anxious and more prone to splenetic depressions. Susceptibility to such diseases, however, was often another matter entirely. Being prone to a disease of civilization could be read as a badge of pride – a sort of corporeal proof of the sufferer's high rank and birth. This is perhaps most evident in a range of nervous disorders which were commonly diagnosed in Britain during the first half of the century and which could instantly associate patients with wealth, luxury, high civility and even political prowess. In George Cheyne's *English Malady* (1733), one of the most popular medical treatises in Britain of the 1730s, the physician explained that such disorders only affected those with particularly fine nerve fibres. 'The common division of Mankind into *Quick Thinkers, Slow Thinkers,* and *No Thinkers*, is not without foundation in Nature', affirms Cheyne, 'persons of slender and weak nerves are generally of the first class' (1733: 182). Recalling Macpherson's Celts and Boulainvilliers' *Germains*, this first class of mankind was also instantly recognizable on account of a tendency towards being blond, pale-skinned and highly intelligent (Cheyne 1733: 101–3). While the sufferers are troubled with vapours and lowness of spirits, they also invariably demonstrate 'a greater degree of sensibility . . . feel pleasure and pain the most readily, and are of most lively imagination' (Cheyne 1733: 105). Those with delicate nerve fibres, wrote Cheyne,

> shall suffer more from the prick of a pin, or needle, from their extreme sensibility, than others from being run through the body . . . none have it in their option to choose for themselves their own particular frame of mind nor constitution of body; so none can choose his own degree of sensibility. That is given him by the author of his nature, and is already determined. (Cheyne 1733: 366)

Only a *real* princess, in other words, can feel the peas hidden under the mattress. At the other end of the spectrum, Cheyne notes, 'fools, weak or stupid persons, heavy and dull souls' did not seem to suffer from these conditions at all. Instead, their 'intellectual faculty, without all manner of doubt, has material and animal organs, by which it immediately works' (1733: 52). Common causes of weak nerves, Cheyne records, included fine breeding and excessive lifestyles, or, in certain cases, an excess of charity, piety and an over-dedication to parliamentary duties (1733: 268, 277). In fact, wealth and high birth are usually the only unifying factors in Cheyne's plethora of catalogued disorders. Few of his patients manifest exactly the same symptoms; some have ostensibly inherited their problems, while others have induced them through artificial means. All their conditions, however, conceptually isolate the elite body as physiologically distinct. All, too, rely on the increasingly common conviction that only wealthy white Europeans could experience the full spectrum of human emotion, while the lower orders and inferior human varieties experienced simpler, duller feelings. Silvia Sebastiani (2000: 224) points to the *Encyclopaedia Britannica*'s entry on 'Love', which notes that

> among savages the affection of love is seldom felt. Even among the lower orders in civil society it seems to be a very gross passion, and to have in it more of the selfishness of appetite than of the generosity of esteem ... savages in general and ... the great body of the labouring poor, are incapable of studying that rectitude of mind and that delicacy of sentiment. (*Encyclopaedia Britannica* 1788-97: 10.298-9)

Such ideas should be understood in a context wherein poverty and low rank were becoming increasingly medicalized. Kevin Siena has examined how social and economic status was inscribed onto the bodies of the poor by early modern physicians (2019: 45, 116–22). By the second half of the eighteenth century, crowded institutions such as jails had become widely recognized as unsanitary, not simply because of their abysmal levels of hygiene but also because of their high concentration of immorality (Siena 2019: 229). The poor were thought to be predisposed to fever, notes Siena, owing to a 'so-called "taint" in the blood, the remnants of a disease imperfectly cured that lingered to reignite or spark new diseases years later, and which could be inherited by one's parents or grandparents' (2019: 232–3). By the mid-century, physicians at the Paris medical faculty (where some of the most pioneering studies into hereditary disease were being conducted) had increasingly begun to discuss hereditary disease as symptomatic of moral decline on a national scale (López-Beltrán 1994: 226; Quinlan 2006: 651–8). The physician Antoine Le Camus (1753: 271–3, 279) blamed the practice of wet nursing for introducing vicious germs into healthy family lines, while his Swiss contemporary Jacques Ballexserd (1762: 23–7) asserted that hereditary degeneration explained why modern Europeans no longer boasted the magnificent anatomies depicted in ancient sculpture. The French physician Charles-Augustin Vandermonde, for his part, saw the management of hereditary traits as key to 'perfecting' the human species, urging people with physical disabilities not to marry one another so as to avoid proliferating undesirable features in future generations (1756: 1.85; see Quinlan 2006: 658–63). Crucially, Siena asserts, the same notions of inherited 'taint' were also used within the field of human variety to define one type of human being from another (2019: 236). The British colonial administrator Edward Long, for instance, claimed that the 'openness of [negroes'] pores gives a free transpiration to bad humours', leaving them more vulnerable to chills and the cold; their skin and lungs, meanwhile, allowed for the 'quicker evaporation of perspirable matter', rendering them more suitable than white Europeans to labour all day in the scorching sun (1774: 412, 533). Towards the end of the century, adds Siena (2019: 238), the Scottish surgeon Colin Chisholm observed that certain diseases emanating from Africa chiefly targeted the 'lower classes of [white] men, and those most especially of loose and debauched manners' (Chisholm 1799: 94).

The most notorious hereditary disease to be linked with the noble body was the affliction of gout. A painful form of arthritis that typically affects the feet, gout had been associated with luxury and excess since antiquity. The Dorset physician Thomas Sydenham rehearsed a common refrain when he described the affliction as a badge of divine favour at the end of the seventeenth century. It was a disease of 'kings, princes, generals, admirals, philosophers, and several other great men', he wrote in his *Treatise on the Gout* (1683), '[it] destroys more rich than poor persons, and more wise men than fools, which seems to demonstrate the justice and strict impartiality of Providence' (Sydenham 1683: 426). Almost a century later, in his *Observations on the Origins, Progress, and Method of Treating the Atrabilious Temperament and Gout* (1779), the Scottish physician William Grant explored the role of genealogy, civility and ethnicity in the onset of this disease. The ailment seems to originate, Grant claimed,

> from some very remote cause, lurking in the constitution long before the disease is developed ... [these] may be called constitutional diseases; and this is the reason why so many of them are hereditary ... as the constitutional diseases are often hereditary, so the hereditary diseases are always constitutional; and that the whole body, solids as well as fluids, is affected or diseased. (Grant 1779: 1.1–2)

This constitutional disposition, Grant proposes, was not only evident in certain family lines but in entire ethnic groups. Echoing Macpherson's *History*, he points to the isolated Scottish Highlanders as a prime example of physiological distinction. 'When I was a young man in the Highlands of Scotland', Grant recounts, 'I hardly ever saw a man able to breed the gout; there is not a word for it in the language of that country' (1779: 1.4). Though the Highlanders regularly 'debauched themselves', he admits, even for years at a time, and though they lived to the same advanced age as might be expected of a southern Englishman, they never once encountered gout, instead being plagued by a completely different range of ailments (Grant 1779: 1.4).

Grant pursues his study with an investigation into the precise physiological differences that can be observed between those of high and low social rank. The enquiry is notable not only for its corporeal interpretation of traditional rank signifiers but also for its parallels with ethno-historical descriptions of the small, dark, dim-witted barbarian and the tall, fair and mentally astute conqueror. A man 'brought up in a rude state', Grant claims, will be instantly recognizable to a physician:

> [T]his man is lean and lank-faced, [with] stout limbs, and no belly; his skin is loose, harsh and hairy; the skin of his head is very movable, so that he has a great deal of motion in his nose, forehead, and ears; he has high cheek-bones, and all his muscles are hard, prominent and unequal; his veins are large and rolling, his bones are short, solid and hard; his joints are small but his limbs are thick in proportion to his bulk and stature. (Grant 1779: 1.11)

Were one to open up the body of such a man, he continues, it would easily be seen that his intestines were shrivelled and his heart and lungs were abnormally large; he would have a swollen brain and 'thick' nerves. These toughened body parts, it seems, would also have affected his mind. Labouring men have keener than usual senses, notes Grant, such as sight and smell, but 'their feelings are blunt, and their nervous system not easily moved . . . hence they are often indolent, ignorant, and contented; their mental faculties are rather solid than quick . . . all their passions are low, equal, and permanent' (1779: 1.12–13). When Grant goes on to describe the anatomy of a 'man born and brought up in a confined life', each of these physical characteristics is systematically inverted. His skin and flesh are soft and tender, his stomach and intestines are noticeably large (presumably from excessive eating) and his lungs and heart peculiarly small (presumably from want of breathing); his capacity for feeling, consequently, has developed entirely differently from the labouring specimen:

> his feelings are so keen, and his wants so many, that his desires are unbounded, and of course his mind is dissatisfied: hence, he is impatient, discontented, industrious, and ingenious; his apprehensions are quick, his knowledge extensive, he is enterprising, and often very daring. (Grant 1779: 1.16)

Grant's parallel study of the differences between a 'rude' and a 'sophisticated' woman offers a further insight into the implications of this discourse. While the lifestyle of a man 'brought up in a rude state' renders him mentally and physically limited, his female counterpart is optimally designed for producing children. The body of a rustic woman, Grant records, is stocky and plump, of a healthy complexion and enjoys regular, light and short periods of menstruation, which cause her no 'pain or inconvenience' (1779: 1.42). Her pregnancies fall easily and often, and she suffers so little from carrying a child that no outward signs of pregnancy are visible until after at least six months. Her deliveries are uncomplicated and swift: 'she is taken in labour, with smart pains at short intervals . . . after [the birth] she is quite composed' (Grant 1779: 1.42–3). The 'woman of fashion', on the other hand, has become physically ill-fit for procreation. While the sophisticated man's delicate nerves had rendered him 'enterprising', the same sensitivity has rendered the sophisticated woman fragile, feeble and vulnerable to strong passions. Born to 'delicate, not to say unhealthy parents', her dainty physique is shaped by her constrictive clothing and her diet of 'tea and hot victuals', and her wearing of high-heeled shoes and tight-laced stays renders her nerve fibres soft.

> Her limbs are long and small, her waist is long and slender, her neck is long and small, her breasts are flat, and her skin a dead white . . . [she] is very susceptible of tender feelings, and those passions that agitate weak nerves. Although her powers are not great, her desires are strong. (Grant 1779: 1.47)

The pregnancies of a sophisticated woman, laments Grant, were therefore not the regular, even casual experiences that they seemed to be among the lower orders, and often led to fatalities in both the mother and infant. This passage has an important resonance. It might be recalled that easy childbirth was routinely cited as a characteristic of inferior human varieties at this time. Goldsmith had recently compared the 'women of savage nations' to the 'wives of the peasants amongst ourselves', before dismissing traumatic childbirth as a feature of nations where women were 'enfeebled by luxury or indolence' (1774: 2.224). In Grant, as in Goldsmith, the assertion serves to create a misogynistic double-bind: uncomplicated childbirth is ascribed to savage women with the implicit aim of dehumanization; at the same time, difficult births are attributed to civilized women as evidence that they have become *too* cultivated and that their bodies have become perverted through material excess.

It is indeed a curious dimension of hereditary disease that it provided a powerful discourse with which to consider genealogical purity as a negative thing. When the Edinburgh physician William Buchan published his immensely popular catalogue of home remedies, *Domestic Medicine* (1769), he scorned rather than simpered to the elite nature of gout and other hereditary maladies. The 'delicate female', he declares, 'who lives on tea and other slops', will be lucky if she can bear a child at all, and if she does, 'it will hardly be fit to live'. The irregular lives of the children's fathers, moreover, could not but hurt their constitution

(Buchan 1769: 441). Engendering family lines with gouty constitutions, he warned, was certainly not something to be admired:

> [W]hat a dreadful inheritance is the gout, the scurvy, or the king's evil, to transmit to our offspring! How happy had it been for the heir of many a great estate had he been born a beggar, rather than to inherit his father's fortune at the expense of inheriting his diseases! A person labouring under any incurable malady ought not to marry. (Buchan 1769: 441–2)

The medicalization of blood purity thus had a significant impact on the form and scope of anti-noble sentiment. The more that genealogical bloodlines could be considered in terms of the physical human body, the more that those very same bodies could be used as a critique of hereditary power. Erasmus Darwin, one of the most notable proto-evolutionary thinkers of the eighteenth century, was quick to recognize the implications of genealogy as a corporeal process. The consistent recurrence of certain diseases in noble families was, for Darwin, not a validation of their blood purity but an indication of steady physical degeneration with each successive heir. In his *Temple of Nature*, probably composed in the mid-to-late 1790s and published posthumously in 1804, he posits that all living things, plants and animals, are in a perpetual state of 'improvement or degeneracy' and that, if the latter be true, 'it becomes a subject of importance to detect the causes of these mutations' (Darwin 1804: 50). Thus, from Darwin's point of view, the 'noble' character of diseases like gout provided a perfect physiological argument against supposed genealogical superiority. 'As many families become gradually extinct by hereditary disease', he warns his readers, 'as by scrofula, consumption, epilepsy and mania, it is often hazardous to marry an heiress, as she is not unfrequently the last of a diseased family' (Darwin 1804: [note 11] 52).

* * *

At first glance, the ethno-histories of Boulainvilliers and Macpherson may seem remote from the medical tracts of Cheyne and Grant and still further removed from the world of equine thorough-breeding. Yet, in their interaction with ideas of noble race it quickly becomes evident that these discourses are inextricable from one another. For one thing, these texts were being published, read and disseminated at the same time. The reader who might have learnt of tall, blond, inherently virtuous nobility from Boulainvilliers' *Essais* in 1732 could have picked up a copy of Cheyne's *English Malady* the following year only to read that shapely, fair-haired members of the social elite were possessed of singularly sensitive physiques and exceptional mental finesse. Another reader, in

1779, could have laid a copy of Macpherson's history of pure-blood Caledonian elite side by side with Grant's description of the sophisticated man, whose quick wit and industry were observable in the shape of his internal organs. A decade later, the same reader might have learnt from Thomas Bewick that the most anatomically 'noble' horses represented 'a pure and ancient race, purer than milk', precisely because their genealogies had been preserved with such care (1790: 5). Each discourse approaches its subject matter from an extremely different standpoint but ultimately comes to a remarkably similar conclusion. Namely, they are all fundamentally contingent on the idea that there is something physically discernible and constitutionally inheritable *in* the elite body; the physicality and mental state of the better sort can, if examined correctly, be observably distinguished from that of other people. More than this, these discourses essentially present objective 'facts' – the mechanics of inherited traits, the history of the nation and the precise dimensions of the human body – through a political narrative that serves to reinforce received ideas of natural difference between pure-blood elites (national or noble) and their inferiors. In equine breeding, ethno-history and medical discourse, these assertions of superior blood represent a highly important dimension to the racialization of noble tradition in eighteenth-century Britain and Ireland. It was a cultural trope, moreover, that would soon find sinister echoes in the expanding fields of human-variety theory.

7

Mankind's new nobility
The rise of genealogical race theory

While the previous chapter examined three developing models of heredity in the eighteenth century, it is important to remember that this evolving idea had little if anything to do with the actual processes of trait transmission. The genealogical operations that ostensibly created elite 'horses of blood', or that maintained an ethnically noble over-class of *Germains*, or that underpinned the difference between 'polished' and 'rustic' anatomies, were invariably grounded in the cultural construct of untainted blood – a state which, on these terms at least, does not exist in molecular genetics. Rather, untainted blood is essentially a political fantasy, predominantly nourished and sustained by hereditary elites. Ultimately, it is this purity model of heredity, and not the actual dynamics of trait transmission, which would go on to influence the concept of human race. That is to say, it was not just any version of heredity that came to uphold the idea of major human races at the end of the eighteenth century, it was the specific and completely fictional interpretation that had been long deployed as a power strategy by nobility. Moreover, within race theory this idea of heredity was used in exactly the same way and for exactly the same reasons: to create an illusion of natural hierarchy, whereby all human beings would have to compare themselves to an arbitrary standard of excellence defined by the self-proclaimed elite of white Europeans. The minute gradations of this hierarchy would have to be constantly performed and paraded to reinforce the natural power of those at its apex. We must keep in mind that the very reason we use the word 'race' to describe the new schema of human hierarchy that emerged towards the end of the eighteenth century is because it was built around bloodline and blood purity. Likewise, the fact that varietal 'hybridity' would become so pivotal to the delineation of these human races, as will be seen in this chapter, underlines quite how much race theory depended on a pre-existing notion of bloodline as an indicator of political and social status. This chapter explores how the noble version of heredity permeated the discourse of human-variety theory during the last decades of the century and how humanity was thereby reimagined as a set of lineal families with its own, self-evident nobility of white Europeans.

* * *

While human-variety theory traditionally relied on observable similarities rather than kinship, the cultural construct of genealogical race had always overlapped to some degree with the taxonomies of natural history. Proliferating alongside discourses of climatic adaptation was the highly tenacious theory of preformation, which held that tiny preformed humans existed inside the body of the mother or the father (which one, exactly, being a matter of debate). What is more, by the turn of the eighteenth century the theory of preformation increasingly incorporated the doctrine of pre-existence, which surmised that *all* entities in Creation must logically already exist in infinitely miniature form (Hoffheimer 1982: 121; Quinlan 2010: 143). Every unborn human being, that is, was already contained within the body of its future parent, successively nestled inside one the other like a 'Russian doll' (Pinto-Correia 1997: 3). Such ideas were useful in so much as they could reconcile the biblical precept of universal descent from Adam with the stratification of Adam's descendants into natural hierarchies. 'Preformation 'scientifically' established that all men were, in fact, brothers, since they all came from the same gonad', notes Clara Pinto-Correia, yet it also explained why it was 'inevitable that servants would always originate from servants, just as kings would always originate from kings' (1997: 4). Preformation also faced its share of scrutiny, however. The French polymath Pierre Louis Moreau de Maupertuis challenged the very basis of the doctrine when he discovered that hereditary defects could be passed down through both male and female lines – suggesting that preformed embryos could not exist solely in the bodies of either men or women (1752: 136–7). Five years later, the German physiologist Caspar Friedrich Wolff substantially destabilized preformationism in his *Theoria Generationis*, reasserting the ancient theory of epigenesis (not to be confused with the modern discipline of epigenetics), whereby unborn organisms began as relatively amorphous matter and gradually developed a complex form (1759: 73, no. 168). The revival of epigenesis, indeed, is indicative of the rapidly rising interest in the mechanics of intergenerational trait transmission from the mid-century onwards.

Others were sceptical that all human beings really did come from the same gonad. For many, notes Colin Kidd, particularly after the ontological disruptions of the Protestant Reformation, questions of 'racial filiation' were far more important than questions of varietal diversity (2004: 263–4). The prevailing doctrine of eighteenth-century climate theory was monogenism, which held that all humans were descended from Adam and Eve. For monogenists, human diversity therefore had to be the result of environmental influence, since Edenic descent meant that they were all sprung from the same parents. Polygenists, on the other hand, sometimes conjectured that certain human varieties did not form part of the original Edenic bloodline and potentially constituted a separate species. Monogenists and polygenists also took a markedly different perspective on the process of intergenerational trait transmission. For monogenists, heredity was effectively understood as a catalyst for diversity – one part of a larger process by which different environments shaped the human body. For polygenists, heredity was more commonly framed as evidence of anatomical exclusivity, with each putative group proliferating a particular set of characteristics and remaining relatively homogenous over time.

It is all too easy, however, to oversimplify these ostensibly opposing viewpoints. Eighteenth-century monogenists were somewhat conspicuous in their denunciation of polygenist theory, vociferously asserting 'monogenism versus polygenism' as a great dividing line in the field of human variety. Linnaeus, for instance, made certain to dissociate his taxonomy from any intimation of polygenesis in the 1758 edition of his *Systema Naturae*, reiterating that his species *Homo troglodytes* did not represent a separate species (1758: 24). Buffon, too, devotes the entire closing paragraph of his *Variétés dans l'espèce humaine* to refuting the possibility of polygenesis, claiming that 'mankind [is] not composed of species essentially different from each other . . . there was originally but one species . . . [which] produced only individual varieties' (1780–5: 3.206; 1749–88: 3.529–30). Johann Friedrich Blumenbach, for his part, denounced polygenists as sensationalist atheists in his 1775 edition of *De generis humani varietate nativa*: 'The idea of the plurality of human species', he remarked,

> has found particular favour with those who made it their business to throw doubt on the accuracy of scripture . . . such is the subtlety of the human intellect, and such the rush for novelty, that many would rather accept a new, though insufficiently considered opinion, than subscribe to ancient truths which have been commonly accepted for thousands of years. (Blumenbach 1775: 98)

These sentiments have largely shaped the historiography of the monogenist-polygenist debate, which sometimes tends to overestimate the influence of polygenesis on subsequent race concepts. In reality, monogenism overwhelmingly dominated the field of human-variety theory, with polygenesis remaining a relatively peripheral theory throughout the century (Wheeler 2000: 37; Seth 2018: 167). Polygenist theories, after all, arguably constituted heresy, and more often than not they amounted to little more than thinly veiled apologies for the slave trade. Monogenists' performative denunciations, meanwhile, often seem to attack polygenesis primarily for its perceived accessibility, framing it as the conclusion of dullards or amateurs who had not taken the time to properly understand established climate theory. Most importantly, polygenesis was not always constructed in opposition to monogenism. In fact, the two models of human variety could significantly overlap.

The early modern theory of multiple origin is commonly traced back to Isaac de la Peyrère's *Praeadamitae* (1655), which suggested that populations of 'Pre-Adamites' resided on earth before God created Man. By the eighteenth century, however, polygenism had come to uphold a surprisingly diverse range of theories. The infamous polygenist Edward Long posited that other variety theories had misread the pattern of the Great Chain of Being. The orang-outang, he claimed, was more similar to Man than it was to other apes, and Black Africans were more similar to orang-outangs than they were to white Europeans; therefore, the gradations between all three categories evidently needed to be revised (Long 1774: 2.358). It is a curious feature of Long's polygenism, notes Suman Seth, that instead of lowering Black Africans 'to the level of beasts ... he raised orangutans to the level of men, offering a three-level ranking of human species within *genus homo*' (2018: 766). In this respect, Seth suggests, Long's polygenism 'presumed less fixity' than some schemes of monogenism such as those of Immanuel Kant (discussed later). The English physician Charles White made a similar argument at the end of the century in his *Account of the Regular Gradation in Man* (1799). White meticulously chronicled the supposed differences between Africans and Europeans in terms of features such as brain size, foot shape, genital size, arm length, life expectancy, menstruation and perspiration, concluding that the Black African was anatomically closer to the orang-outang than the white European in every respect and should thus be considered on a lower rung of the *Scala naturae* (1799: 50–9). A more conventional example of polygenism can be found in the work of the Scottish philosopher Henry Home, Lord Kames, whose *Sketches of the History of Man* (1774) became one of the best-known examples of the theory in Britain. Anyone who had the common sense to distinguish different animals as a child, Kames declared, could instantly see that the major climate theorists of the day had 'wandered wonderfully far from nature' in their classificatory systems (Kames 1774: 1.2). Climate theory, he claimed, could not account for the consistency of skin colours found across the Americas, nor could it explain why some populations had remained at a hunter-gatherer stage of human development. 'Adam and Eve might have been the first parents of mankind', he proposed, 'without being the first parents of the Americans' (Kames 1774: 2.75). In 1786, the German-British natural historian and political radical Georg Forster, whose role on James Cook's voyage to the South Seas will be examined in Chapter 9, made a polygenist argument in his *Noch etwas über die Menschenraßen* (Something More about the Human Races) precisely to undermine monogenist theories of 'major races' (particularly Kant's theory). Monogenists, Forster claimed, were simply forcing empirical evidence into a Christian narrative of Creation, and ultimately they could produce no more evidence for their doctrine than polygenists could for theirs (1786: 55–7).

Monogenists' proscription of their polygenist counterparts rang increasingly hollow from the 1770s onward, as their own theorists drifted inexorably towards a model of discrete and immutable human type: race. For most of the century, traditional race discourse had functioned as a kind of conceptual 'bridge' in human-variety literature, to be crossed when observation failed to account for anomalies such as intergenerational variation or interspecies diversity. In a certain sense, to invoke the supposed effects of lineal bloodline as a support for observational classification was simply to fall back on received wisdom, turning to intuition and cultural precedent in order to fill causative gaps in empirical observation. As monogenist climate theory became increasingly complex, however, its proponents came to rely more and more on bloodline to lend coherence to their varietal schemas. This is noticeable in Buffon's *Variétés dans l'espèce humaine*, in which the author systematically used the French word *race* to describe human anatomical type. Buffon's use of the term was partly designed to undermine Linnaean taxonomy. 'Race', as will be remembered, was an extremely broad term, and, to Linnaeus's frustration, the French theorist often divided his *races* into sub-categories like *espèce*, *nation* and *peuple* (Sloan 1995: 134). At the same time, it is no accident that Buffon chose a piece of vocabulary that related primarily to lineal families. While Linnaeus's *varietates* left little room for change or development, notes Nicolas Hudson,

> 'race', on the contrary, suggested a family lineage of animals or humans that was by no means permanent or inflexible, but formed a veritable 'history' of traits passed down through generations in innumerable different forms . . . Negroes, Americans, Lapps, Orientals, Europeans and so forth represented particular stocks whose members, like those of great families, showed a considerable degree of resemblance, yet were in a state of constant variation. (Hudson 1996: 253–4)

Not only did the cultural concept of 'race' not contradict Buffon's theory of climatic influence, but it became essential to it. His notion of individual gradation depended on the continuity of climatic conditions over multiple generations, which necessarily meant that with each generation the parents must have been passing down some of their externally acquired anatomical traits to their offspring. This perpetual reinforcement of the climate's actions, Buffon held, went to explain why corporeal differences were so pronounced. The alterations of the human body, he states in the *Variétés*,

> were rendered more general, more strongly marked, and more permanent, by the continual action of the same causes; that they are transmitted from generation to generation as deformities or diseases pass from parents to children. (Buffon 1780–5: 3.207; 1749–88: 3.530)

Lineal succession upheld Buffon's theory of species formation, explaining how individual gradation settled into distinct groupings of similar entities. This, in turn, echoed the English botanist John Ray's highly influential definition of 'species' as a taxonomic unit in the late seventeenth century, denoting groups of organisms that could only produce fertile offspring with members of their own kind (1693: 1.40). Unlike Linnaeus then, who had defined a species simply as a group of creatures with a set of shared characteristics, Buffon linked the coherence of a species with its temporal succession: members of a single species not only had to resemble one another but also had to be capable of generating more beings like themselves. 'The reality of species was to be found only in material connections', explains Sloan, 'two beings are members of the same species not because they "look alike" or even because they share essential defining properties ... [but] only if they have a material relation to one another' (1995: 132). This principle was notably employed in Buffon's discussion of hybridity and fertility in donkeys and mules in the *Histoire naturelle*:

> It is neither ... the number nor the collection of similar individuals, but the constant succession and renovation of these individuals, which constitutes the species.... It is by comparing present individuals with those which are past that we acquire a clear idea of species ... we can draw a line between two species, that is, two successions of individuals who reproduce but cannot mix. (Buffon 1780–5: 3.406; 1749–88: 4.384–5)

The monstrous peoples of the world, claims Buffon, had clearly bred accidental defects among themselves, and these had proliferated in their isolated populations. Any human trait can be continued, he claims, if it is sufficiently isolated within one lineage, and thus it can be explained how certain monstrous features were 'propagated from generation to generation like hereditary diseases' (Buffon 1780–5: 3.408; 1749–88: 4.388). Buffon, notes Sloan, 'provided a means by which the contingencies of geography and climate, acting upon the molecules, could affect the actual reproductive lineage of the species' (1995: 133).

In the wake of Buffonian theory, the inheritance of acquired traits took on a renewed significance within monogenist human-variety discourse, not least in relation to the propagation of different human varieties. Goldsmith, for instance (again, applying his own logic to contemporary systems of natural philosophy), noted that in areas where human varieties tended to interact, a certain hybridity of skin colour occurred over time. 'In those places where trade has long flourished', he observes,

> the races are usually found blended . . . in the islands of the Indian Ocean . . . the inhabitants appear to be a mixture of all the nations upon the earth; white, olive, brown and black men, are all seen living together in the same city, and propagate a mixed breed. (Goldsmith 1774: 2.231–2)

Goldsmith's assertions were undoubtedly influenced by the intense focus on skin-colour caste systems in the colonial Atlantic at this time (discussed later). In some respects, too, they seem to approximate John Hunter's 'hereditary principles' by isolating intergenerational trait transmission from the effects of climate. At the same time, for Goldsmith the phenomenon of human 'hybridization' is entirely compatible with the inheritance of acquired characteristics. 'We find nothing more common', he explains,

> than for children to inherit sometimes even the accidental deformities of their parents . . . I myself have seen a child, distinctly marked with a scar, similar to one the father had received in battle . . . from this, therefore, may have arisen the small eyes and long ears of the Tartars . . . the flat noses of the blacks . . . and the flat heads of the American Indians. (Goldsmith 1774: 2.238–9)

In his naïve interpretation of Buffonian theory, Goldsmith manages to lay out the multiplicity of dogmas that could feed into ideas of inheritable human type at this time. His work reminds us that these diverse notions were not necessarily approached as mutually incoherent. Rather, they represented a heady mix of ancient tradition and pioneering observation, constantly being shaped and reshaped by cultural bias and expectation.

One of the most influential voices to advocate the influence of lineage within human-variety theory was Immanuel Kant, whose *Von der verschiedenen Rassen der Menschen* ('Of the Different Human Races', completed in 1775 and expanded in 1777) would eventually become a foundational text of race theory. Every division of species and genera, Kant asserted, must be in accordance with the Buffonian law of common propagation (Kant 1777: 8). In other words, two beings must be able to breed and produce an identical being together in order for them to be properly considered a species. Thus, Kant proclaims, it is useless to classify animals according to their similarities; instead, it is necessary to focus on the descending bloodlines which attend physiological distinctions (1777: 8). The law of common propagation also confirmed monogenesis as the only possible theory of human origin, since all human varieties could produce offspring with each other. Kant, however, places far more emphasis than Buffon did on the role of races as representative of inbuilt human differences. While accepting climate theory as the foundation of human variety, he constructs his races (*Rassen*) as subspecies based on lineage. If a species represents two entities who can generate fertile offspring together, Kant claims, a race denotes two individuals who will propagate a specific set of human characteristics together. Kant's races, like Buffon's species, exist only in their own successive generation – if a member of one race was to 'breed into' another racial group, he suggests, the skin colour and anatomy of their progeny would quickly assimilate into the dominant racial lineage. As an example of his propagation-based race construct, Kant points to the selective breeding practices of nobility: 'Features ultimately become rooted in reproductive power', he asserts,

> this development has presumably been observed in the old Venetian nobility, especially the women. At any rate, all of the noble women on the recently discovered island of Tahiti do have longer noses than is common. – Maupertuis[1] believes that we may cultivate a noble stock of human beings in any province, a stock in whom understanding, diligence, and probity were hereditary . . . [any] stock would always be recognisable and might even be called a race, if their characteristic feature does not seem too insignificant. (Kant 1777: 10–11)

Noble blood here comes to represent the epitome of human selective breeding, whether it be in a Persian concubine, a Tahitian princess or a Venetian *dogaressa* – essentially isolating an elite strain of humanity with a desired set of physical/moral/political traits. Kant's example of physical traits in noble lines (or selectively bred lines which imbue noble attributes) is extremely appropriate for his subsequent assertion of 'pure blood', which can define the degree to which one belongs to any one of his four 'major' varieties of mankind – White, Hindu,

---

1 Kant alludes to Maupertuis's *Vénus Physique* (see Maupertuis 1745: 2.110–11).

Hun and Negro (1777: 11). Even within these varieties, he holds that some races are purer than others, again depending on their lineage. The Hindustani, he suggests, are purer and more ancient than other Hindus, as are Kalmucks among the Huns. Just as in the tradition of noble race, this genealogical 'purity' is evaluated according to the ancientness of a people's direct line of descent. Even the effects of climate, for Kant, are limited to their effects on the reproductive potency of the inhabitants.

Within Kant's racial theory, notes Bruce Baum, one can identify 'three properties that would remain basic to racial thought for most of the next two centuries' (2006: 72). The first of these was an idea of race as being primarily defined by a handful of characteristic physical features (such as skin colour or hair texture) which were reproduced across generations. The second was that race was different from more occasional and inconsistent bodily variations (such as the sporadic occurrence of red hair), which did not seem to persevere over successive generations. The third is the most important: this was the idea that individuals born from two different races would automatically constitute 'half-breeds'. Kant's essay asserts that all peoples who do not fit into one of his four human types have resulted from interbreeding between them. Through this he invents his races through a process of exclusion: by defining all those who did *not* fit into his four major races as 'half-breeds', Kant automatically reinforces the reality of his arbitrary race categories. His handful of characteristics, through becoming the rule that is defined by exceptions, can be reconceptualized as the hereditary identity of an entire set of global populations. Like noble families, his pure races depend on this constant threat of contamination to exist. Hybridity, likewise, consolidates Kant's arbitrary parameters of hereditary excellence (whiteness), helping to characterize all deviance from that master-template in terms of gradational inferiority.

Here we can see how the theories of an arch-monogenist like Kant can quickly begin to overlap with those of his polygenist rivals. A year before Kant's *Rassen der Menschen* was published, Edward Long had similarly mediated on varietal 'hybrids', going so far as to suggest that they were born naturally sterile. Mulattos, Long notes, only seemed to produce children with either Black or white spouses. '[S]ome few of them have intermarried here with those of their own complexion', he remarks, 'but such matches have generally been defective and barren. They seem in this respect to be actually of the mule kind' (Long 1774: 2.335). While taking a different perspective from Kant, Long ultimately has the same endgame in sight. By downplaying the existence of people whose anatomy conforms to neither Black nor white stereotypes, he endeavours to reinforce blackness and whiteness as mutually exclusive states of being. They are not merely hazards of climate, which may wax and wane over time, but immutable conditions which will always re-establish themselves as naturally separate from one another. The polygenist Charles White also concludes that weather must not have much to do with skin colour after all. Without an 'intermixture of blood', he stated in his *Account of the Regular Gradation in Man* (1799), 'it has never been ascertained that blacks have a tendency to become white, or whites to become black, in any part of the earth' (1799: 117).

Interest in skin colour seemed to escalate alongside interest in blood-based human variety. It might be recalled that Blumenbach (1775: 108) had contrasted the swarthy skin colour of working men with the 'brilliancy of the higher class of European', that Goldsmith (1774: 2.236) had attributed white skin among the upper ranks of Europeans to their mode of life or that Samuel Stanhope Smith (1787: 22) had observed working men in America degenerating to just 'a few shades lighter than that of the Iroquois'. Likewise, it will be remembered that Boulainvilliers characterized his Germanic nobles as blond and white-skinned, that Macpherson's elite *Celtae* were yellow-haired and white-fleshed and that Cheyne's diseases of civilization affected the pale and fair-haired most of all (Boulainvilliers 1732: 337; Macpherson 1771: 203; Cheyne 1733: 101–3). These tropes are all the more remarkable when it is considered that skin colour was, at this same time, being directly grafted onto complex schemes of social hierarchy. Staffan Müller-Wille and Hans Jörg Rheinberger have noted the profound influence of colonial Latin America's *casta* tradition, wherein one's exact skin colour, paired with one's parentage, could decide one's precise social and legal rights (2012: 66). The contemporary genre of *casta* painting, the first complete series of which has been dated to 1715, seems to have exerted a considerable influence on how skin colour was discussed (Bethencourt 2013: 163). These paintings, depicting various ethnic couplings and the children produced therein, were mostly produced in Mexico City and served to identify minute caste distinctions in local society. They typically formed a series, with each scene attributed a number 'to highlight a hierarchy of purity of blood: generally from one to sixteen' (Bethencourt 2013: 163). Francisco Bethencourt has noted that this system was built around local ethno-social hierarchies and was not designed to delineate a universal system of skin-colour hierarchy (2013: 171). Nevertheless, the world view contained in these paintings resonated widely within the field of human-variety theory, most especially through their captions which systematically asserted classificatory identities based on specific genealogies, such as *mestizo*, *quinterona* or *requinterona* (Bethencourt 2013: 168). As will be seen later, the language of *casta* certainly appears to have permeated the work of key race theorists like Buffon, Blumenbach and Charles White.

One of the reasons that skin colour became so central to racial identity at this point was that it could be held up as an exact indication of genealogy. Buffon had mediated on the bodily mechanics of skin colour in 1749, noting that some theorists believed it was not the skin but the membrane beneath which turned black in Africans, while he himself was more convinced that different populations had differently coloured blood (1749–88: 3.524). In 1777, however, he returned to his *Variétés dans l'espèce humaine*, making a new note to acknowledge the *casta* categories, as recently reported by Dutch philosopher Cornelius Franciscus de Pauw. According to de Pauw's *Recherches philosophiques sur les Américains* (1768), Buffon noted, different hereditary combinations could reliably be counted upon to result in specific sub-varieties, including the *Mulâtre*, the *Quarteron* and the *Octavon* (Buffon 1777: 4.504; de Pauw 1768: 1.180–1). Buffon's mention of de Pauw is significant: in his *Recherches philosophiques*, de Pauw had also written about black skin colour as a literal 'stain', which could physically tarnish the white body, remaining in a single lineage for at least four generations before it could be bred out again (1768: 1.180). Tissues composing the brain matter, blood and semen of Black Africans were darker than those of Europeans, claimed de Pauw, and this highly tenacious colouration would inevitably pass via spermatic fluid onto the next generation (1768: 1.179). De Pauw's ideas, in turn, drew on the work of French surgeon Nicolas Le Cat in his *Traité de la couleur de la peau humaine* (Le Cat 1765: 55–63), who had himself taken inspiration from the theories of seventeenth-century Italian physician Marcello Malpighi. Similar theories had surfaced in the field of hereditary disease, with physicians like Charles-Augustin Vandermonde not only cautioning against intermarriage between people with disabilities (see Chapter 6) but also denouncing alliances between 'whites' and 'negroes', which would 'bastardize' and 'adulterate' the skin colour of future generations (1756: 1.91). The notion of blackness as a literal stain had become so widespread by the mid-century, note David Bindman and Henry Louis Gates Jr (2011: 7), that William Hogarth even referenced it in his book of aesthetic theory, *The Analysis of Beauty* (1753). 'When the upper skin is taken away', Hogarth proclaims, one will find a set of 'tender threads like network, fill'd with different coloured juices . . . [including] black [in] the negro' (1753: 114).

In the 1795 edition of his *De generis*, Johann Friedrich Blumenbach identified the 'seat of colour' in the reticulum, by which he meant a second layer of skin. Under the skin of all humans, he asserted, lay a white mucous called the corium. In 'clear complexioned men', he continues, 'where they are stained with no pigment' the 'natural roseate whiteness of the corium' would typically shine through (1795a: 207–8). Darker reticula, however, were found in both exotic human varieties and the lowest orders of European society. In the first edition of his work, Blumenbach reported that the physician Christian Gottlieb Ludwig had recently dissected one of the 'lowest sort of men' who was 'blacker than an Ethiop', while Blumenbach himself had

> dissected at Jena a man's corpse of this kind, whose whole skin was brown, and in some parts, as in the scrotum, almost black. . . . Haller [the Swiss natural historian Albrecht von Haller] observed in the groin of a woman the reticulum so black that it did not seem to differ much from that of an Ethiopian; one as dark in the groin of a man was in the possession of B.S. Albinus [the Dutch anatomist Bernard Siegfried Albinus]. (1775: 109)

Like Kant, Blumenbach contends that skin colouring originally stemmed from exposure to harsh environments but eventually settled into family lines where it was propagated thereafter through hereditary action. The agency of climate 'appears most clearly', he continues, 'in the unions of people of different tints, in which cases the most distinct and contrary colours so degenerate, that white men may sensibly pass and be changed into black, and the contrary' (1775: 111).

The 1795 edition of Blumenbach's *De generis* has since gained him a somewhat outsized reputation for his perceived role in the inception of racial pseudoscience – despite the fact that he often disapproved of subsequent theorists' adaptations of his ideas (Andrew Curran 2011: 173). That legacy is partly built on his extensive use of craniometry or skull measurement. Skulls, notes Bindman, were particularly interesting to race theorists partly because they were understood to have been shaped by the brain (thereby reflecting character) and partly because they were relatively difficult to attain (2002: 209–10). Another tenacious element of Blumenbach's legacy was his terminology, inscribed in the 1795 edition's highly influential taxonomy of human variety. This taxonomy had been significantly influenced by another Gottingen academic and major figure in the history of race: Christoph Meiners. Ten years previously, Meiners's *Grundriss der Geschichte der Menschheit* ('Outline of the History of Mankind') divided humanity into two main varieties: the virtuous, beautiful 'Caucasians' (or 'Tartars') and the servile, ugly 'Mongolians' (1785: 6, 30, 26; see Baum 2006: 84–7). Caucasians, according to Meiners, were stronger in body and mind than their 'Mongolian' counterparts but were also divisible into two further *Racen* [*Rassen*]: the more sophisticated *Celtische* (Celtic, again, representing an ambiguous catch-all term at this point) and the less sophisticated *Slawische* (Slavic) (1785: preface, n.p. [xx]). In Meiners's view, human variety was inherent and inherited, with the civilized nations of earth being descended from the superior peoples of the Caucus mountains (1785: preface, n.p. [xx–xxi]; see Baum 2006: 85). In Blumenbach's varietal taxonomy, this same word 'Caucasian' comes to stand in for the lighter-skinned peoples of the world, taking both climate and descent into account in their formation. His categories included:

1. The *Caucasian* (white), encompassing Europe, North Africa and parts of Asia (as far east as the river Ganges).
2. The *Mongolian* (yellow), which represented populations in the rest of Asia as well as the Laplanders.
3. The *Ethiopian* (black), encompassing sub-Saharan Africa.
4. The *American* (copper), comprising all Amerindians 'except the *Esquimaux*' (which belonged to the Mongolian variety).
5. The *Malay* (tawny), which represented Pacific islanders (Blumenbach 1795a: 264–6).[2]

While maintaining the Latin word *varietates* as a classificatory title for these groups, Blumenbach increasingly makes use of the term 'gens' (clan, or nation) in a way that effectively corresponds with the contemporary use of 'race', as exemplified in his chapter titled *varietates coloris gentilitae* (Blumenbach 1795b: 119) which Bendyshe translates as 'racial varieties of colour' (Blumenbach 1795a: 209). A decade later, in an 1806 revision of his *Beyträge zur Naturgeschichte* ('Contributions to Natural History'), Blumenbach returned to his taxonomy and renamed his varieties as *Hauptrassen* or major races (1806b: 1.67). There was now no doubt that all men were the same species, he announced, and so we should think about human varieties 'in the same way as we classify races and degenerations of horses' (Blumenbach 1806a: 303). As with Kant, the most striking aspect of Blumenbach's racial classification is how he interprets subjects who ostensibly fall *in between* his major groups. In both the 1775 and 1795 editions of his *De generis*, he made special reference to the hybrids of the *casta* tradition, recording 'the constancy with which offspring born from parents of different colours present a middle tint made up as it were from that of either parent' (Blumenbach 1775: 112 and 1795a: 216). Unlike de Pauw, Blumenbach does not limit this theory of hereditary skin colour to a single caste system but instead draws evidence from a range of English, German and Spanish sources (including Edward Long's *History*

---

2 Blumenbach includes these English terms for his skin-colour variations in the original Latin text (1795a: 120).

of Jamaica), recording the names which had been variously attributed to these racial 'hybrids'. The first generation of intermarriage between the major varieties, Blumenbach affirms, produces the following sub-varieties:

1. A *European* and an *Ethiopian* will produce a *Mulatto*.
2. A *European* and an *American* will produce a *Mestizo*.
3. An *Ethiopian* and an *American* will produce a *Zambo* (Blumenbach 1795a: 216–17).

In the second generation, the genealogical schema becomes more complex:

1. Two *Mulattos* will produce a *Casquas*; two *Zambos* will produce a *Cholo*.
2. A *Mulatto* and a *European* will produce a *Terceron* (also called, Blumenbach notes, a *Quateron* or a *Morisco*).
3. An *American* and a *Mestizo* will produce a *Tresalvi*; an *Ethiopian* and a *Mulatto* will produce a *Griff* [*grifo*] (Blumenbach 1795a: 217).

By the third generation, Blumenbach has created whole networks of genealogical identity, wherein each subject bears a specific relation (and breeding potential) to the others:

1. A *European* and a *Terceron* will produce an *Octavon*.
2. A *Terceron* and a *Mulatto* will produce a *Saltara*.
3. A *Quarteron* and a *Mestizo* will produce a *Coyota*; a *Griff* and a *Zambo* will produce a *Givero* (Blumenbach 1795a: 217–18).

Like Kant's *Rassen*, Blumenbach's major races depend on genealogical purity in order to exist. His catalogue of hybridization demonstrates that, by definition, members of a major race must be born from two members of that same race. It follows that his 'hybrids' can only be understood according to their exact genealogical relationship with a member of one of those major races. As in a noble family, genealogical purity acts as a natural barrier, with those of mixed blood being relegated to various degrees of impure status depending on their precise degree of proximity to the dominant racial lineage.

It is sometimes remarkable to see how established this decidedly race-based discourse of varietal hybridity had become by the end of the eighteenth century. The third edition of the *Encyclopaedia Britannica* vehemently defends climate theory, but then provides its own schema of varietal bloodlines in a footnote under the entry for 'negro', explaining:

> A white man with a quadroon woman, or a negro with a quadroon woman, produce a mestizo, seven eights white and one eight black, or seven eights black and one eight white ... there being no visible difference between the fair quinteroons and the whites ... the children of a white and quinteroon consider themselves as free from all taint of the negro race. (*Encyclopaedia Britannica* 1788–97: footnote a, 7.796)

While both Blumenbach and the editors of the *Encyclopaedia Britannica* openly ridicule polygenist theory, their monogenist networks of blood identity are almost indistinguishable from some contemporary polygenist theories. In 1774, the polygenist Edward long had already referred to varietal bloodlines in terms of 'drops' and 'stains'. He points out that the Spanish colonies assign a certain social status to each degree of parentage, noting that 'a Quateron will hardly keep company with a Mulatto' and that 'the Giveros lie under the imputation of having the worst inclinations and principles' (2.261). The Dutch, Long continues, actively try to breed out this black 'stain' from their colonies. '[T]hey add drops of pure water to a single drop of dusky liquor', he explains,

> until it becomes tolerably pellucid. But this needs the apposition of such a multitude of drops, that, to apply the experiment by analogy to the human race, twenty or thirty generations, perhaps, would hardly be sufficient to discharge the stain. (Long 1774: 2.261)

Not only was skin colour hereditary, Long claims, but it would be theoretically possible to completely eliminate black skin from the human species through a controlled scheme of breeding. Like Blumenbach, Long provided a visual map of varietal bloodlines in his *History of Jamaica*. Racial descent, he asserted, could be 'mediate', meaning that one's descendants eventually changed from Black to white or *vice versa*; or it could be 'stationary', meaning that descendants remained in a state of racial hybridity (Long 1774: 2.260–1). Moreover, he once again invokes the logic of De Pauw to counter climate theory. 'The particulars wherein [black Africans] differ most' from white Europeans, he notes, include 'the dark membrane which communicates that black colour to their skins, which does not alter by transportation into other climates, and which they never lose' (Long 1774: 2.351–2).

The English physician and polygenist Charles White's *Account of the Regular Gradation in Man* (1799) offers a prime example of how these multiple and often mutually incoherent arguments could be called upon simultaneously to support the pre-existing biases underpinning race theory. In order to prove his thesis that Black Africans were immutably separate from the rest of humanity, White invokes a dizzying array of racialist arguments that had been put forth over the course of the century. First, he relates human variety to the Great Chain of Being, situating different human populations within the providential 'gradation from man to animals' (White 1799: 39). At the same time, however, he recalls the tradition of human–ape interbreeding, reminding his readers that orang-outangs 'have been known to carry off negro-boys, girls, and even women . . . and it has been asserted by some, that women have had offspring from such connections' (White 1799: 34). He goes on to provide a detailed craniometric analysis of different skull samples, referencing the diagrams of Dutch physician Petrus Camper, whose compiled *Works* had been published in English in 1794, as well as those of Swiss physiologist Johann Kasper Lavater, which had illustrated contrasting facial angles in Europeans, non-Europeans and animals (White 1799: 41–51; Bindman 2002: 211). He reiterates recent theories of inheritable black tissue, noting that 'the cuticle, including the reticulum, is much thicker and harder in black people than in white ones' and utilizes contemporary medical theories on human variety, stating, for instance, that Black Africans were considerably more susceptible to 'lockjaw' than Europeans (White 1799: 71, 73). Later on, he subscribes to the 'sixteen-fraction' model of the *casta* tradition, meticulously recording the precise blood purity of offspring issued from different varietal combinations (White 1799: 117). Like Long, White eventually concludes that blood trumped environmental influence in the formation of human type, declaring that 'no general and permanent affection of colour is produced by climate' (1799: 132). Perhaps most striking is his reference to the inferior nerve fibres in the black African body. Echoing the conviction that the upper orders were more physically and emotionally sensitive than working people, Charles White suggests that white people are similarly more sensitive than Black people, claiming that 'negroes have not that lively and delicate sense of touch that the whites have, since both the cuticle and the rete mucosum are thicker in them' (1799: 71). He supports his argument with reference to the English physician Benjamin Moseley, who had claimed some ten years previously that '[negroes] are void of sensibility to a surprising degree. They are not subject to nervous diseases . . . they bear chirurgical operations much better than white people; and what would be the cause of insupportable pain to a white man, a negro would almost disregard' (Moseley 1787: 472; White 1799: 74).

* * *

The steady rise of genealogical race in eighteenth-century human-variety theory at once signals an ontological revolution and a return to something familiar, even intuitive, in European traditions of human hierarchy. The power strategies of the noble paradigm were, after all, ideally suited to racialized discrimination. They had already been tailored over centuries to fit a schema of human hierarchy, implicitly aligning with the Great Chain of Being and confirming the natural dominance of those who already held the reins of power. The noble paradigm offered a mode of hierarchy that began with the assumption that those who controlled its parameters sat at its apex. White Europeans would never have to actively *do* anything in order to prove their natural superiority. For as long as they controlled the discourse of race, anything that deviated from their own arbitrary parameters of excellence was automatically classed as a degree of non-excellence. By this reasoning, other human 'races' were indeed human, but their genealogical status relegated them to an inferior rung of that humanity. Their lowness, like the lowness of servants or criminals, was part of the natural order. Unlike servants and criminals, however, nature had bred them into specific genealogical lines, the exact degree of which could now be ascertained by observing their physical anatomy and charting the purity of their blood. White Europeans, meanwhile, by assuming their natural superiority in terms of lineal race, became a natural elite by proxy: they alone possessed the exclusive *eugeneia* of the white race; they alone could pass this privilege down through the generations; and they, like scions of a noble line, intuitively understood that they had to protect this privilege by maintaining their genealogical integrity. In a word, genealogical race theory seized and exploited the tried and tested power strategies of the noble paradigm, creating a system in which white Europeans could demonstrably confirm their status as natural rulers.

8

Ireland's imposter aristocrats

The nobility of Ireland has thus far been largely absent from this study and for good reason. The very idea of an 'elite' in eighteenth-century Ireland was inseparable from the island's all-pervasive colonial context, rendering it markedly distinct from anything that might be found on the neighbouring island of Britain. By the eighteenth century, successive waves of colonization had left Ireland with a complex and volatile set of allegiances: the island remained within the orbit of British control but continued to exist outside the Union; its small colonial establishment was both loyal to the crown and increasingly hungry for legislative autonomy; and the bulk of its peasantry was split between a vast, deeply resentful Catholic majority and a progressively radical faction of Dissenting Protestants. The ethno-cultural patchwork created by experimental plantations in Ireland meant that to speak of a rightful 'Irish nobility' was almost impossible: one first had to define who the Irish *were*.

This chapter will explore how crude attempts to force British-style nobility onto an Irish context undermined the paradigmatic basis of the island's official peerage, thereby allowing other groups to usurp the paradigm for themselves. At the same time, it can be seen how the racialization of the 'native' Irish resulted in an unprecedented wave of cultural cohesion. Irish Catholics, having been defined by their ostensibly inferior bloodlines, were able to recentre the hierarchical discourse around the purity of their own 'race' by harnessing the noble paradigm on their own terms.

* * *

In eighteenth-century Ireland, one's family name would have automatically suggested adherence to one or more of the island's four major cultural groups. An Ó Flaithbheartaigh or an Uí Néill almost certainly hailed from the indigenous Gaelic majority. More typically Scottish surnames, such as Lindsay or Creelman, likely indicated descent from seventeenth-century colonial planters, who had mainly settled the northern province of Ulster during the previous century. A de Burgo or a Fitzgerald, meanwhile, spoke of descent from the 'Old English' – the erstwhile Hiberno-Norman elite who had, until recently, held power over much of the island for centuries. A Swift or a Sackville, conversely, might boast connections to the 'New English', an epithet given to the post-Cromwellian settlers who had seized vast tracts of Catholic land. These four cultural groups, already distinguished by way of their traditions, their language and their politics, were further segregated by entrenched religious differences. The Gaelic natives largely held firm to the Catholic faith; many descendants of Ulster planters adhered to Dissenting Protestant sects; the Old English represented a heady mix of Catholics and converts; and the New English were mostly Anglican. The sectarian penal laws (active c. 1652–1829), which denied basic civil rights to the Catholic majority (and, to a lesser extent, Dissenting Protestants), rendered these group distinctions even more complex. On one level, those laws profoundly consolidated ethnic segregation, enshrining religious, linguistic and cultural differences in a harsh and punitive legal code. On another level, they offered opportunities for advancement to those who were willing to hop the divide, especially when it came to securing land or inheritance. While in theory these groups remained markedly distinct, in practice they could also be extremely heterogeneous, having bled into one other to varying degrees over multiple generations. To further complicate matters, the island's colonial establishment promoted an idea of 'nation' that generally excluded the vast majority of Ireland's inhabitants. Even though Catholics represented somewhere in the region of 75–80 per cent of the population in the eighteenth century, the 'Irish nation' at this time generally referred only to the Protestant minority (Bartlett 2014: 521). The native Irish Catholics, much like indigenous Americans or Australians, were commonly treated as an irksome aboriginal presence on the island – an obstacle standing in the way of the nation, rather than an integral part of it. In fact, for the best part of the century, as noted by the emancipationist political writer Denys Scully in 1812, the island's Catholic majority remained somewhat existentially questionable. The Lord Chancellor of Ireland, Lord Bowes, records Scully, had firmly declared in 1759 that 'the law does not suppose any such person to exist as an Irish Roman Catholic' (Scully 1812: 334). All the 'effective inhabitants of Ireland', Scully asserts, were 'presumed to be Protestants, and . . . therefore Catholics, their clergy, worship &c., are not to be supposed to exist, save for reprehension and penalty' (1812: 333). When Jonathan Swift addressed the 'whole people of Ireland' in his *Drapier's Letters* (1724–5), claims Thomas Bartlett, it would thus have been understood that he was referring only to the small fraction of the population who adhered to the Protestant faith (Bartlett 2014: 518). In this respect, suggests Colin Kidd, the Anglo-Irish had built an identity for themselves which was not dissimilar to the 'celebrated *thèse nobiliare* by Boulainvilliers' (1999: 179). Perhaps unsurprisingly, the precise ethno-religious make-up of the country was never fully documented during the eighteenth century. Partly, claims Bartlett, because it might have highlighted the extreme minority status of the Protestant population, but also because it may simply have seemed irrelevant – 'quality, not quantity counted', and when it came to landownership and political authority, 'Protestants were the quality' (2014: 521).

This profound chasm between settler and indigene was exacerbated by contemporary understandings of Irish Catholics as morally and corporeally degenerate. The Irish body had long constituted a subject of discussion among human-variety theorists and colonial commentators alike. Johann Friedrich Blumenbach not only referred to the reported similarities between the 'pendulous' breasts of native Irish women and Hottentots but also noted comparisons between their reportedly large legs and those of the Māori people (1795a: 248–50). Even the attribution of painless childbirth, which William Grant ascribed 'rustic' peasant women in 1759 and Oliver Goldsmith reported in the barbarous nations of India in 1774, finds precedent in an earlier text on the Irish by the travel writer Fynes Moryson, who claimed in 1617 that

> [Irish] women within two hours after they are delivered many times leave their beds to sop [i.e., gossip] and drink with women coming to visit them. . . . Some say that commonly the women have little or no pain in child-bearing, and attribute the same to a broken bone. (319)

Such fantasies, in turn, were fuelled by a colonial attitude that leant heavily on dehumanization. In 1596, during the early colonial plantations, Edmund Spenser had suggested that Wesminster might speed up land clearances in Ireland by way of enforced starvation. That way, the natives, who were reported to be cannibals, would hurry along their own extermination by eating each other. Spenser based his advice on the very real effects of mass starvation he had recently witnessed in the southern province of Munster, after which 'in short space there were none almost left, and a most populous and plentiful country suddenly left void of man or beast' (1596: 510). After the Gaelic rebellion of 1641, English propaganda seized once again upon the Irish cannibal trope. Richard Lawrence's *Interest of Ireland* (1682), though published some forty years after the rebellion, described a scene of 'miserable old women and children', squatting by a campfire to watch 'a dead corpse broiling, which as the fire roasted, they cut off collaps and eat' (1682: 2.86, 87). Such ideas seem to have provided ample excuse for Cromwell's 'state-sanctioned and systematic ethnic cleansing' of the native Irish in 1649. 'The fact that [Cromwell's campaign] did not include 'total' genocide in its remit', notes Mark Lavene, 'says less about the lethal determination of its makers and more about the political, structural and financial weakness of the early modern English state' (2005: 56). Even by the turn of the nineteenth century, the Irish monster trope was still being deployed in loyalist propaganda. In 1808, the Reverend James Bentley Gordon warned that if Ireland's Republican rebels had succeeded in overthrowing British rule in 1798, cannibal scenes like those described by Lawrence more than 100 years earlier would have been all but inevitable (1808: 346).

The parallels between the racialization of the Gaelic Irish and that of more distant colonial subjects are still more interesting when we consider that Ireland and especially its Ascendancy was simultaneously implicated in the transatlantic slave trade. While the absence of 'an active and interested West Indian lobby' in Ireland meant that few records have survived, W. A. Hart estimates that the Black population in Ireland probably stood somewhere between 1,000 and 3,000 during the second half of the eighteenth century, which would have represented a significant number in relativity to other Western European countries at the time (1964: 22). The majority of surviving references allude to Black domestic servants, which appear to have been as fashionable among the Anglo-Irish elite as they were in Britain (Hart 1964: 24, 26; see Chapter 10). 'Race', then, in all senses of the word, was strangely ubiquitous in eighteenth-century Ireland: on an island that was actively involved with Britain's greater colonial projects, four major ethno-religious groups were underpinned by their lineal race, with the taboos (and legal prohibitions) of inter-community marriage ensuring a substantial degree of genealogical segregation. These genealogical identities, in turn, were entwined with ideas of social and corporeal hierarchy, marking the difference between the treacherous, savage indigene and the virtuous, instructive civilizer. Meanwhile, the Protestant 'Irish nation' remained a decidedly ambiguous construct, at once asserting its difference from Britain while maintaining a distinct remove from native Irish culture. Thus, what should have been the dominant template for pure-blood 'race' – the nobility – was, in Ireland, deeply fractured. The penal laws ensured that a British-style social hierarchy could never exist in Ireland. Nobility and gentry alike were subsumed by this greater sectarian elite known as the 'Ascendancy' – an ill-defined oligarchy based around the Dublin parliament, which was decidedly heterogeneous in its social composition (Malcomson 1978:

xix; Foster 1988: 170). 'The definition [of the Ascendancy]', notes R. F. Foster, 'revolved around *Anglicanism*', which meant that it comprised both professional and landed elites from Old English, New English and sometimes even Gaelic backgrounds (1988: 170). For most of the century, it was by virtue of being born a Protestant that one could enjoy the right to purchase land, to enter the military, to bear arms, to access or provide education, to hold office or to enter the legal professions. Some of these penal laws were gradually reformed during the last decades of the eighteenth century, but their effects nonetheless lingered on in Irish society for generations. Effective repeal was not achieved until 1829, and definitive repeal would have to wait until 1920. Consequently, even minor Protestant landlords in eighteenth-century Ireland (about 5,000 of whom possessed 95 per cent of Irish land by 1776) often wielded a brutal authority over their tenants that would have been unthinkable for even the most powerful landowners in Britain (McCracken 1986: 34). In 1776, the travel writer Arthur Young echoed the sentiments of countless astonished observers when he reported:

> A landlord in Ireland can scarcely invent an order which a servant, labourer or cotter dares to refuse to execute. Nothing satisfies him but unlimited submission . . . a poor man would have his bones broke if he offered to lift his hands in his own defence. Knocking down is spoken of in the country in a manner that makes an Englishman stare. It must strike the most careless traveller to see whole strings of cars whipt into a ditch by a gentleman's footman, to make way for his carriage; if they are overturned or broken in pieces . . . were [the tenants] to complain they would perhaps be horsewhipped. (Young 1776: 2.128)

Legally, Irish nobility referred to the Irish peerage – an institution that could be traced back to the earliest days of Norman settlement. Separate from the English and Scottish peers who sat at Westminster (having united into a single peerage after the 1707 Acts of Union), Irish peers had their own House of Lords in Dublin, where they theoretically represented the social and political apex of Irish society. Theory aside, the reality for Irish peers was not quite as eminent. In both Britain and Ireland, the eighteenth-century Irish peerage had long been synonymous with absenteeism, corruption and cynical political ambition, and it was regularly touted as a domain of 'new men' who could boast few meaningful links with ancient noble dynasties. It was 'a purely legal concept', notes A. P. W. Malcomson, 'and Irish peers were not necessarily characterized by birth, residence or lordship in Ireland, or even by the common denominator that their patents of peerage had all passed the great seal of Ireland' (2000: 293). Originally, notes Tony Barnard, the Irish peerage, along with an attendant system of squires, yeomen and primogeniture, had been established 'to bring the island closer in character to England' (2003: 7). Yet, by the eighteenth century, Dublin's House of Lords had almost become a parody of that at Westminster, wielding less power than any of Britain's other colonial assemblies and ultimately existing at the whim of London rule (Bartlett 2004: 6; Malcomson 1978: 306).

In their performance as social representatives of hierarchical cohesion and moral authority, the Irish peerage was nothing short of catastrophic. Malcomson notes that fewer than half the peers of Ireland made for a clear-cut example of 'Irish' nobility – that is to say, individuals who took a seat in the Irish House of Lords, who could boast at least some Irish ancestors or who had landed estates in Ireland (1978: 294). Instead, vast numbers of Irish noble titles belonged to Englishmen, many of whom had never set foot in the country. This obliviousness or disdain for Irish lands and titles had moreover persisted as a tradition among claimants to the Irish peerage for generations. The early seventeenth-century Wilcote baronet Sir William Pope had already accepted his Irish earldom before deciding on a location to suit his title. 'I am sertan that ther is such townes as Lucan and Granard, but can not find it in the mape', his son Thomas wrote him in 1628, 'but divers teles me for sertane there is such a places . . . if it is posible [sic] we will change Granard for a [w]hole countie' (Pope 1628: 16–17). Sir William's wish was granted: he subsequently became the 1st Earl of County Down. By the mid-eighteenth century there was 'a distinctive dearth of temporal peers in the Irish House of Lords, because [so] many of the then Irish peers were Englishmen, absentees, or bad attenders' (Malcomson 2000: 299).

Ireland's artificially stunted economy represented yet another impediment to noble performance. Successive embargoes had been imposed on Ireland at the close of the seventeenth century to ensure that it bolstered, rather than rivalled, English economic expansion. A ban on the exportation of cattle and dairy products in 1680 was followed by a ban on colonial trade in 1696 and a ban on the exportation of wool in 1699, all contributing to endemic poverty and frequent famines (Lecky 1892: 1.173–80). Absentee peers, whose fragile Irish incomes were tasked with financing a fashionable life in London, were often crippled with debt. That made for an uncomfortable contrast with Ascendancy professionals such as William Connolly, the son of an innkeeper, who was Ireland's wealthiest man on his death in 1729, or the tradesman Joseph Leeson, a brewer's son who built Ireland's largest private house in 1755 before being hastily ennobled the next year (Barnard 2003: 26). Worse still, the embarrassing poverty of Irish peers was, along with their titles, fully inheritable. In 1720, Lord Blayney had to be bailed out of debt by George I, who finally acquiesced in order to uphold the dignity of his peers (Barnard 2003: 26). The seventeenth-century Earls of Cavan and Roscommon amassed so much hereditary debt that they ended up totally at the mercy of charity from the state, with their descendants still asking the government for money, and receiving it, in 1744 (Barnard 2003: 27).

In Britain there was little question that an Irish title made for a drastically less favourable honour than an English or Scottish equivalent. 'For [many] Englishmen', notes McCahill, 'the Irish peerage constituted a sort of middle passage . . . it consoled them until they finally attained the great object of their ambitions – a British peerage' (1981: 265). In 1776, Horace Walpole lamented the vulgarities of an Irish title:

> If I would stoop to artifice, I could insert [in this letter] a list of so many new Irish Lords that there would be no room to sign my name. But what would you care for a beadroll of mushrooms, half of whom . . . will not be gentlemen under a generation or two? They are like the Lord Bateman, whom George I made an Irish peer to avoid making him a Knight of the Bath; for, said he: 'I can make him a lord, but I cannot make him a gentleman'. (1776: 6.357)

The American revolutionary wars saw a huge escalation in Irish ennoblements, largely as a precautionary measure against a copycat revolution in Dublin. In 1776 alone, notes F. G. James, 'Lord North's ministry created twenty-two Irish peers, eighteen of them within a two-day period' (1995: 89). Thus, depending on the circumstances, the granting of an Irish title could just as well have been considered a demotion, rather than an elevation, in one's political career. When William Pitt the Younger attained an Irish marquisate for Richard Wellesley, then the governor general of India, Wellesley reacted with outrage rather than gratitude. 'As I was confident there had been nothing *Irish* or *pinchbeck* in my conduct, or in its result', Wellesley raged, 'I felt an equal confidence that I should find nothing *Irish* or *pinchbeck* in my reward'. His letter is signed 'ever, dear Pitt, yours most affectionately . . . (*not having yet received my double-gilt Potatoe*)' (1800: 3.233).

In a word, the peers of Ireland had failed to successfully harness the noble paradigm: the devaluation of their titles had exposed the superficial nature of their honours, their chronic absenteeism prevented them from adequately performing their natural excellence and, worst of all, any excellence that might have been noted among them did not appear to stem from anything resembling *eugeneia*. Since the Irish peerage was widely considered to be composed of New English families, critics from all backgrounds derided it as a vulgarly recent construction, thrown together from the disparate descendants of Cromwell's barbarous army (Barnard 2003: 448–9). Since the peerage also incorporated a number of Old-English and even Gaelic family lines, it was simultaneously open to the accusation of contamination with 'mere Irish' blood. As titled peers lost their grip on the noble paradigm, however, other groups – with their own, far less fragile claims to *eugeneia* and *nobilitas* – were waiting patiently in the wings. For, the Dublin peerage was not the only group to assert noble status in eighteenth-century Ireland. The largely dispossessed Old-English dynasties still maintained a profound cultural authority and were central to a swelling rhetoric of anti-establishment sentiment over the course of the century. What is more, the seventeenth and eighteenth centuries witnessed a revived interest in Gaelic nobility, whose order had declined irrevocably after the Tudor conquests and Stuart plantations. For the Old English, notes Colin Kidd, Gaelic Ireland and its ancient dynasties promised a substantial measure of authority and they accordingly 'adopted the Gaelic past as the core element in their identity' (1999: 147). Even the Protestant Church of Ireland was now turning to the Gaelic past, carefully appropriating native Irish culture in order to obscure its conspicuous lack of historical tradition on the island (Kidd 1999: 165).

A prime example of this Gaelic revival is the seminal text of Irish history *Foras Feasa ar Éireann* ('A Foundation of Knowledge on Ireland'), originally composed in 1634 by the Old-English cleric Geoffrey Keating (Seathrún Ceitinn), with English translations still appearing in Dublin and London in 1734 (Cunningham 2001: 14). The work is notable first because it reasserted the 'natural' leadership of ancient Irish dynasties and second in that it resurrected the defunct Irish term *Éireannach* (Irish person) to mean exclusively an Irish Catholic (Bartlett 2014: 518). It was the ancient high-king Brian Ború who had 'appointed sirnames of distinction, to all the several branches of the Milesian race', reads one 1723 Dublin edition, 'in order . . . that the genealogies might be better preserved with more regularity' (Keating 1634: 90). The translator of this edition was certainly aware of the work's political significance, describing it in his dedication as

> a most sacred refuge . . . from the centuries of illiterate and unjust men who insolently attempt to vilifie and traduce the lineal descendants of the great Milesians (a marshall, a learned, and generous race), as a nation ignorant, mean-spirited and superstitious. (Keating 1634: 10–11)

Keating's careful association of Gaelic lineage and Catholic faith with 'true' Irishness thus added another layer of racialized identity to early modern Irish society. By uniting the Catholic Irish around their shared Gaelic lineage, *Foras*

Feasa automatically excluded the Protestant Irish by reason of their supposed British descent. According to this reasoning, the New English could not possibly claim 'Irish' nobility because they were not of the Irish race. A convenient exception was made for the Catholic Stuart Kings, it might be noted, whom Keating allows to claim rightful authority over Ireland because of their 'Scotic' ancestors (Cunningham 2001: 16).

Keating's interpretation of Irish history also delineated a valuable element of proto-nationalist rhetoric by emphasizing the common ground between the Old-English and Gaelic nobilities: a shared history and identity which markedly distinguished them from their New English successors. The Old English, after all, had long ago earned a reputation for 'going native'. Since they had first arrived in Ireland in the twelfth century, Hiberno-Norman settlers had tended to become absorbed into the sociopolitical framework of Gaelic Ireland. To Westminster's immense frustration, wave after wave of these settlers failed to anglicize the native population and instead fell victim to the phenomenon of *Hiberniores Hibernis ipsis* (becoming 'more Irish than the Irish themselves'), adopting Gaelic dress, language, law and tradition. By the early modern period, many of the most prominent Old-English families in Ireland had become thoroughly Gaelicized, and proudly boasted a uniquely Hiberno-Norman identity. In 1612, the poet and member of parliament Sir John Davies pinpointed these Old-English renegades as the reason why Ireland had never been properly subdued. Not only did English colonists 'forget the English Language, & scorne the use thereof', but they 'grew to bee ashamed of their very English Names, though they were noble and of great antiquity; and tooke Irish *surnames* and *nicke-names*' (emphasis in original) (Davies 1612: 182). The Condon dynasty of Waterford, Davies reported with dismay, had renamed itself 'Mac Maioge' and the once-stately Bourkes had become 'Mac William Eighter'. '[T]his they did in contempt and hatred of the English name and nation', Davies continued, 'these degenerate families became more mortal enemies, then the mere [i.e. Gaelic] Irish' (Davies 1612: 183–4). This reputation, coupled with centuries of intermarriage into Gaelic aristocracy, allowed the Old English to seamlessly claim legitimacy as natural rulers of the Irish. By the eighteenth century, it was becoming clearer than ever before that they and their Gaelic counterparts enjoyed access to a brand of noble authority that existed only in the dreams of many a titled peer seated in the colonial parliament.

Keating's writings provided the foundation for a whole movement of Gaelic revival rhetoric in the mid-eighteenth century. The antiquarian and Catholic emancipationist Charles O'Conor, for example, who claimed descent from the

Gaelic kings of Connacht, used his extensive study of ancient Irish manuscripts to vindicate native Irish political systems as not only equal but superior to those imposed by Britain. In his *Dissertations on the History of Ireland* (1753) he deploys the old trick of the noble paradigm by asserting that ancient kings of Ireland came to their thrones by merit of great actions, unlike the 'modern monarchs' who were empowered by primogeniture and addicted to luxury and pomp (O'Conor 1753: 46). Moreover, he claims, 'government which prevailed in *Ireland* was a mixed monarchy', far predating the similar yet structurally inferior system in neighbouring Britain (emphasis in original) (O'Conor 1753: 56). In a clever inversion of established ethno-histories, O'Conor intimates that Britain's comparatively deficient mode of government is partly a result of their having been ruled by backwards and illiterate Goths. It took troops of Irish Monks to finally teach 'the *Saxons* and the *Normans* the use of letters', he reminds his readers. 'When Europe groaned under the servitude of Gothic ignorance, *Ireland* became the prime seat of learning to all Christendom' (O'Conor 1753: 204).

In London, these increasingly loud assertions of true Irish nobility were hastily showered with anxious ridicule. Bombastic pride in family names is an element of anti-Irish caricature that can be found throughout the literature of eighteenth-century Britain. Tobias Smollett's *Expedition of Humphry Clinker* (1771), for example, sends up the typical Irish gentleman at Bath in the heiress-hunting figure of Master Macloughlin:

> My name (said he) is Master Macloughlin; but it should be Leighlin O'Neale, for I am come from Tir-Owen the Great; and so I am as good a gentleman as any in Ireland; and that rogue, your sarvant, said I was a taylor, which was as big a lie as if he'd called me the pope. I'm a man of fortune, and have spent all I had. (Smollett 1771: 2.47)

This scene, interestingly, possibly satirizes the dramatist Charles Macklin (discussed later), whose real name (Mac Lochlainn) really did have connections with the Gaelic Uí Néill dynasty, erstwhile rulers of the Ulster kingdom of Tír Eoghain. Earlier in the text, the idea of treacherous Irishmen using phoney genealogy to manoeuvre their way into English high society is given a somewhat sinister edge, when the main character's young nephew, Jery, describes some of his new acquaintances:

> The Irishman is a political writer, and goes by the name of my Lord Potatoe. He wrote a pamphlet in vindication of a minister, hoping his zeal would be rewarded with some place or pension ... [then] he published an answer to his own production. In this he addressed the author under the title *your Lordship*

with such solemnity, that the public swallowed the deceit. (Smollett 1771: 1.181–2)

Ireland's imposter aristocrats commonly manifested in the British imagination as fortune hunters, who would woo gormless English heiresses with fantastical stories of their illustrious families and grand estates back home. Henry Fielding's *Tom Jones* (1749) recounts the story of an Irish *callabro* who travels to Bath and convinces a young gentlewoman to run away with him, only to reveal himself as 'an absolute wild Irishman' (1749: 3.80). The Irish fortune hunter was still being lampooned in 1779, when James Gillray published a satirical print titled *Paddy on Horseback* (see Figure 10). The image depicts a ragged Irishman riding backwards on a bull in the direction of London (referencing a contemporary genre of absurdist humour known as the 'Irish bull'). Beside him rests a sack of potatoes, a book entitled *A New System of Fortune Hunting* and a list detailing the names, addresses and finances of the capital's eligible heiresses, beginning with 'Lady Mary Rotten Rump, St. James Square, £30,000' and descending in order of income.

In his 1759 London stage play *Love-à-la-Mode*, the Irish playwright Charles Macklin (born Cathal Mac Lochlainn) rehearsed the trope of bombastic family pride through the medium of farce. Macklin's main character, Sir Callaghan O'Brallaghan, at once denotes the barbarity of the 'wild' Irish natives and the

Figure 10 'Paddy on Horseback' by James Gillray (1779), London: William Humphry. © National Portrait Gallery.

administrative incompetence of the Protestant Ascendancy, while deriving his main dramatic motivation from the ostensibly preposterous conviction that an Irish surname was not only as good as but better than a British noble title. As the female lead is informed near the beginning of the play, '[y]ou may laugh madam, but [Sir Callaghan] is as proud of his name as any of your lovers are of their titles' (Macklin 1759: act 1, p. 7). The farcical nature of Sir Callaghan's parochial airs, however, is also transgressive – particularly in that it actively extols 'pure' Gaelic nobility: 'My moder's side', he announces, 'is a little upstart family that came in vid one Strongbow . . . my father's side are all the true old Milesians, and the O'Shoknesses and the Mac Loughlins . . . and all the tick blood of the nation' (Macklin 1759: act 1, p. 21). 'Strongbow' (Richard de Clare, 2nd Earl of Pembroke), whose marriage to a Leinster princess in 1170 was the founding myth of Anglo-Irish supremacy on the island, represents a claim to nobility that is quintessentially colonial; in stark contrast, Mac Loughlin (Mac Lochlainn, meaning 'Son of the Lakes') is the Gaelic original of Macklin's own anglicized name – denoting a much more ancient blood hierarchy that was hiding in plain sight.

Far more explicit was Macklin's later play *The True-born Irishman* (1762), which, tellingly, had to be re-titled *The Irish Fine Lady* before it was allowed to go on stage in London. Here, Macklin presents the rusticity of the Irish gentleman as inherently *superior* to the superficial trappings of British-style peerage. When Murrough O'Dogherty, the titular true-born Irishman, learns that his wife wishes him to vie for a peerage, he replies with disdain for the whole institution:

> She would have me desert my friends and sell myself, my honour, and my country, as several others have done before me, merely for a title . . . and sink the antient name of Dogherty in the upstart title of Lady Thingum. (Macklin 1762: act 1, p. 9)

'[W]hat are your Jones and your Stones . . .', he declares later, when he has convinced his wife to recognize the value in her Gaelic lineage,

> and a parcel of little pimping names that a man would not pick out of the street, compared to the O'Donovans, the O'Callaghans [etc.] . . . for they come out of the mouth like a storm; and are as old as the Bog of Allen, though they have been dispossessed by upstarts and foreigners. (Macklin 1762: act 2, p. 46)

The 'foreigners' O'Dogherty refers to are the Anglo-Irish 'nation' and their British cousins, here judged by a cultural standard which holds Gaelic nobility as a touchstone of social value. Ireland's legally recognized peers, meanwhile, are not only dismissed as faux-nobles but repudiated as mediocre hacks in comparison with the true-born hereditary elites of the island. Unsurprisingly, London audiences were not amused when Macklin brought *The True-born Irishman* to Covent Garden in 1767 – despite the fact that he had vigorously edited the text for smoother consumption by the British public. An attempted revival of the play at Bath over thirty years later in 1801 saw it cancelled after just one night (Goring 2002: 64).

The rhetoric of superior Gaelic nobility only grew in popularity during the 1780s and 1790s as Ireland fell rapidly into political turmoil. In 1782, the Irish Patriot Party succeeded in winning an unprecedented degree of legislative independence from Westminster, rendering the colonial parliament more autonomous than it had been for centuries. This, paired with the fallout of American independence and the outbreak of revolution in France, had facilitated an acute weakening of the penal laws – especially evident in the rise of interdenominational militias like the Irish Volunteers. Ideas of the 'Irish nation' at this time can be seen to increasingly shift away from the Anglo-Irish establishment and to instead centre more squarely on an idea of shared heritage between the Gaelic Irish and the Gaelicized Old English. In one little-known novel of 1797, Mrs F. C. Patrick's *The Irish Heiress* (1797), the author identifies the unrecognized Gaelic and Old-English nobility as the Catholic saviours of British social order, while the Westminster peerage, ruined by fashionable excess and superficial morals, is linked with the anarchy of the French Revolution. Augusta O'Flaherty, the novel's protagonist, is born to an Irish Catholic squire and an English Protestant noblewoman, yet it is her Gaelic lineage that primarily defines her sense of nobility. Describing her family history, she explains:

> My grandfather was offered a title by the late Duke of Bedford, on condition of rising his influence at an election – his answer was an Irish one, for it was a question, 'Is it me, honey? Me, Terry O'Flaherty that you would make a lord? Me, that am descended from the kings of Connaught? . . . everybody knows me and mine these four thousand years, nor will they forget those after me as long as they keep up their names, but if we take up titles, then we shall mix with all the new lords that nobody knows, nor anybody wants to know'. (Patrick 1797: 1.5–6)

Those who profess true Gaelic blood in Patrick's novel do not shy away from proclaiming themselves Ireland's real hereditary rulers. They are presented, in effect, as a clandestine nobility, whose natural claim to power has been waiting patiently in the wings of colonial Ireland for centuries. Their reassertion of hereditary power, the novel suggests, will go hand in hand with a revolution against the yoke of British subjugation. Their Gaelic lineage, meanwhile, supersedes all the traditions of British honorary titles, representing a purely genealogical identity into which one cannot simply be ennobled. When Augusta's English father-in-law, Lord Mostyn, questions the value of 'Irish blood', her outraged father replies in kind: 'it is not withstanding . . . the purest [blood]', he roars, 'for Ireland has been once betrayed, while England has been often conquered' (Patrick 1797: 1.9).

The very idea of untainted Irish blood turned the noble paradigm on its head. In Britain, isolated bloodlines usually worked in opposition to the plethoric descent of the non-noble, with the unchecked breeding of the lower orders diffusing and negating any potential for hereditary privilege. In Ireland, however, noble and even royal bloodlines could be claimed by anyone with the right surname. Those who were beginning to reassert their Gaelic lineage also reasserted their ancient seats of governance, their illustrious ancestors and their age-old political allegiances, making for an awkward contrast with the absentee coterie of 'new men' who were perceived to dominate Dublin's colonial peerage. This paradoxical situation was further complicated by Britain's racialized view of the native Irish. The juxtaposition of the term 'Irish' (denoting Catholicism, barbarism and disloyalty) with the term 'nobility' (here denoting British civility and parliamentary fidelity to Westminster) invoked a set of cultural anxieties that were difficult to ignore. Even the most anglicized of the Anglo-Irish nobility in eighteenth-century British literature are invariably stained with the negative associations of Irish identity. Nor were these negative associations entirely symbolic. The tradition of *Hiberniores Hibernis ipsis* could, in many respects, be interpreted as the literal effects of an Irish environment on the bodies and minds of the high-born. Such notions are frequently echoed in late-century depictions of Irish peers in literature, as exemplified in the character of Lord Newry in Elizabeth Blower's 1785 society novel *Maria*. A villainous rake, Lord Newry, represents a character whose noble body and blood have been possessed by the treacherous spirit of the native Irish. When he is first introduced in the novel, entering into a drawing room full of wellborn ladies, the duplicity of Newry's character almost envelops his physical presence:

> Lord Newry was a native of the Kingdom of Ireland, about the age of five and twenty; his figure was tall and manly; his eyes were dark and had a fire and wildness bordering on ferocity; his complexion was florid, his features prominent and masculine; and his profile of the Grecian turn . . . render[ing] his

person generally pleasing to the ladies; though his manners had more ease than elegance, and his conversation displayed a greater degree of spirit and vivacity, than wit or solid understanding. (Blower 1785: 1.137)

Terms like 'native', 'wildness' and 'ferocity' here leave little doubt about Newry's decidedly Irish constitution, almost boiling over into his 'florid' complexion and 'easy' manners. What is most interesting about this description, however, is the veneer of exotic beauty which masks his true nature. Even his civility seems not quite right, presenting all the expressions of well-bred disinterestedness while appearing to tend towards 'spirit' and 'vivacity' which can be understood in the given context as intemperance and extravagance. Unsurprisingly, Newry is soon revealed as a cruel tyrant and a sexual profligate, using his title not to uphold the dignity of his rank but to pursue his own immoral pleasures.

No literary peer, however, could match the very real and dramatic exploits of eighteenth-century Ireland's most infamous nobleman: Lord Edward Fitzgerald. Son of Ireland's highest-ranking family, Lord Edward boasted noble credentials which qualified him within each competing tradition of hereditary rule on the island. First, the Fitzgeralds were perfect paragons of the Protestant Ascendancy and the official peerage of Ireland. In 1766, Lord Edward's father, James Fitzgerald, became the country's premier peer when he was titled Duke of Leinster while also maintaining an esteemed English peerage as Viscount Leinster of Taplow. The elder Fitzgerald was highly popular, making a point of remaining in Ireland instead of decamping to England and 'commanding a sizeable block of MPs' in the Ascendancy parliament (Tillyard 1998: 8). Second, the Fitzgeralds were a quintessentially Old-English family, tracing their line right back to the very first generations of Norman settlers. Their ancestors, furthermore, included some of the most iconic figures of Old-English resistance to London rule. Gearóid Mór Mac Gearailt, the fifteenth-century Lord Deputy of Ireland, had shown sufficient infidelity to the crown that he was sent to the Tower as a traitor, while Tomás Mac Gearailt, also known as Tomás an tSíoda (Silken Thomas), had denounced allegiance to the English monarch in 1534 and led a full-scale rebellion against the loyalist stronghold of Dublin castle. As their Gaelicized names suggest, the Fitzgeralds were also an exemplary product of *Hiberniores Hibernis ipsis*, with multiple generations having adopted the Irish language and culture and assimilating into Gaelic dynasties. In the fourteenth century, Gearóid Iarla Mac Gearailt, Earl of Desmond had gone so far as to explicitly claim the patronage of Áine, the Gaelic sovereignty goddess of Munster, dubbing his late father 'the King of Áine' and himself the 'Son of the cavalier of bright Áine' (Ó hÓgáin

2006: 8). The young Lord Edward, however, brought an entirely new dimension to the Geraldine tradition. Young, handsome and immensely popular, he scandalized Dublin and London alike when he denounced the institution of nobility entirely and took up arms against the British crown. Having been introduced to Revolutionary politics in Paris in the early 1790s, Fitzgerald had become deeply invested in the idea of an independent, secular Irish republic. In 1792, he renounced his title for the epithet 'citizen' and was consequently expelled from the army. Thereafter, he became a notorious figure on the streets of Dublin, reportedly abandoning his horse and carriage to walk the streets in a tricolour cravat, cropping his hair short in the revolutionary style and attending Ascendancy functions uninvited – only to hiss at 'God Save the King' (Bartlett, Dawson and Keogh 1998: 91–3; Tillyard 1998: 205–66).

It was during this same time that radical revolutionaries were preparing for what would become one of the bloodiest and most devastating uprisings Ireland had ever seen: the 1798 Rebellion. This rebel movement was chiefly inspired by the American and French Revolutions, and its architects (principally Theobald Wolfe Tone, a Protestant barrister) saw extreme potential in the rising doctrines of secular republicanism. The Society of United Irishman, formed in 1791, capitalized on the deeply held resentments in every quarter of Ireland's fragmented society by calling on Catholics, Protestants and Dissenters to form a united front against British rule. While this dream was never fully realized, the significant inter-religious cooperation that characterized the rebellion was enough to threaten a total breakdown of Ireland's sectarian order. British propagandists went to great lengths to portray the uprising as a purely Catholic phenomenon, but they were at pains to obscure the fact that it actually derived its greatest impetus from Dissenting radicals in Ulster and a conglomeration of Dissenter and Anglican republicans in Dublin – with both groups only later calling upon the Catholic majority for support (Bartlett, Dawson and Keogh 1998: 18). Lord Edward Fitzgerald's multifaceted credentials made him an ideal figurehead for the United Irishmen. With his bloodline inescapably linking him to the highest nobility of Ireland, Fitzgerald represented an open and high-profile defection from the colonial establishment, all the while lending the United Irishmen 'a glamour and an instant pedigree of centuries of Geraldine resistance' (Tillyard 1998: 205). Furthermore, the rejection of a noble title by this Hiberno-Norman nobleman made for a profound validation of an Irish identity that was definitively opposed to the colonial 'Irish Nation'. The promised leadership of a true-born Irish noble – albeit promoting the establishment of an Irish republic which would presumably retain neither peerage nor House of

Lords – reinforced the idea that Irish nobility existed in spite of the colonial establishment, not because of it. Noble blood in this country, it seemed, was independent of colonial order, rather forming an inherent and ineffaceable element of the 'Irish race'.

Lord Edward ended his life as one of the 30,000 casualties of the rebellion in the summer of 1798 – adding to a greater death count, notes Susan Egenolf, than that of the French Reign of Terror (2009: 49). Long after the calamitous defeat of Fitzgerald and the United Irishmen, however, and for generations after the subsequent induction of the Irish parliament and peerage into the United Kingdom in 1801, this notion of true Irish nobility – along with its various (and variable) associations with Old-English dynasties – remained a powerful element of the Irish nationalist tradition. The very idea of 'true-born' Irish nobility not only fractured the hegemonic paradigm of noble race, but in doing so it presented a direct challenge to the integrity of British hereditary privilege and thus to the authority of the colonial elite in Ireland. Irish nobility offers a uniquely intricate vision of the racialized body in the eighteenth century, because it does not simply oppose a noble-caste of 'super-humanity' against a slave-caste of 'sub-humanity', but – by its very essence of racialization – allows the slave-caste to independently assume a race-based superiority while permitting an invalidation of the noble-caste on account of its perceived lack of racial integrity. In eighteenth-century Ireland, that is to say, noble race became almost indistinguishable from ethno-varietal identity – offering multiple, competing communities a power strategy of inborn excellence which promised to bolster and protect anyone who could manage to control its discourse.

9

The South Seas

Laboratory of the noble physique

The influence of nobility on the shape of emerging race theory is perhaps nowhere as evident as in the South Seas, where wave after wave of eighteenth-century natural historians suggested that the hereditary elites of certain Oceanic islands demonstrated a different varietal type from their social inferiors. What these observers were actually witnessing, as will be seen, was usually quite different from what they imagined. What is striking, however, is their consistent tendency to project the paradigm of hereditary nobility onto these racialized bodies, not only framing emerging racial categories according to European social codes of bloodline and civility but interpreting the ostensibly superior physique of the South Seas islanders as evidence that the 'true' noble body was recognizably different after all. This chapter analyses the observations of Joseph Banks, James Cook, Johann Reinhold Forster and Georg Forster during their expeditions to the South Seas, before following them back to London and charting how the discovery of a 'noble physique' in Oceania was received at the British court.

* * *

When the English ethnologist James Cowles Prichard published his *Researches into the Physical History of Man* in 1813, he included what had by then become a routine observation about the populations inhabiting the South Seas islands. There were two principal types of islanders in this region, he recorded: the first was 'universally in that rude unimproved state', with the rudest 'form and complexion approximate to those of the Negro'. The second type of islander, however, was apparently quite different. It incorporated:

> an elevated rank of people who are distinguished in many respects from the lower orders, and particularly in the physical description of their persons. Their form and complexion approach considerably towards those of Europeans, while

the aspect of the inferior class borders closely on the rude and uncultivated constitution of the races arranged in the first division. (Prichard 1813: 250)

Prichard was drawing from decades of established tradition. Since the European arrival in Tahiti in the 1760s, observers had consistently distinguished the South Seas islanders for their highly advanced system of social hierarchy and, most especially, for the ostensibly 'European' beauty of their ruling castes. Successive commentators had not only asserted that the Tahitians' precise social status had transformed their physical bodies but frequently interpreted these physical differences as the manifestation of distinct human varieties. In other words, the process of varietal diversification was understood to have taken place *within* Tahitian society, with social rank being the primary agent of physical transformation. More than this, those at the upper reaches of this society were portrayed as being at the upper reaches of varietal hierarchy; as they climbed the ladder of civility, their bodies became whiter. In many ways, these theories about Tahitian society simply bore out the base logic of contemporary human-variety theory. After all, the idea of a society wherein rank and race were visibly correlated had been implicit right across the spectrum of eighteenth-century human-variety theory, from Cheyne's distinction of nerve fibres and moral sensibility, to Buffon's physiological differentiation between the urban rich and the rural poor, to Goldsmith's and Blumenbach's observations of skin colour degeneration in the lower ranks and 'brilliant whiteness' among the established elite. The racialized ranks of Tahiti simply provided a forthright example of a race/rank dynamic that had long been presumed. Furthermore, this was an idea of race and rank which involved the reinterpretation of Tahitian ritual and religion in terms of 'feudal' social structures, constructing a schema of corporeal race around an equally constructed schema of Eurocentric political hierarchy.

Kathleen Wilson has noted that Captain James Cook's three voyages to the South Seas – first aboard the *Endeavour* from 1768–71 and twice more aboard the *Resolution* during the years 1772–5 and 1776–80 – fell during a period of 'political, cultural and imperial crises [which] had raised urgent questions about empire, "race" and [Britain's] relationship to national identity' (2003: 56). In the backdrop of growing turbulence in the American colonies and fortifying opposition to the transatlantic slave trade, Wilson suggests, Cook's Pacific voyages constituted a certain rehabilitation of English national character on the colonial stage. An endless series of biographies, dramas and paintings, she notes, constructed an image of Captain Cook as a modern and enlightened English explorer, bringing British art, government and civility to the most remote corners of the world. The voyages were noted for their dedication to empirical research, receiving sponsorship from the Royal Society, the king and the admiralty for the commission of 'trained naturalists, astronomers and artists' who were to collect vast new banks of data on Pacific civilizations (Wilson 2003: 56–61).

The idea that there were numerous and distinctive 'races' in the islands of the South Seas had already been established well before Cook set out on his first voyage. George Robertson, who had briefly anchored at Tahiti in 1767, recorded in his journal that there were 'three distink colours of people here',

> which is a thing most difficult to account for of anything which we have yet seen, the red people are ten times more numerous nor the mustees, which is a medium between the whitest sort and the red or Indian colour, and the mustees are near ten times as numerous as the whitest sort. (Robertson 1948: 179)

There were also, notes Robertson, 'a great many familys of jolly fatt well made people', on the island, 'mutch fairer nor any that we ever saw before', and these families seemed to form 'the people of the first rank' (1948: 204). All of the servants who paddled these families from place to place in canoes, he observes, '[were] of a coper colour and their masters and mistresses seemd to have a great power over them, the whole of the fair people sit under the canopys' (Robertson 1948: 227).

It was Louis Antoine de Bougainville, on claiming Tahiti for France under the name *La Nouvelle-Cythère* in 1768, who probably had the greatest influence on how this island hierarchy was to be conceived. Bougainville presumed that island society would be egalitarian but soon identified distinct ranks within the local social structure, which he recorded in his *Voyage autour du monde* (1771) as *les rois, les grands, les gens du peuple, les esclaves and les valets* (1771: 229). In 1772, Johann Reinhold Forster, soon to take over as natural historian on Cook's second voyage, published an English translation of Bougainville's account titled the *Voyage Round the World* (not to be confused with similarly titled volumes by Forster and his son published in later years). 'The distinction of ranks is very great at Tahiti, and the disproportion very tyrannical', Forster transcribed,

> the kings and grandees have the power of life and death over their servants and slaves, and I am inclined to believe they have the same barbarous prerogative with regard to the common people, whom they call *Tat-einou*, vile men.... The grandees have liverees for their servants. In proportion as the master's rank is more or less elevated, their servants wear their sashes more or less high. This sash is fastened close under the arms, in the servants of the chiefs, and only covers the loins in these belonging to the lowest class of nobility. (Bougainville 1772: 269–70)

The very notions of 'grandees', 'liveries' and 'servants' here establish an important sense of contemporary European social organization. Even though the servant Bougainville observes is very nearly naked, he does not interpret the 'sash' (*pièce d'étoffe*) as a symbol of moral degeneracy as he might have done with the Hottentots or Bushmen. Instead, Bougainville understands the servant's garment as a ceremonial declaration of the precise social rank of his master in the gradations of Tahitian nobility. Tahiti's hereditary elite, that is, informs Bougainville's perception of that society's national character. Notably, he employs the French term *race* to describe the island's different social groups – a word which implied inherited rank while also importing a Buffonian dimension of varietal hereditary succession. Forster, accordingly, translates the term directly to English as 'race':

> The inhabitants of Tahiti consist of two races of men. . . . The first, which is the most numerous one, produces men of the greatest size; it is very common to see them measure six feet. . . . I have never saw men better made and whose limbs were more proportionate: in order to paint a Hercules or a Mars, one could nowhere find such beautiful models. Nothing distinguishes their features from those of the Europeans: and if they were cloathed; if they lived less in open air, and were less exposed to the sun at noon, they would be as white as ourselves. . . . The second race are of a middle size, have frizzled hair as hard as bristles, and both in colour and features, they differ but little from mulattoes. (Bougainville, J. R. Forster trans. 1772: 249)

Here, Bougainville has set the groundwork for a thoroughly racialized vision of the upper and lower orders of Tahiti. Each rank is assigned a different mode of varietal causality: the first race, already aligned with classical beauty ideals, is so little affected by climate that its complete transformation into a full 'European' variety requires no more than studied avoidance of the midday sun; those of the second race, conversely, are characterized by those features which deviate from European beauty ideals and denote varietal ignobility. Their comparison to mulattos, moreover, identifies their darker skin colour not with climate but with the hereditary effects of miscegenation.

The first natural historian to accompany Cook aboard the *Endeavour* was Sir Joseph Banks. A dedicated follower of the Linnaean method, Banks was intrigued by the physical differences between ranks in Tahiti, though he was rather less impressed by the physique of the 'superior sort' than Bougainville. The tall and handsome upper orders, he notes, could not truly accede to the beauty of Europeans because of their generally 'broader' noses. The 'inferior sort', however, were certainly much smaller in stature – probably owing to their 'early amours', to which he believed they were 'much more addicted . . . than their superiors' (Banks 1768-71: 1.334-5). For Banks, the islanders' skin colour mainly reflected their respective daily activities:

> those of inferior rank . . . are obliged in the exercise of their professions, fishing especially, to be much exposed to the sun and air are of a dark brown; the superiors again who spend most of their time in their houses under shelter are seldom browner (the women especially) than that kind of brunette which many in Europe prefer to the finest red and white. (Banks 1768-71: 1.334)

Most notable is Bank's interpretation of the Tahitian form of government, which he identifies as an 'early state of feudal laws by which our ancestors were so long governed' (Banks 1768-71: 1.432). The superior rank the Tahitians called the *Earee ra hie*, he claims, answers to the European rank of 'king', being always the male head of the best family in the country. Ranking directly below the *Earee ra hie* are a set of about 100 important figures known as *Earees*, each of whom represents an individual district of the island and whom Banks likens to the rank of 'baron'. These baron figures appear to rent their land to a middling rank of islanders, known as the *Manahounies*, whom Banks dubs as 'vassals' since they offer their service to the local *Earee* in return for military protection. Each *Earee*, he notes, also presided over a kind of court, at which their younger brothers held distinguished positions and where they could display the splendour and riches of their estate. Between the ranks of *Earee* and *Manahounie*, Banks identifies two additional median grades, the *Erate* and *Towha*, whom he believed answered to the ranks of 'Yeoman' and 'Gentleman', respectively. At the very bottom of Tahitian hierarchy were the *Toutous*, 'who are almost on the same footing as the slaves in the East Indian Islands, only that they never appeared to us transferable from one [island] to the other' (Banks 1768-71: 1.433).

Much like the comparable tendency among observers to compare Oceanic islanders with figures from Greek and Roman antiquity, this attribution of feudal-style titles should be understood as conscious cultural interpretation – a kind of translation of this incredibly exotic civilization using terms and concepts that a European reader could better comprehend. Yet, by situating this remote island community at an advanced stage of civil progress, there is also an implicitly historicizing element to Banks's descriptions. The conventions of stadial theory are here used to portray the Tahitians as living in a golden age of feudal hierarchy, wherein rank is natural, uncontested and imprinted onto the bodies of the islanders. At the same time, this historicized view of social order is overlaid with the contemporary language of varietal hierarchy. Banks's reference to 'slaves in the East Indian Islands' most likely alludes to the tens of thousands of African slaves who had been transported to the island of Sumatra to work on the British East India Company's pepper factories around this time (Allen 2018: 156). The *Toutous*, then, are directly aligned with contemporary chattel slavery, and Banks seems surprised that in Tahiti they are not bought, sold and traded from one island to another.

Alongside this nascent form of European social structure, Banks recognizes a surprising degree of 'civility' in the way the Tahitians dress and present themselves. The custom of tattooing, he notes, though at first abhorrent to European eyes, often served the very same purpose for Tahitian women as black felt patches did for 'our European ladies'. Tattoos were a more extreme cosmetic recourse, he suggests, because even the best Tahitian complexions were not so brilliantly white as those of European women, yet their similar employment nonetheless demonstrated that 'whiteness is [here] esteemed the first essential in beauty' (Banks 1768–71: 1.339). Likewise, the superior ladies of Tahiti, just like their counterparts in Europe, derived 'gentle amusement' from sewing, dying and constructing new clothes from bark cloth. Their dress is 'often very genteel', he notes, and is composed of 'a kind of petticoat (*parou*) wrapped around their hipps', made from a single piece of cloth two yards wide and eleven yards long, 'for the rich seem to show their greatest pride in wearing a large quantity of cloth' (Banks 1768–71: 1.340). Atop all this, he records, they wear wigs of human hair, plaited in coconut oil, which are then wrapped around the head, 'the effect of which if done with taste was most becoming' (Banks 1768–71: 1.342). Banks insists that all Tahitian islanders are remarkably hygienic, taking care to remove excess body hair and always perfuming themselves with a special coconut lotion infused with flowers and herbs. Though he warrants that the smell of coconuts was quite unappealing to the European sense of smell, once one had adjusted to the aroma, 'it must be preferred to the odoriferous perfume of toes and armpits so frequent in Europe' (Banks 1768–71: 1.343).

The colonial projection of European civility and governmental systems is all the more pertinent when contrasted with what the colonists seem to have been actually observing. Douglas Oliver has noted that what visitors interpreted as hierarchy and deference in island society usually referred to the extremely complex system of *tapu* (taboo), which marked out certain members of the community (often hereditarily based) as sacred and/or proscribed from normal social interaction from a very young age (1974: 158). One of these ritual practices, for example, was the system of *ha'apori*, which translates as 'to make fat and delicate by keeping out of the sun' and which undoubtedly resulted in certain islanders being significantly taller, more corpulent and paler than others (Oliver 1974: 158). The physical bodies of those who underwent *haʻapori* were themselves considered *tapu* and were subject to a range of ritualistic treatments: sometimes the subjects could not walk on common ground, as they would render it *tapu* in their wake and thus forbidden to others, so they were often carried from place to place or ferried in canoes; in other instances, they were not permitted to feed themselves, so they had to be hand-fed by devotees; and, in the aim of bleaching their skin and developing as much body fat as possible, they were sometimes confined to their dwellings for months at a time, while others brought them food and provisions (Oliver 1974: 157–9). As J. C. Beaglehole explains, 'The *arii* commanded and was obeyed',

> he was addressed in special forms; his person, his clothing, his possessions were protected by *tapu*; he had his officials – his priest, his war-leader, his orator, his executive assistants ... he had his mountain, his promontory, his gathering place for assemblies; he had his symbols of authority, his staff and spear ... if he were an *arii nui* or *rahi* his sanctity extended to his house, his canoe, the ground on which he trod; his body and his head especially was sacred, or *tapu*. (Beaglehole 1967: clxxix)

It is little wonder that such treatment, coupled with the pre-existing biases of previous reports, might be misinterpreted as a mode of rank deference. Moreover, notes Jonathan Lamb, at the very moment Europeans were exploring the South Seas, Tahiti's *Ari'i* were increasingly involved with a flourishing religious cult, the *Arioi*, which was 'characterized by epicureanism and spectacular celebratory displays' (2001: 150).

One of these lavish ceremonies may well feature in Georg Forster's later *Voyage Round the World* (1777), which anticipated his father Johann's better-known publication of a similar name (discussed later). Georg Forster provides an interesting description of what he assumes to be a pantomime performed by the chief's daughters and wherein bark cloth and other offerings are hung from the waist of female *Ari'i*. What he was really witnessing, notes Oliver, was probably a standard island ceremony used to validate agreements (Oliver 1974: 158–9). In Georg's eyes, however, the young noblewomen, as he sees them, are presenting him with a strangely exotic version of European court fashion:

> Their dress was remarkably different from the usual fashion of these islands. It consisted of a piece of brown cloth ... [or] a piece of blue European cloth, closely wrapped around the breasts so as to resemble the close dresses which our ladies

wear; a kind of ruff of four rows of their cloth, alternately red and white, rested on their hips . . . and from thence a great quantity of white cloth descended to their feet, forming an ample petticoat . . . the neck, shoulders and arms were left uncovered, but the head was ornamented with a kind of turban, about eight inches high, made of several skains [lengths] of plaited human hair. (Forster 1777: 1.399–400)

This is a description, it might be noted, which bears close similarity to the genteel dresses Banks had so admired among the 'superior' women he had encountered during Cook's first voyage. The artist James Webber, who accompanied the second sailing of the *Resolution*, appears to have illustrated a similar ceremony some years later, with his female subject donning a Tahitian version of European court attire and her single exposed breast imparting a sense of classical decorum to the scene (see Figure 11).

Figure 11 *A Young Woman of Otaheite Bringing a Present*. Engraving by Francesco Bartolozzi after a painting by John Webber. From James Cook and James King (1784), *A Voyage to the Pacific Ocean*, London: John Stockdale, pp. 358–9. Wellcome Collection. Public domain.

The influence of Bougainville and Banks runs deep in Johann Reinhold Forster's *Observations Made during a Voyage Round the World* (1778), which would eventually become one of the most famous ethnographical works on Tahiti of the eighteenth century. Forster was, in fact, a last-minute choice for Cook's second expedition on the *Resolution*, with Banks unexpectedly withdrawing shortly before the voyage (Gascoigne 1994: 10). Dour, irritable and already disliked by many in the Royal Society (including Banks), Johann Reinhold Forster was so difficult to work with that he soon alienated the *Resolution*'s crew and its sponsors (10). Nevertheless, this former Dissenting minister, born in Prussia to a Scottish family, had built such an outstanding reputation as a professor of natural history in London that Carolus Linnaeus personally wrote to congratulate him on his appointment to Cook's expedition (Hoare 1982: 53). Every bit as prodigious as his father was Forster's eldest son Georg, who accompanied him aboard the *Resolution* as draughtsman and artist and who ended up publishing his own account of the voyage a full year before Johann Reinhold's *Observations*. Together, this remarkable pair documented the flora, fauna, language, rituals and geography of the Pacific archipelago in exhaustive detail.

One of the most notable elements that Johan Reinhold Forster adopted from Bougainville was the term 'race' itself, which he employs to describe ostensible subsets of Oceanic populations. There were two principal 'races' of people in the South Seas, he claimed: the first was 'fair, athletic, of a fine size, and a benevolent temper' and the most beautiful among them were to be found mainly in Tahiti; the second was 'blacker, the hair ... woolly and crisp ... the body slender and low' and could be found mainly in New Caledonia, Tanna and the New Hebrides (Forster 1778: 228). Each race could be divided into a number of varieties, whose specific anatomical features were associated with individual islands but also with certain social stations. That is to say, while the most beautiful of the first race lived on Tahiti, the lower orders on that island had ostensibly degenerated in such a fashion that they resembled the islanders of New Caledonia and so forth:

> Each of the [first] two races of men, is again divided into several varieties, which form gradations toward the other race; so that we find some of the first race, almost as black and slender as some of the second ... [O-Taheitee and the Society Isles] no doubt contain the most beautiful variety of the first race ... the common people are most exposed to air and sun; they do all kinds of dirty work; they exert their strength in agriculture, fishing, paddling, building of houses and canoes; and lastly, they are stinted in their food. From these causes, they degenerate, as it were, towards the second race, but always preserve some

remains of their original type; which in their chiefs or *Arees*, and the better sort of people, appears in its full lustre and perfection. (Forster 1778: 228–9)

There thus seem to be several different layers of degenerative influence at work in Forster's racial system. First, there is a basic geographic division of body type, maintained through successive generations. This geographic division also encompassed ostensible migratory patterns. Bougainville, for instance, had suggested that darker-skinned women from other islands had been taken to Tahiti as tokens of war, subsequently darkening the skin of the lower orders (Bougainville 1772: 253–4). At the same time, Forster's system asserts the powerful effects of civilization, which seem to resurface on every island in the same way, though not to the same degree. The inhabitants of the Friendly isles were generally 'of a darker hue' than neighbouring islands, he notes, but 'many among them, especially the better sort of people, and the greater part of their women, approach near to the complexion of the O-Taheitean fair ones' (Forster 1778: 234). Implicit in these basic observations is a strange congruence of rank and racial formation: light skin, according to Forster, is a direct consequence of the islanders' polished mode of life, yet this lightness has also become a racial characteristic of the whole island of Tahiti, barring its lowest ranking members. There comes a point, it would appear, when the body type engendered by civility becomes general to an entire nation, with only slight gradations of skin colour – as in Blumenbach's swarthy peasants and brilliant-white elites – characterizing the social hierarchy of a community. In the *Observations* it seems that the Tahitian population must be engaged in constant battle with the effects of climate and incivility to maintain this general whiteness of their race. Moreover, the 'better sort' seem to be *aware* that their race and their rank are connected, notes Forster, and they thus deliberately avoid degenerative climatic influences. The lower ranks of people 'who all go naked', he claims, 'are much exposed to the air and sun: hence they become thin and slender; for even their bones are not strong, but solid and hard', but the 'better sort of people . . . who carefully study and endeavour to keep themselves cool, and avoid as much as possible, an exposure to the heat of the sun, are succulent, fleshy, and fat' (Forster 1778: 266–7). Likewise, he claims that the island women maintain their superior physiques by wearing the 'genteel' European-style clothing that Joseph Banks had so admired:

[t]he breasts of the women of O-Taheitee, the Society Isles, Marquesas and Friendly Isles are not so flaccid and pendulous as is commonly observed in Negro women . . . and some of the women of the lower sort at the Society Isles. . . . [t]he women of the *Aree* never have them so pendulous and long. I should rather

ascribe it to the greater relaxation of the body in the women of the lower class, who are more exposed to the air and sun, than those of the *Aree* tribe. The gentle constriction of the upper part of the body, by the finer sorts of cloth in which the O-Taheitean women of quality gracefully wrap themselves, contributes likewise to keep the breasts high. (Forster 1778: 269–70)

Forster is here concentrating on the same social practices that Banks had found redolent of European aesthetics and relative to a polished, feudal society – yet in this passage such practices become a causative factor in the formation and maintenance of European varietal type. His observations are clearly evocative of Linnaeus and earlier travel writers, who had linked the form of the female breast with tight-fitting clothing and had matched the undress of African women with genital 'relaxation', distended, 'simian' breasts and excessive lactation. It might also be recalled that Oliver Goldsmith had directly linked constrictive, European-style clothing with quickness of mind and industry. Here, the better sort of Tahitians manifest visible varietal superiority as a direct consequence of their acting in a civilized and European manner. This is not unique to them. The civilized behaviour and Western dress of Europeans, Forster warns his readers, is actually a fundamental safeguard for their own 'racial' integrity:

> If two Europeans, equally fair, are removed to the same hot climate, and the one is well-dressed and avoids, as much as possible, being exposed to the action of the air, and the power of the sun; whilst the other finds himself obliged to work in the open air, and has hardly any rags to cover his skin; they will, of natural consequence, become widely different in colour; moreover, if this diversity in the mode of living be kept up for several generations, the character of both must of course become more strikingly different. (Forster 1778: 273)

When Forster later describes the physical effects of hard labour, he references not the Tahitians but the labouring ranks of Europe. '*Violent labour* is equally hurtful in regard to the increase of the body', he warns, 'for too long an exertion of muscular fibres in young men causes a rigidity. . . . Let us only cast an eye on the wretched objects, who, from their infancy, toil in confinement, and observe their distorted, disproportionate limbs, their ghastly faces, and their puny, stinted size' (Forster 1778: 266). The British, in short, are no more immune from degeneration towards a 'second race' than the Pacific Islanders.

British perceptions of race and rank in Tahiti intensified in 1774, when Captain Tobias Furneaux of the *Resolution*'s consort vessel, the *Adventure*, returned to London with a young man named Mai. 'Omai', as he was commonly known in England, was met with acclaim at the London court, and his portrait would even go on to represent the Malay race in Blumenbach's scientific atlas, the *Abbildungen naturhistorischer Gegenstände* (1796–1810). This same work recounts that the islander's manner was so refined that, while momentarily dazzled by the light from a window, Dr Johnson mistook him for the nearby Lord Mulgrave (Blumenbach 1810: n.p. [19–20]). It became an almost fashionable trope, notes Harriet Guest, for all those who met Omai to contrast his 'natural civility with the barely equal or even inferior charms of a European man' (2004: 321). The *Westminster Magazine* reported in 1774 that 'Omiah' was a man of 'some estate in his native land' of Ulatea (the island of Raiatea), before local unrest obliged him to flee to Tahiti and assume the humble life of a fisherman (1774: 427). By consequence, his deportment was so 'genteel, and resembles so much that of the well-bred people here' that it was difficult to imagine he had so recently arrived from the South Seas (*Westminster Magazine* 1774: 427). Frances Burney, who had the pleasure of dining with Omai, thrilled at his tall figure and fine countenance, proclaiming that he appeared like a visitor from a foreign court 'with an understanding far superior to *us cultivated gentry*' (1774: 325). 'He makes *remarkable* good bows', she admired, 'not just for *him*, but for *any-body*' (Burney 1774: 323). Compared to the 'pedantic booby' Mr Stanhope (Lord Chesterfield's nephew), she jibes, who had benefitted from 'the best education that any man can receive', Omai 'with no tutor but nature ... appears in a new world like a man who had all his like studied *the graces*', so much was his manner '*politely easy*, and *thoroughly well bred!*' (Burney 1774: 326; see also Guest 2004: 321).

Omai was just one of many exoticized visitors to the London court who found themselves at the centre of a 'native prince' narrative – a cultural fable, notes Laura Brown, which permeated literary representations of such encounters throughout the century (2001: 180). The 'native prince' narrative usually revolves around a refined, yet exotic, visitor to London who displays a brand of 'native sensibility and natural gentility' that puts the foppish British courtiers to shame (Brown 2001: 180–1, 193). In one respect, the native prince imports elements of the 'noble savage' trope, standing as 'the embodiment of that Rousseauist abstraction, "natural" man' (Brown 2001: 192). On the other hand, he is a politically recognized member of the elite and relatively equivalent (or, rhetorically, superior) in status to his admirers in the London court. Like the slave kings with whom he shared this cultural narrative (discussed in Chapter 10), Omai was by definition *not* a noble savage: he was distinct from other Tahitians precisely because he was both socially sophisticated and politically authoritative (Weller 1992: 69). This confluence of 'natural man' and 'natural nobility' allowed the putative native prince to show Europe's upper orders what real, virtuous nobility looked like – unsullied with mercantile ambition or modern effeminacy, and conveniently accessible to studious observation on account of his racialized body.

John O'Keefe's 1785 pantomime *Omai, or a Trip around the World*, offers a fascinating insight into this figure's paradoxical implications. The show, notes David Worrall, was tremendously successful, attended by an estimated 110,000 people within one year (2007: 139). With celebrated scenery based on etchings from Cook's expedition, the pantomime followed a contemporary tradition of highly exoticized representations of colonial adventure. Yet, not all characters in *Omai* were exoticized in the same way. By comparing the stage conventions of *Omai* with similar productions such as George Colman's *Inkle and Yarico* in 1787 and Isaac Bickerstaff's *Padlock* in 1768, Worrall concludes that the eponymous lead would almost certainly not have been played in blackface (2007: 158–65). His servant, however, would most likely have been 'blacked up' in vermillion or burnt cork as was the convention for black 'sables' in similar dramas. In fact, argues Worral, the servant character in this play essentially presented a forerunner to the black-faced minstrel, ending one of his songs with the lyrics 'cry, get out dam negar' (O'Keefe 1786: 41; Worrall 2007: 165). The spectacle of a white-faced, noble Omai and his black-faced, lowly servant would thus have performed multiple facets of racialized nobility at once. For the London audience, Omai's whiteness could be taken to represent his high rank, while his servant's blackness could be inferred to represent rank inferiority. That received idea of rank and race takes on an extra dimension when it is remembered that the very same alignment of white skin with noble birth and dark skin with servile rank had already informed the varietal categories of Banks, Bougainville and the Forsters back in Tahiti.

Omai's actual social status, however, was rather more complicated. While literary representations and public interest alike relied on him being one of Tahiti's famed *Arees*, Johann Reinhold Forster and his son Georg felt they knew better. Omai, Georg Forster proclaimed, was a *Tow-tow* (a member of the servant rank, equivalent to Banks's *Toutou*) and, worse still, he displayed all the physical features of his low race (1777: 211). The *Westminster Magazine*'s curious explanation as to why this 'man of some estate' had been working as a fisherman when he encountered the crew of the *Resolution* hints at a wider circulation of such rumours. Even Captain Cook had wondered at Furneaux's choice of this particular ambassador, who, he argued,

> was not a proper sample of the inhabitants of these happy islands, not having any advantage of birth or acquired rank, nor being eminent in shape, figure or complexion; for their people of the first rank are much fairer, and usually better

behaved, and more intelligent than the middling class of people, among whom Omai is to be ranked. (Cook 1784: 187)

Eric H. McCormick suggests that Omai was in fact a member of the *Raatira* order in Raiatea, which corresponded to the second order of society, and – as the Forsters suspected – would have ranked him inferior to the *Ari'i* (1977: 1). Whatever the case, David Bindman notes that this curious disparity of perception became starkly evident in visual representations of Omai (2002: 136). Joshua Reynold's noted 1776 portrait of a stately and pointedly light-skinned Tahitian Prince, donning pseudo-oriental robes and an intelligent, soulful expression, seems a world away from the clinically ethnographic sketches of William Hodges, Cook's official artist (see Figure 12). Omai's whiteness, it seems, was directly contingent on whether the artist had known him as a *Tow-tow* in Tahiti, or as an *Aree* in London (Bindman 2002: 136). While Cook eventually succumbed to Omai's charms at court, Georg Forster remained outraged at the praise and

Figure 12 *Omai, a Man from the Island of Raiatea*. Mezzotint by John Jacobé, after original painting by Joshua Reynolds (1777). Wellcome Collection. Public domain.

admiration this ostensible imposter had received. If Omai really was a prince, he remarked bitterly in 1777, he had certainly never mentioned as much in Tahiti – or, at least, not before he was offered the chance to return with Cook's fleet to London. On the contrary, Omai was in every way 'one of the common people'; and even aboard the *Adventure* 'he did not aspire to the captain's company but preferred that of the armourer and the common seamen' (Forster 1777: 1.388). For Georg, it was clear that Omai's 'features did not convey an idea of that beauty which characterizes the men at O-Taheitee. . . . His colour was likewise the darkest hue of the common class of people, and corresponded by no means with the rank he afterwards assumed' (1777: 1.388–9).

Johann Reinhold, who had originally planned to bring a high-born *Aree* to London in order to demonstrate the varietal attributes of Tahitian nobility, was profoundly disappointed at Omai's immense popularity – which, for him, indicated a European elite which had lost all sense of racial integrity. In the profligate and corrupted bloodlines of modern Europe, he announced,

> the guiles of art and deceit are so great in one sex, and curiosity, levity and lewdness, are so common in the other, that they contribute still more to make the preservation of races precarious. This depravation prevailed so far, that even OMAI became the object of concupiscence of some females of rank. (Forster 1778: 247)

Johann Reinhold Forster, it seems, expects the European elite to instinctively understand Tahitians as an inferior variety of human being, but also to be able to recognize – through the object-body's degree of anatomical similarity to European physical type – precisely what *rank* he belongs to, and if this rank is equivalent to their own race-based social status. A sexual attraction to Omai, not as a Pacific Islander but as a *low-ranking* Pacific Islander, is here conceived as a symptom of racial degeneracy in the very same way as dark skin is perceived to be a symptom of racial degeneracy in the islanders themselves. What is more, the culprits of this degeneracy are 'females of rank' who, it can be inferred, are the supposed guardians of the highest genealogical lines in Britain, just as the *Arees* were in Tahiti. For Georg too, the British upper orders' blindness to the fact that they were celebrating a servant in place of a prince only evidenced their own degeneration: 'O-mai has been considered either as remarkably stupid, or very intelligent, according to the different allowances which were made by those who judged his abilities', he remarked snidely in the preface to his *Voyage*,

> upon his arrival in England he was immediately introduced into genteel company . . . and presented at court amidst a brilliant circle of the first nobility.

> He naturally imitated that easy and elegant politeness that . . . is one of the ornaments of civilized society . . . [though] he was not able to form a general comprehensive view of our whole civilized system . . . his senses were charmed by beauty, symmetry, harmony and magnificence . . . his judgement was in its infant state and therefore like a child he coveted almost everything he saw. (Forster 1777: xiv–xvii)

* * *

The work of Bougainville, Banks and especially the Forsters had a profound impact on the development of modern race theory at the end of the eighteenth century. In fact, Johann Reinhold Forster's empirical documentation of the racial impact of civilized behaviour – essentially confirming a hypothesis that had long been assumed but seldom satisfactorily demonstrated – became an academic benchmark of racial theory. In a 1781 revision of his *De generis*, Blumenbach (who was in regular correspondence with Banks and the Forsters) changed his *four* principal human varieties to *five* by weight of these new reports from the South Seas (1781: 52). His fifth human variety, which would eventually come to form the Malay race, was further divided into two 'tribes' – the first black and the second brown (1781: 52), meaning that '[J. R.] Forster's dual classification of South Sea Islanders was thus firmly inscribed in metropolitan scholarly awareness within three years of its publication' (Douglas and Ballard 2008: 107). Later, note Bronwen Douglas and Chris Ballard, Blumenbach personally commissioned the extensive 'Cook-Forster Ethnographic Collection' at the University of Göttingen and regularly exhibited the Forsters' findings during his lectures on natural history there (2008: 106–7). Six years later, when Samuel Stanhope Smith asserted racial differences between domestic and field slaves in North America in his *Essay on the Causes of the Variety of Complexion in the Human Figure* (1787), he used the example of the Forsters' 'Eerees' as a documented example of race being moulded by civilized behaviour (1778: 85). By the time John Cowles Prichard, cited at the beginning of this chapter, referenced the well-established corporeal differences among ranks in Tahiti in 1813, he could rest assured that the greater community of natural historians in Britain would largely agree with him. 'Civilisation', wrote one anonymous reviewer of Prichard's work in the *Monthly Review*,

> appears indeed to be the most permanent cause of change in the complexion . . . the most savage tribes [of the South Seas] are quite black, with wooly hair; while the more civilized communities are nearly of the same complexion as

Europeans, and have long hair, with the same anatomical structure. ('Researches into the Physical History of Man' 1814: 132; see also Augstein 1996: 87)

What racial investigations of the South Seas demonstrate, then, is that high rank – and a physical ideal attached to that idea of high rank – was an essential element in the construction of the basic racial phenotypes that went on to underpin modern racial divisions. In this instance, the idea of light skin being specifically associated with hereditary elites was just as important to this racialization process as was dark skin being associated with slavery and servitude. The human-variety theory of Tahiti reveals, perhaps more than anywhere else in the canon of eighteenth-century human-variety theory, a steady correlative between colonial human-variety discourse and the domestic traditions of genealogical hierarchy.

10

'Royal slaves'

Abolitionism and fantasies of slave nobility

The 'Royal Slave' trope provides an intriguing example of old race (lineal family) interacting with new race (discrete human type). Largely stemming from the literary tradition of Aphra Behn's *Oroonoko; or, The Royal Slave* (1688), this cultural trope transformed over the course of the eighteenth century, demonstrating changing ideas of both nobility and human variety along the way. The typical Royal Slave is a hereditary elite in his own nation, recognizably superior in body and mind to the rest of his countrymen and instinctively responsive to the standards of European civility. As the noble paradigm of race increasingly influenced varietal categories, however, representing the noble physique through a racialized African body began to take on very different connotations. This chapter looks at the place of Black servants in noble households during the eighteenth century, before exploring the legacy of Aphra Behn's Royal Slave through an analysis of *Oroonoko*'s successive interpretations, and, in particular, a little-known but highly revealing novel from the later century, Anna Maria McKenzie's *Slavery; or the Times* (1792).

* * *

'Am I not a Man and a brother?' The kneeling, shackled slave of Josiah Wedgwood's iconic medallion, adopted in 1787 by the Society for Effecting the Abolition of the Slave Trade, posed his question to the British public at a time when the transatlantic slave trade was being criticized on an international scale. The impact of Wedgwood's medallion lies in the simplicity and directness of its question, and yet its answer, from whatever quarter it might be received, was likely to be anything but simple. In the racialized discourse of human-variety theory, ideas of humanity and brotherhood invariably came with certain conditions: for Linnaeus, the Black slave was indeed a Man, though, taxonomically, he was primarily a brother to those who shared his skin colour, habitat, humours and social structure; for Buffon, this Man's degree of brotherhood depended on the climate, the terrain and the society in which he was raised, recreating him according to his exact longitude, latitude and elevation; for Goldsmith, this brother had drifted far from the Edenic original of Man, and his colour and physique bespoke indolence, laziness and sexual depravity; for Kames, the African was one among multiple species of Man, and thus a brother to none but his own kind; for Kant he was a brother in blood to those of his own lineal race, and a Man only in so far as his genealogical line would allow; and, for Monboddo he was at once more than Man and less than Man, brother both to the orang-outang one step below him and to the white European, one step above him.

Human-variety theory was essential to those who would defend the slave trade, especially during the second half of the eighteenth century. Both monogenist and polygenist theories – whether based on climate, civility, bloodline or divine providence – were complicit in a culture that linked non-Europeans with servitude. If global populations were discussed in terms of natural hierarchy, the oppression of those at the bottom of this hierarchy could thus be projected as inevitable. Most importantly, ideas of human variety supported the central paradox at the core of slavery: slaves were valuable, notes George Boulukos, precisely because they were *human*, and could perform complex tasks that only humans could; yet the continuance of slavery nonetheless depended on the constant and systematic *negation of this humanity* (2008: 1). Human-variety theory offered various forms of ranked humanity, all of which reinforced an arbitrary Chain of Being hierarchy which always placed high-born, white Europeans at its apex. Slavery apologists could therefore liberally pluck tenets from different theories in order to support their arguments, since they all fed into the same 'common sense' logic of universal order. In opposition to this, Abolitionists in Britain and America often drew on non-conformist traditions of social equality. The Quakers, who had long condemned the practice of slavery in the American colonies, actively distributed anti-slavery literature in Britain from the 1760s onward (Carey 2006: 397). Following the landmark James Somerset case of 1772, when the Abolitionist advocate Granville Sharp successfully set the precedent that no individual had the right to forcibly remove an enslaved person from English soil, 'a unified pro-slavery position began to coalesce', which had not existed previously in Britain (Appiah and Gates 2005: 5.42; Swaminathan 2009: 130). As positions continued to polarize, more and more religious groups began to organize into an active Abolitionist front in the 1780s and 1790s. This movement was further fuelled by Thomas Clarkson's economic arguments against the endemic torture of slaves in his *Essay on the Impolicy of the African Slave Trade* (1788: 96–107) and William Wilberforce's seminal parliamentary bill of 1791 (Carey 2006: 397). Nevertheless, much of the rhetoric at the heart of the Abolitionist movement was deeply enmeshed in its own brand of race thinking. One of the primary aims of the movement, notes David Brion Davis, was to lend a positive image to 'the negro's cultural difference', motivating its supporters to trawl through travel literature for 'examples of man's inherent virtue and creativity' (1966: 222). By the 1770s, Brion Davis notes, Europeans such as John Wesley and the Abbé Raynal were portraying the African slave as 'a man of natural virtue and sensitivity who was at once oppressed by the worst vices of civilisation and yet capable of receiving its greatest benefits' (1966: 24). While Abolitionist rhetoric commonly emphasized the shared humanity of both master and slave, then, this sense of humanity tended to be directly contingent on the slave's manifestation of European virtues. Wedgewood's kneeling Man and Brother is an unthreatening suppliant. He not only asks the European observer to recognize him as a human being but to recognize him as a 'good' human according to their cultural standards. He firmly belongs to the iconographic tradition of the Grateful Slave, which aimed to communicate the equality of Black Africans with white Europeans by projecting white European values onto the Black African body (Boulukos 2008: 2–3). In one of those paradoxes so common to racialized discourse, the Black African's full assumption of European humanity thus involved his acceptance of a hierarchical tradition in which he was a quintessentially inferior human being.

Similar ironies permeated the fetishization of Black servants in eighteenth-century Britain as symbols of exotic royalty. Young men and boys, especially, made for highly fashionable additions to the homes of the nobility, gentry and urban elite. They were commonly included at the periphery of family portraits, such as those by the genre painter George Morland, investing the domestic scene with connotations of colonial wealth and status (Oldfield 1995: 20–1). At the same time, a Black servant's presence in the household was a quotidian reminder of slavery and the racialized hierarchy upon which it increasingly depended. The fact that these servants were frequently renamed for grand figures of antiquity, notes Kathleen Chater, might at best imply that they were patronized by their employers as 'pets', and at worst might have constituted a deliberate form of mockery (2009: 197). Fanciful slave names such as Caesar, Titus or Scipio also served as a reminder of what Orlando Patterson has called the slave's 'natal alienation' (1982: 7). While family names were the very foundation of elite hereditary privilege, slaves' names were deliberately taken from them, alienating them 'from all formal, legally enforceable ties of blood' (Patterson 1982: 7, 55). The name of a Roman emperor would certainly have made for a cruel contrast with the decorative silver collars that many slaves, especially children, were made to wear during the first half of the century, oftentimes 'stamped with the owner's name, initials, and coat of arms' (Aravamudan 1999: 38). One such collar can be seen in the anonymous group portrait of *Elihu Yale, William Cavendish, 2nd Duke of Devonshire, Lord James Cavendish, Mr. Tunstal and page*, dated to around 1708. In this image, the inherited slave status of the black page is brutally contrasted with the inherited authority of his masters and the inherited freedom of the white children who play behind him. His metal collar is fastened with a padlock and appears to be notched so that it can expand as the child grows (see Figure 13).

While Black servants were foremost among the 'exotic' faces on the streets of Britain, population estimates vary considerably. Chater notes that while the *Gentleman's Magazine* reported a Black population of 20,000 in London in 1764, documentation exists only for 550 individuals during the 30-year period between

Figure 13 *Elihu Yale, William Cavendish, 2nd Duke of Devonshire, Lord James Cavendish, Mr. Tunstal and page* by unknown artist (*c.* 1708). Yale Centre for British Art, accession no. B1970.1. Public domain.

1742 and 1772 (2009: 26–7). Norma Myers, for her part, concludes that the Black population in London had probably reached upwards of 5,000 by 1780, with figures of at least 10,000 for Britain as a whole (1996: 35). Whatever the case, the typical domestic functions of Black servants rendered them disproportionately visible to the public in a city like London. 'Wherever they went, upper- and middle-class people must have seen blacks', notes Chater, '[t]hey opened doors to visitors, they served meals, they drove coaches in the streets' (2009: 26). Until the Somerset case of 1772, no clear parliamentary legislation had ever been passed regarding slave status in England, and for long afterwards the line between fashionable servant and dehumanized commodity remained considerably blurred. The 'free' Black servants of the later eighteenth century, notes Norma Myers, continued to live in constant fear of enslavement through kidnapping or other means, and their position remained extraordinarily precarious (1996: 62). When presented as a pastiche of exotic nobility, these Black servants thus made for a sinister juxtaposition of 'slave race' and 'noble race' discourses, highlighting a sense of racialized identity that ran all the way through the social hierarchy. On one end of this hierarchy there was a racialized underclass, linked with servitude, corporeal deviance and barbarity; on the other was a racialized social elite, linked with natural governance, superior physicality and high civility. Both had found themselves in their respective conditions because of their birth and circumstance; both were held up as examples of the universal order and its expression in the physical body; and both would pass on their own position in the natural order of things to their progeny.

The strange intimacy between those who had been condemned to the very bottom of the social order (owing to their birth), and those who had long claimed their place at the very top (again, owing to their birth), was not lost on those critics who ventured to suggest that, in their shared expressions of 'race', the two extremities of British society might not be so different after all. Felicity Nussbaum has noted a fascinating convergence of noble tradition and the racialized black body in one of William Austin's well-known satirical plates from 1773, representing Catherine Hyde, the third Duchess of Queensbury, fencing with her Black servant 'the Creole Soubise' (2003: 7–9; see Figure 14). The eccentric Duchess, a famous beauty and friend to Pope, Gay and Swift, is depicted lunging towards her opponent, who in return thrusts his lance towards her heart (he has landed a *touché*), making for clear undertones of the pair's rumoured sexual relationship (Nussbaum 2003: 8). Though described in Austin's caption as her 'black servant', Julius Soubise played a rather more ambiguous role in the Duchess's life. Having been brought to England as the

Figure 14 'The Duchess of Queensbury playing at foils with her favourite lapdog Mungo after expending near 10,000 to make him a — ', by William Austin (1773). Soubise quotes the Black servant of Isaac Bickerstaffe's 1768 play *Padlock*: 'Mungo here mungo dere, mungo ev'ry where, above, & below Hah! Vat your Gracy tink of me now[?]'. Library of Congress, reproduction no. LC-USZ62-102368. Public domain.

child of a slave and 'gifted' to Catherine Hyde in 1764, he was raised more like a ward, growing up to become something of a celebrity among the London quality (Nussbaum 2003: 8). Alongside his Roman name, Julius, the Duchess named him 'Soubise' after the French courtier Charles de Rohan, Prince de Soubise and hero of the Seven Years' War – thus associating him with both the idealized *nobilitas* of the ancient world and a comfortably 'foreign' symbol of contemporary military *virtus*. She also took delight in dressing him in extravagant clothing as a boy, which was a trait that he would later harness in his adulthood by styling himself as a bona fide Macaroni. In fact, Soubise went on to become a prominent figure of fashion in London, exhibiting the latest and most ostentatious trends, practising oration with David Garrick and Richard Sheridan, becoming renowned for his 'shapely legs' and handsome face, and holding court to an endless succession of admirers at Vauxhall, the Opera, and Hyde Park (Millar 2009: 62). In his public persona, and, indeed, in his filial/servile/erotic relationship with his noble mistress, there is a curious conflation of varietal degeneration (as embodied in his non-European physique) and perceived moral degeneration brought on by luxury, wealth and vice. In many ways, Soubise could be seen as a superlative symbol of elite luxury because his very body was perceived as a decoration, an item of fashion and the accessory of a magnificently wealthy noblewoman. It is interesting, then, that the resounding criticism of William Austin's satire is one of racialized transgression. In the 1773 print, notes Nussbaum, Soubise is deliberately caricatured to resemble Tyson's Pygmie, heightening the incongruity of the clothes and status of this Duchess's favourite 'lap dog' (2003: 8). The Duchess, in turn, appears to have undergone a certain racial degeneration through her transgression of social order: her fencing mask is shaded so as to mirror the colour of Soubise's skin, her headscarf mimics his caricatured hair and her defeat implies hierarchical as well as sexual submission to her opponent. By lowering herself to his company, or, indeed, by raising him to hers, the Duchess appears to have sacrificed the integrity of her own noble race. In the image, then, Soubise's incongruously fine clothes represent racial impurity invading the ranks of nobility, while the Duchess's blackened visage indicates the rapid degeneration of pure-blood nobles to a state of racialized inferiority.

Perhaps the most striking conflation of noble race and racialized slave discourse is to be found in the Royal Slave motif, which remained a popular cultural trope throughout the century. This peculiar construct at once reinforced the Chain of Being world view, the noble tradition of *eugeneia* and the intimate relationship between racialized body hierarchies and European social order. Though the 'Royal Slave' trope is sometimes asserted as part of the 'Noble Savage' tradition, notes Barry Weller, it actually represents the exact opposite: 'the point about the royal slave is of course that he is precisely not a savage, but rather occupies (or has occupied) a place in a highly articulated and hierarchical society' (1992: 69). The cultural fantasy of the Royal Slave is perhaps better understood in terms of the 'Native Prince' narrative, which, as will be remembered from the previous chapter, also extended to figures like Omai (Brown 2001: 180). The Royal Slave motif imagines an African socio-spiritual hierarchy, whose leaders are noticeably more competent, more physically beautiful and essentially of higher human worth than those lower down the social scale. By consequence, it implies one basic criticism of the slave trade: that it has upturned the Chain of Being by enslaving those who were born to rule. The standard mould for the eighteenth-century Royal Slave narrative was largely cast in Aphra Behn's 1688 novella, *Oroonoko; or, The Royal Slave*. Following Behn's template, the plot invariably revolves around a male protagonist of high birth who begins his narrative in a pastoral pseudo-African setting ruled by patrilineal royalty. He usually has a female counterpart, to whom he is undyingly constant; he is betrayed into slavery, endures its brutalities and then dies with a 'grand gesture' (Sypher 1942: 9).

Behn's work also established the most significant aspect of this narrative in relation to anatomically based variety theory: the slave's physical beauty. It must be remembered that Behn's much-studied depiction of a Black African prince, whose nobility manifests itself through white, European and 'heroic' physical features, predates the development of Linnaean or Buffonian human-variety templates. The eponymous Oroonoko's black body exists in a context of morality rather than natural history, expressing virtue, vice and spiritual providence rather than attesting to generations of climatic influence. 'In Behn's novella', notes Laura Brown, 'Oroonoko represents a European aristocratic ideal, associated with the Stuart monarchs and the Roman heroes and distinguished from the common sort who surround him' (2001: 195). This aspect alone is highly significant considering later reprisals of the Oroonoko story: Behn's hero represents a sense of 'moral corporeality' that not only continued to exist alongside 'varietal corporeality' in the eighteenth century but which would remain a standard trope of noble superiority. His anatomy, that is to say, expresses his rank in the Great Chain of Being in the just same way as that of any true nobleman, and in this it liberally traverses the boundaries that would later be established by 'varietal' race thinking. Consider, for instance, Behn's famous introductory description of Oroonoko:

> He was pretty tall, but of a shape the most exact that can be fancied; the most famous statuary could not form the figure of a man more admirably turned from head to foot. His face was not of that brown rusty black which most of that nation are, but a perfect ebony or polished jet. His eyes were the most awful that could be seen, and very piercing; the white of them being like snow, as were his teeth. His nose was rising and roman, instead of African or flat. His mouth, the finest shape that could be seen; far from those great turned lips, which are so natural to the rest of the Negroes. The whole proportion and air of his face was so noble and exactly formed, that, bating his colour, there could be nothing in nature more beautiful, agreeable, and handsome. (Behn 1688: 20–1)

Oroonoko's physique is that of a nobleman above all, incarnating physical ideals of heroic antiquity which allow him to manifest a quintessentially 'white' tradition of excellence despite being Black. At the very same time, Oroonoko's 'polished jet' blackness implies that he is a prince among Africans rather than a prince among all men: in this dimension, his superlative blackness functions as a pastiche of white European tradition – it is a mark of the prince's purity,

Figure 15 *Bust of a Man* by Francis Harwood (*c.* 1758). J. Paul Getty Museum, item no. 88.SA.114. Public domain.

a distilled quality of his nation, unsullied with later associations between this same blackness and anatomical degeneration. He 'is not just black', asserts Catherine Gallagher, 'but very, very black. His blackness is, moreover, luminous, beautiful, wonderful' (1996: 2). This is essentially the same, exoticized kind of nobility that can be read in some eighteenth-century art pieces, such as Francis Harwood's *Bust of a Man*, probably commissioned by Hugh Percy, Earl of Northumberland around 1758. The bust ostensibly depicts an African warrior whose 'head can be read as noble' but who also displays signs of 'savagery' in his nakedness and the 'jagged scar on his forehead' (Bindman and Gates 2011: 40; Figure 15). Oroonoko's body, similarly, plays out the traditional narrative of noble superiority as expressed through physical appearance while, at the same time, maintaining a parallel racialized significance. This depiction of corporeal virtue via racialized features would, moreover, come to undermine the reasoning of later variety theorists, who, it will be remembered, focused heavily both on the idea of uniform anatomy within each variety and the moral/mental/social limitations imposed by this anatomy in order to consolidate the 'reality' of those varieties.

Pro-slavery human-variety theorists depended on homogeneity *within* their varieties in order to justify the indiscriminate exaltation or subjugation of entire populations. Oroonoko's noble beauty assumes a dramatically different significance when considered alongside Edward Long's description of sub-

Saharan Africans almost a century later in 1774. The Inhabitants of 'Guiney, or Negro-Land', Long declares, are distinguished by their

> covering of wool like bestial fleece instead of hair . . . the roundness of their eyes, the figure of their ears, tumid nostrils, flat noses, invariably thick lips, and [the] general large size of the female nipples as if adapted by nature to the peculiar conformation of their children's mouths. . . . In general, they are devoid of genius, and seem almost incapable of making any progress in civility and science. . . . They have no moral sensations; no taste but for women; gormondizing and drinking to excess; no wish but to be idle. . . . They are represented by all authors as the vilest of the human kind, to which they have little more pretention of resemblance than what arises from their exterior form . . . a general uniformity runs through all these various regions and people . . . it being a common known proverb that all people on the globe have some good as well as ill qualities, except the Africans. (Long 1774: 2.352–3)

Long's insistence that all Guineans share a uniformly savage physique, that they alone among global human populations are invariable in their inferiority, seems to address (and negate) the possibility of a real Oroonoko figure. When directly contrasted with descriptions such as the above, it is easily seen how Behn's archetype of the Royal Slave took on an anti-slavery position all by itself.

In its various incarnations, notes David Brion Davis, 'the tale of Oroonoko became one of the most internationally popular stories of the eighteenth century', showcasing a certain racial evolution, so to speak, of the Royal Slave character (1966: 473). Thomas Southerne's 1696 dramatic interpretation was by far the most popular of these, becoming one of the most frequently performed theatrical pieces in Britain for the next one hundred years and consolidating the Royal Slave trope as a standard feature of eighteenth-century drama. Though mostly uncritical of slavery as an institution, Southerne's play (also named *Oroonoko*) helped to establish what Barry Weller has called the 'Oroonoko effect' (1992: 65). That is, the singling out of a genealogically distinguished slave (whose nobility is expressed through an affinity with Western virtue and a Europeanized anatomy) as representative of human dignity degraded (Weller 1992: 65; Oldfield 1995: 23; Boulukos 2008: 44). It is a device that only works when the few are contrasted with the many; the Royal Slave is, by definition, an exception to the rule of the otherwise inferior African body. In both Behn's and Southerne's works, by virtue of the fact that Oroonoko is an exceptional noble shining forth amid an unexceptional commonality of Black Africans, the Royal Slave can make a case against the abuse of slaves while remaining complicit in the continuance of slavery. Maximillian E. Novak and David Stuart Rodes point out that Southerne's Oroonoko deals openly with slave traders, 'and he sees nothing inherently wrong with the idea of slavery itself', while at the same time he is set apart from white commoners, implying that 'men like Oroonoko are natural rulers and the planters typical subjects, incapable of either ruling or selecting a ruler' (Novak and Rodes 1976: xxxv, xxxiii).

One of the most notable aspects of Southerne's interpretation is that Oroonoko's lover, Imoinda, described in Behn's novel as 'female to the noble male; the beautiful black Venus to our young Mars', is recast as a white woman (1696: 23). This transformation, notes Nussbaum, may well have been more practical than anything else. As far as is known, Black women had never performed on stage in England at the time Southerne published the play, and the spectacle of a white woman in blackface would possibly have distracted from the seriousness of Imoinda's role (Nussbaum 2003: 158). A white female lead may also have drawn favourable comparisons with *Othello* as well as 'positing a white European femininity in opposition to the developing stereotypes of black womanhood such as Jezebel' (Nussbaum 2003: 157). In any event, suggests Laura Brown, the Native Prince tradition was more invested in Black masculinity than Black femininity. 'The native prince is programmatically male', she asserts, and the 'fable focuses on a masculine ideal'. While non-white female characters commonly constituted a major element of these stories, 'the sensibility attached to an elite, public, male figure posed a different problem and produced a different imaginative response from that evoked by the vulnerable domestic female protagonist' (Brown 2001: 181). These considerations aside, the 'whitening' of Imoinda has a very real effect on the narrative's racial discourse. Behn's original Imoinda was besieged by white suitors (providing evidence of her beauty and worth), and in Southerne's play this dynamic arguably works in the opposite sense. Oroonoko's union with a white woman could be read as another inherently noble quality of his character. As 'female to the noble male', her feminine beauty is a direct reflection of his masculine nobility, and by becoming visually white, Imoinda could be seen as further whitening Oroonoko's rank.

While the standard Royal Slave motif remained mostly unchanged over the course of the eighteenth century, its message was transformed in the context of Abolitionism. The typical plot, notes Wylie Sypher, which gradually gained popularity along with the rise of religious anti-slavery movements in the mid-century, subsequently merged with 'a great stream of egalitarian theory' in the wake of the 1772 Somerset case (1942: 10). Overt anti-slavery sentiment had already begun to noticeably infiltrate the Royal Slave tradition in successive revisions of Southerne's play, which reflected the changing significance of the plot for mid-century audiences. In 1759, the London editor John Hawkesworth staged what was to become one of the most popular adaptations of Southerne's *Oroonoko*. Much of the text remained the same – in fact, Hawkesworth did not even put his name to early editions of the adaptation – but among the significant alterations was a replacement of Southerne's unremarkable introductory scene with a damning depiction of colonial planters. The play is thereby immediately reframed in the context of a corrupt slaving industry, one symptom of which is a failure to recognize innate nobility. 'Squire Blandford has one that they say is not of their complexion', one planter remarks about Imoinda. 'The lieutenant governor has taken a fancy to her', come the replies, 'and yet, wou'd you believe it, she gives herself airs and will scarce speak to him . . . 'tis a wonder . . . his honour don't buy her' (Hawkesworth 1759: act 1.1, 2). Oroonoko's eventual rebellion and death, here, becomes not only the tragic case of a prince who has been unjustly enslaved but a case of a degenerate slave-holding caste, who display neither respect for, nor understanding of, his high birth and rank. This, in turn, casts a dual 'racial' scrutiny on the white as well as the Black characters. The vulgar (prose) speech of the planters, meanwhile, makes for a direct contrast with the eloquent (iambic) verses of Oroonoko and his retinue, exemplified in the speech of his companion Aboan:

> O Royal Sir, remember who you are,
>
> A Prince born for the good of other men:
>
> Whose God-like Office is to draw the sword
>
> Against Oppression and set free mankind. (Hawkesworth 1759: act 3.2, 31)

The first explicitly Abolitionist rendering of the Oroonoko plot was put forth in John Ferrier's *Prince of Angola: A Tragedy*, published in 1788 at the behest of the Manchester Committee for Effecting the Abolition of the Slave Trade (Iwanisziw 2006: 203). Once again maintaining much of Southerne's original dialogue, Ferrier further enhanced the degenerative aspects of the slave traders in order to highlight the superior rank of the African princes. The worthy, noble slaves here become spokespeople for European nobility, the decline of which is expressed through the moral corruption, verbal vulgarity and social inversion of the white characters. Aboan's speech, above, is altered so as to make the African nobles more overtly aware of European ignobility:

> By what enchantment is my prince beguil'd
>
> Again to trust European honesty?
>
> . . .

Whose accursed arts

Corrupt th'ingenuous Negro, and inlay

Our honest black with Christian wickedness.

...

Who proud perhaps to own a royal slave,

May suffer you to get young princes for him

...

The last of your illustrious lineage, born

To pamper up his pride and be his slaves. (Ferrier 1788: 28–9)

To consolidate his point, Ferrier supplements his play with an entire appendix detailing the abuses of the contemporary slave trade.

The Royal Slave trope was not always confined to fiction. In the late 1740s, all of London was aware of an ostensibly real-life Oroonoko: William Ansah Sessarakoo, the so-called 'Prince of Annamaboe'. Sessarakoo was the son of Eno Baisie Kurentsi, one of the most powerful traders on the Gold Coast, who had been courting competitive trade agreements with Britain and France since the 1730s (Hanley 2002: 331). Kurentsi had previously sent an elder son to Paris, where his hosts – eager to encourage business relations with the French – had lavishly celebrated their young visitor at court, showering him with expensive gifts, providing him with tuition in European manners and introducing him to Louis XV (Hanley 2002: 332). When Kurentsi agreed to send his younger son to London a few years later, therefore, he was no doubt expecting a similar reception. Instead, Sessarakoo was kidnapped and transported to Barbados by corrupt slave traders, resulting in a grave diplomatic incident. The British Royal African Company (RAC), who helped secure the young man's emancipation in 1748, blamed the debacle on moral debasement caused by deregulated markets. Despite having forcibly transported more human beings across the Atlantic than any other single institution during the era of the slave trade (Pettigrew 2013: 11), the RAC could nonetheless condemn lesser traders for their inability 'to recognize social rank as a legitimate security from slavery' (Hanley 2002: 334). When Sessarakoo finally arrived on British shores, notes Ryan Hanley, the British commentariat implicitly associated him with the 'sentimentalized image of the royal slave' by emphasizing 'cultural markers of nobility' – including his introduction to the monarch, his interaction with high society and his immensely fine clothes (2002: 330). Gabriel Mathias's 1749 portrait of Sessarakoo, observes David Bindman, presents its subject in a stance often assumed by sea captains, holding his hat beneath the arm of his richly embroidered coat (2002: 45). Such stately presentations, Bindman suggests, reframed Sessarakoo's history of enslavement and allowed him 'to show his true mettle and overcome circumstances that might have condemned his less well-born fellows to resign themselves to a life of servitude' (2002: 45–6). Sessarakoo accordingly made a sensational appearance at Covent Garden to attend a performance of Thomas Southerne's *Oroonoko*. Journalistic accounts of this highly publicized event liberally dimmed all distinctions between the prince on stage and the prince in the audience, concluding that Sessarakoo's and his companion's reaction to the play offered an authentic glimpse of the Royal Slave in action:

> The seeing persons of their own colour on stage, apparently in the same distress from which they had been so lately delivered . . . strongly affected them with that generous grief which pure nature always feels. . . . The young prince was so far overcome, that he was obliged to retire at the end of the fourth act. His companion remained, but wept the whole time; a circumstance which affected the audience yet more than the play, and doubled the tears which were shed for Oroonoko and Imoinda. (*Gentleman's Magazine* 1749: 90; see also Nussbaum 2003: 189)

Sessarakoo's ordeal, including this trip to the playhouse, became the subject of still more Royal Slave narratives. William Dodd's poem 'The African Prince' (1749a: 323–5) even provided Sessarakoo with a fictional heroine, Zara, who chimes in with a poetic reply from her own perspective (Dodd 1749b: 372–3).

By the late century, the Royal Slave trope had become so well established that it seemed to underpin practically every representation of 'exceptional' Black Africans who disproved the varietal assumption of uniform inferiority. Even Gustavus Vassa's benchmark autobiography, the *Interesting Narrative of Olaudah Equiano* (1789) takes many cues from the Royal Slave plot: Vassa too claims to have been born into a hereditary elite, notes Weller (he remarks at the beginning of his history that 'my father was one of those elders and chiefs . . . styled *Embrenché* . . . importing the highest distinction, and signifying in our language a mark of grandeur'), and throughout the narrative he consistently stands out as special, more capable and more competent among his peers, both to his fellow slaves and his European masters (Vassa 1789: 4; Weller 1992: 71). As part of his self-mythologization, even Julius Soubise had reportedly claimed descent from African royalty (Millar 2009: 62).

Other works of prose fiction utilized the 'Oroonoko effect' by incorporating the Royal Slave trope with more general criticisms of social transgression in

British society. One of the most intriguing of these is Anna Maria Mackenzie's little-known *Slavery; or, The Times* (1792), which weaves the Royal Slave plot into an epistolary novel of manners. The novel recounts the story of Prince Adolphus of Tonouwah, who has been sent to the home of the kindly Mr Hamilton in London's Finsbury Square to receive an English education. The prince soon falls in love with the young Mary Ann St. Leger, before being betrayed by a rival suitor, reunited with his father in England and eventually winning the heart of his beloved. The 'manners' that the novel commends follow the conventions of the literary Royal Slave tradition. The 'good' characters of the novel all recognize the value and desirability of Adolphus's and Mary Ann's relationship, since they value the pair's shared nobility over their physical differences (Mary Ann, who begins the novel as an orphan, is soon revealed as a daughter of noble stock). The 'bad' characters, conversely, including Mary Ann's rival suitor Francis Berisford and her scheming guardians Mr and Mrs Abrams, confirm their own upstart pretensions by not being able to discern the prince's inherent nobility. They, being unsophisticated, only see his colour. Even worse (and this is one of the main comedic tropes of the novel), they assume that *they* are superior to *him* (Mackenzie 1792: 2.190).

Mackenzie's novel distinguishes the African elite as mentally and physically superior to lower Africans in the same way as the English upper orders are differentiated from the middling ranks. Those at the top of each hierarchy – African and English – here possess a common understanding of natural superiority. Just like his literary predecessors, the seventeen-year-old Adolphus is immediately recognizable to everyone around him as different from his common countrymen. Near the beginning of the novel, when the captain of his ship is taken ill, Adolphus is instantly called upon to take control of the voyage and distinguishes himself by refusing to mistreat the other slaves on board (Mackenzie 1792: 1.18). Like his Royal Slave predecessors, too, this Prince of Tonouwah is assisted by a pair of servants, Sambo and Oran, whose constant deference, fear and supplication serve to highlight their master's leadership, bravery and natural virtue. Their constitutional difference from him, furthermore, is again expressed in their respective speech patterns: Adolphus speaks in long eloquent sentences, punctuated sporadically with charming inaccuracies (both he and his father, for instance, sometimes refer to themselves in the third person); Sambo and Oran, on the other hand, speak in the caricatured pidgin of the stage-slave. 'Sambo go England', proclaims the former at the beginning of the novel, '– Live with prince. – No whip, no work, like slave' (Mackenzie 1792: 1.21). Later, when his tutor asks Adolphus why he does not complain about England as his servants do, the prince explains that Sambo and Oran are not Black Africans in the same way that he is a Black African:

> I am neither a servant nor a slave; and the son of a king should not be capricious ... though you continually aim to lessen my ideas of hereditary dignity, yet – do not be angry, sir, – yet I cannot forget that Adolphus is a prince; that Sambo and Oran are but his father's subjects. How should they then think as I do? I know they are my fellow-creatures, claiming all the rights of humanity; but do not, good sir, do not suppose they are my equals, in strength of mind, self-denial, or descent. (Mackenzie 1792: 95)

Adolphus's physical beauty again consolidates his superiority of character, and though he is not given a detailed physical description in the manner of Oroonoko, it is later revealed that he (unlike Oroonoko, and reflecting the 'post-varietal' values of the 1790s) is 'almost as white as a Christian' (Mackenzie 1792: 1.101). Most significantly, Adolphus's 'traditional' sense of social order implicitly casts a critical light on the novel's English characters, whose speech patterns are similarly indicative of their social and moral rank. The genteel Mary Ann and Mr Hamilton speak in a self-effacing and highly decorous register, while the insolent, arrogant jabbering of Mrs Abrams and Francis Berisford is characterized by mispronunciation, stunted cadence and phonetic comedy. Indeed, Berisford's broken elocution oftentimes resembles that of Sambo: 'Slow and sure at setting out', he writes to Adolphus explaining his malicious plan, '– Set off cool. Keep my breath. –Lie by. –Let 'em all get before me. . . . –How d'ye like my plan? Full of mettle isn't it?' (Mackenzie 1792: 2.62).

The difference between Sambo and the Abrams, however, is that Sambo accepts his inferior rank with dignity and grace, while the Abrams – who are obsessed with embezzling Mary Ann's fortune – can think only of rising in society. In case the reader was left in any doubt, the minute particulars of the Abrams' social situation are confirmed through their street address. The novel is careful to mention that they live on Church Street (present-day Fournier Street), in Spitalfields, which not only situates them in the heart of artisan East London but in a conspicuously 'high' part of what was a relatively 'low' district. Having been at the heart of a redevelopment project in the 1720s, Church Street boasted some of the finest houses in the area, mostly occupied by wealthy silk merchants who used the garrets for industry and often converted the ground floor into a shop. The presence of silk waste found packed between the floor joists of these houses, notes F. H. W. Sheppard, suggests that the sound of looms would have been uncomfortably audible from the attic workshops (1957: 199). In the context of this novel, then, Church Street can be taken as an address with ideas above its station. Adolphus certainly seems disgusted with the Abrams' household when he is invited to meet Mary Ann's guardians. After waiting 'a quarter of an hour in a small parlor' he is led upstairs 'by a clumsy black boy in a crimson and white coarse turban' before stepping into a 'large shewy dining room' (Mackenzie 1792: 1.100–1). On being introduced to the prince, Mrs Abrams wastes no time in embarrassing herself by treating her royal guest as a servant: 'Mercy on me!' she exclaims to Mary Ann, 'what's this the young black-a-moor you said was so handsome? Why he is not at all like our Mark Anthony! Laus-a-me, he's almost as white as a Christian!' (Mackenzie 1792: 1.101). Later, it is revealed that Mrs Abrams has built her misplaced sense of superiority on contemporary texts of human-variety theory. Clumsily inviting herself to dine with Adolphus's guardians, she states: 'one coach will hold us all; and as for young Caesar, I have no objection to his riding with us, though he isn't, perhaps, of our own spechus, as the great Mr **** [probably Edward Long] says' (Mackenzie 1792: 1.102). Adolphus – whose noble birth has gifted him an instinctive sense of English decorum while his non-Englishness permits him to openly give vent to these convictions – refuses Abrams's self-invitation with a naïve directness unavailable to his English friends. 'He declared, with a look of the warmest dislike', we are told, 'that Mr Hamilton [his guardian] entertained none but people of fashion, birth, or education; consequently, as Mrs Abrams could not be admitted under either of those claims, she would meet with a repulse' (Mackenzie 1792: 1.103). Mrs Abrams, scandalized, counters him with uncontrolled fury:

> [T]his scrubby negro, cannable, this selvidge, chuses to insult me. –Sir, if he was a Christian, or even a Jew, one would not mind it so much. But when the parlermint house is all up in arms about 'em, when even all Mr Will-by-force can say stands for nothing, though he pretends they're free born like us, is such a puppy as this to chatter? (Mackenzie 1792: 1.103–4)

This scene positions Abolitionism between two opposing forms of race thinking. Mrs Abrams is echoing a distinctly modern form of 'varietal racism' – and seemingly referencing the polygenist variety theorist Edward Long in order to support her point of view. Yet, as emphasized in her earlier mispronunciation of the word 'species', the narrative frames her very belief in such a sensational variety theory as inseparable from her stupidity. On the other hand, the more polite company in the room sits in silent embarrassment, because Mrs Abrams is transgressing the boundaries of an older form of race. She has not only neglected to show deference to the high-born royal before her, whom the 'good' characters have instinctively recognized as inherently superior in body and mind, but is so blind to the ranks of universal order – and, indeed, so waylaid by her modern notions of varietal race – that she places him on a level with her African servant. In short, Abrams's implementation of standard varietal racism, which necessarily requires her to place herself above the Prince of Tonouwah, transgresses the sense of race hierarchy according to which she is low-born and he, owing to his genealogy and hereditary privilege, is her superior. Anti-Abolitionists, according to the narrative, are not only ignorant, they are ill-bred. A true understanding of universal order, it would seem, requires an assessment not only of skin colour but also of station, birth, education and, according to the sartorially sensitive Adolphus, fashion. It is an understanding that Adolphus is not merely a Black African, but a Black African whose exalted rank brings him within the acceptable bounds of white Europeans, and, moreover, of white Europeans who are hierarchically superior to the Abramses. The Abolitionist critique of the Abramses' racism then centres on the idea that it is too simplistic, ignoring the essentially racialized aspects of social rank.

For Wylie Sypher, Anna Maria Mackenzie's *Slavery* represents the 'the apotheosis of the noble Negro'; it is

> a grand total of the deficiencies of 'literary' anti-slavery – the juxtaposition of the noble and ignoble savage, nauseous sentimentality, primitivistic critiques of culture, wilful neglect of fact, the arbitrary selection of an exceptional Negro over whom to weep, and the vicious implication that the ordinary slave deserves his bondage. (Sypher 1942: 287)

The distinction between Royal Slaves and common slaves also speaks volumes about a society that sanctioned a different treatment for each. Not forgetting that this novel was published during the Revolutionary upheavals of 1792, the suggested 'racial' integrity of properly honouring royalty and nobility is even more significant. In an awkward digression from the novel's main action, the characters decamp briefly to Revolutionary France where they come face to face with a merciless Republican regime. The last page of the novel, in fact, is entirely given over to the Frenchman M. Soissons, who apologizes on behalf of his countrymen: 'the liberty we contend for blossoms sweetly in your nation. – Had our mode of government been as mild as yours, the rights of royalty would have been equally secure. –Go then, Sir and enjoy with your friends the pure sunshine of freedom' (Mackenzie 1792: 2.237). This peculiar episode sanitizes the text of any potential sympathies for radical equality, yet it also highlights how the Royal Slave can, at this time, be neatly woven into a particularly English fantasy. By linking Abolitionism with an older sense of noble 'race' and defence of traditional social order, Mackenzie is also linking it with the 'English race'. The recognition of truly noble and worthy individuals, even among slaves, is posited as a celebration of the social order, while the indiscriminate oppression of entire nations is characterized as a potential agent of this order's destruction. The sense of deference that moves the high-born English characters to honour Adolphus, then, can be read as a 'racially' English tendency to honour royalty, and indeed to respect, and protect, every individual's inherited place in the Great Chain of Being.

* * *

The Royal Slave trope stands as a striking reminder of the endemic racism within Abolitionist and reformist rhetoric – demonstrating that there existed a scale of human worth even within contemporary pleas for the compassionate treatment of all human beings. It also demonstrates, however, the sheer resilience of noble templates of race right up until the end of the eighteenth century, which were not only entwined with human-variety discourse but stood alongside it as independent modes of reasoning rooted in social rank and genealogical identity. Most importantly, the Royal Slave trope demonstrates how easily the frontiers of social rank could overlap with those of racialized status. Whether they were literary figures like Oroonoko or Adolphus, or mythologized celebrities like Julius Soubise or William Ansah Sessarakoo, the fact that these Black Africans could be considered at the summit of a Western-style social hierarchy had a profound impact on how their race was conceived. The transformation of the Royal Slave's physical appearance, whether in the heroic identity of Oroonoko or in the varietal identity of Adolphus, ultimately reflects the long association of hereditary nobility with physical excellence. The super-human qualities of the Royal Slave express the reality and validity of social hierarchy through the subject's physical body. The Royal Slave was at once a threat to human-variety theory by highlighting the heterogeneity of ostensibly inferior nations and a buttress to greater ideas of graded human worth – re-imagining the African world as a reflection of Western order wherein the racialized qualities of a hereditary elite reinforced the natural legitimacy of Britain and Ireland's leading families.

11

Noble race in a time of revolution

The noble paradigm's influence on the development of race theory at the end of the eighteenth century did not only affect how 'race' was understood, but it also transformed the very meaning of race in a noble context. The fact that global populations were increasingly being discussed in terms of genealogy meant that, ironically, noble dynasties could now be viewed through the prism of racial ideology. By the time Europe's nobilities faced into the existential crisis of the French Revolution, their critics were already armed with a new discourse of human taxonomy based on blood and heredity, which wielded the power to transform those who were 'born to rule' into little more than an example of blundersome selective breeding. This chapter examines how the genealogical discourse upholding nobility became racialized in a new way during the turbulent 1790s, while the noble paradigm, having been subsumed into race theory, was used to undermine nobility itself.

* * *

When revolution first broke out in France in 1789, notes Amanda Goodrich, many in Britain were left ambivalent (2005: 5). After all, the French monarchy represented an institution of absolute power and Catholic supremacy, poised in direct contradiction to Westminster's parliamentary principles. The fact that it took another three years for the French to 'finally decide what to do about their monarchy', however, and the fact that this intervening period saw the abolition first of noble privileges in August 1789 and then of noble titles in June 1790, unleashed a fresh set of anxieties (Goodrich 2005: 5). In the years leading up to the execution of Louis XVI in 1793, asserts Goodrich, political debate in France and Britain shifted away from the monarchy and gravitated instead around noble institutions. This focus was vigorously renewed during the subsequent Terror of 1793–4 'in which "aristocrats" were sought out and summarily guillotined' (2005: 7). In parallel, the tone of British public debate was undergoing a significant change. The events in France, claims Dror Wahrman, had stirred up a strikingly binary discourse of the 'aristocracy' versus the 'people' (1995: 32). Unlike in previous decades, when political conflict in Britain had centred on disputes between elite factions or the negotiation of concessions from those factions, this divide was about 'the very identity and legitimacy of the elite ... about the foundations of the power structure itself' (Wahrman 1995: 32). The use of the word 'aristocracy' to describe the English peerage or wider nobility in the 1790s is indicative of this discursive shift. Aristocracy, explains Goodrich, described a system of government rather than a group of people, but now British commentators were beginning to employ the term *aristocrate* (a largely derogatory descriptor for the French nobility) to refer to their own hereditary elites (2005: 17). Such characterizations struck a resolute blow to the British peers' careful self-stylization as an integral element of mixed government. The idea that the peerage constituted a British 'aristocracy' allowed them to be directly compared with their French counterparts, who were now being decried as enemies of the people (Goodrich 2005: 167). In short, notes Wahrman, during the debates of the 1790s the political became inseparable from the social; radicals and loyalists set out a binary of high and low, rich and poor, and 'in between, the scene was set for the identity of political moderates to be projected onto a social middle' (1995: 36).

The titanic sense of old and new worlds colliding which characterized the Revolutionary period also had extreme ramifications for contemporary ideas of race and rank. As Blumenbach's *De Generis* left the printing houses of Gottingen in 1795, detailing its seminal schemes of major human races/varieties, Revolutionary France was ushering in its *Constitution of Year III*, which aside from guaranteeing '*la liberté, l'égalité, la sûreté,*' and '*la propriété*' to all men, openly outlawed slavery. 'Any man', it read, 'can offer his time and service; but he cannot sell himself nor can he be sold; his personhood is not alienable property' (*Constitution de la République française* 1795: arts 1 and 15).[1] At the same time, the growing interest in genealogically based human-variety theory was transforming the ways in which 'noble race' could be evaluated. The latter decades of the eighteenth century represented a moment of rapid transformation for the nobilities of Britain and Ireland. It must not be forgotten, notes David Cannadine, that the American and French Revolutions were attended by an industrial revolution and massive demographic shifts,

---

1 My translation: 'tout homme peut engager son temps et ses services; mais il ne peut se vendre ni être vendu ; sa personne n'est pas une propriété aliénable' (*Constitution de la République française*: article 15).

both of which fundamentally altered the nature of landownership (1994: 10). Estates and assets were increasingly concentrated in the hands of the wealthiest landlords, while the squirearchy went into steep decline; concordantly, there was a certain 'internationalisation' of the English, Scottish and Irish nobilities as they effectively began to amalgamate into 'a new, supra-national British aristocracy' (Cannadine 1994: 10–12). Inheritance among the 'propertied classes', asserts E. P. Thompson, had always functioned within a network of interlinked grids, wherein 'inheritance of security, status, power, by a social group, caste, or class', was intertwined with grids of law, landownership, custom and vested interests (1976: 358). By the 1790s, a grid of genealogically determined human variety had been noticeably added to this matrix. Since the mid-century, the race concept had been steadily advanced along the nobiliary principles of lineal, hierarchized, family units, reflective of a natural order and sociopolitical status that was manifest in the human body. Now, the idea of major human races, built on the noble paradigm, would come to constitute the most powerful tool with which to interrogate the 'racial' integrity of nobility itself. Noble race in the 1790s, in other words, faced scrutiny based on new racial parameters that had been constructed around its own fundamental power strategies.

Long before the outbreak of revolution, some radical egalitarians had already recognized human-variety theory's potential to undermine noble tradition. One such figure was Georg Forster, son of Cook's natural historian Johann Reinhold Forster, who had rapidly compiled his own narrative of the journey, the *Voyage Round the World* (1777) on his return to London from the South Seas. The young Forster's *Voyage* became one of the first studies of its kind to compare 'indigenes with one another rather than solely with "civilized" or classical societies', notes Vanessa Agnew, establishing a 'frame of reference for all subsequent eighteenth-century reflections on the question of human diversity' and marking a discursive intersection between close observation of anatomical difference and 'increasingly abstract, speculative and implicit formulations of biological race' (2003: 89–90). While Georg's work largely detailed the same human varieties as his father, the younger Forster took a significantly different perspective on the matter – linking the processes of generation and degeneration with the effects of reason, economic inequality and political tyranny. One of the most important discrepancies between the two theorists is in their deployment and understanding of the term 'race'. Whereas Johann Reinhold used the term to describe his differently coloured ranks of islanders, Georg prefers the term 'class'; in fact, he explicitly rejects the term race and indeed any strict concordance between morality, heredity and physical appearance. Like the 'heroes of Homer', he notes in the *Voyage*, '[t]he Tahitian chiefs, compared to the common people, are so much superior in stature and elegance of form, that they *look* like a different race' (Forster 1777: 2.105–6, emphasis added). Certain theorists, such as Bougainville, he continues in a footnote, have fallaciously been 'led by this difference of appearance to assert that they [the chiefs and common people] *really were* two different races' (Forster 1777: 2.106, emphasis added). By 'race', here, Forster is referring to lineal family. He is not rejecting the idea that the islanders can be separated into distinct corporeal categories, but he questions the factors behind their transformation. Instead, he posits that the Tahitians' anatomies reflect their cultural condition rather than their descent: 'men in a similar state of civilisation resemble each other . . . even in the most opposite extremes of the world', he explains, and thus the Tahitians are beautiful like the Ancient Greeks because they lead a similar lifestyle to the Ancient Greeks (Forster 1777: 2.106). The great feasts of the Tahitian *Arees*, for instance, recalled the famous banquets of the 'men at the siege of Troy'. Likewise, a certain

> simplicity of manners is observable in both nations; and their domestic character alike is hospitable, affectionate and humane. There is even a similarity in their political constitution. The chiefs . . . are powerful princes, who have not more respect for *O-Too* [a local king], than the Greek heroes had for the 'king of men'; and the common people are so little noticed in the *Iliad*, that they appear to have had no greater consequence than the *tow-tows* in the South Sea. (Forster 1777: 2.106)

Forster cautions that although the *Arees* are possessed of a more European physique than the *tow-tows*, this does not necessarily reflect an essential inner virtue. In describing the King of Tahiti, he remarks that the monarch's skin was certainly 'the fairest of his people', that his hair was 'lank' and of 'a light brown, turning into reddish at the tips, or being what is commonly called, sandy', yet the *countenance* of this same king was 'unmeaning [i.e. vacant], and rather expressed some kind of fear and distrust at our first meeting, which suited ill with the ideas of majesty, and yet are often the characteristics of lawless power' (1777: 1.305). The observation that 'the classes of *aree, manahouna*, and *tow-tow* . . . bear some distant relation to those of the feudal system of Europe' is a matter of concern rather than admiration in Georg's *Voyage* (1777: 1.365). For him, the European-style political systems of Tahiti stand in opposition to what he equates with the virtues of antiquity – threatening an idyllic, Homeric existence with the inherent inequality of feudal government.

Jurgen Goldstein notes that it is unclear whether Forster had read Rousseau before he composed the *Voyage*, but that it is probable he had at least encountered ideas of the Noble Savage second hand (2019: 58). Some of Georg's convictions certainly seem 'Rousseauian' in nature, including the assertion that civil inequalities were imprinted on the bodies and minds of the islanders (see Rousseau 1755: 125–6). Rather than seeing the Tahitians as developing through 'stages' towards polished, commercial society, he suggests that they are steadily degenerating from a pastoral golden age to a modern state of economic and social inequality, as already evidenced by the anatomical inequalities among their ranks. For all the strict social hierarchy in Tahiti, he claims, there is not yet 'that disparity between the highest and the meanest man which subsists in England between a reputable tradesman and a labourer' (Forster 1777: 1.366). With time, however, he predicts that this gentle cleft between ranks is destined to widen into a chasm as the islanders develop more effective agriculture and as the idleness of the *Arees*, by consequence, becomes ever greater. 'The indolence of the chiefs is already . . . a step towards its [equality's] destruction', Georg warns, and

> though cultivation is a labour scarce at present felt by the *tow-tows*; to whom it is allotted; yet by insensible degrees it will fall heavier upon them, as the number of chiefs must naturally increase . . . because the chiefs are perfectly unemployed. (Forster 1777: 1.366–7)

While Georg and his fellow shipmen could easily trust the 'middle-ranking' *manahounas*, he takes care to note that they learnt to beware of 'the specious politeness of the court and courtiers, who fed our hopes with empty promises' (1777: 1.307).

Like his father, Georg directly links the corporeal state of the islanders with their exposure to influences that favour European sophistication; unlike his father, he identifies this sophistication with vice and misgovernment. The very existence of a physically distinct *Aree* rank, no matter how closely they might emulate the elegance of the European upper orders, is, for Georg, a sign of their debasement into a state of degenerate inequality. Georg portrays the idea of anatomical hierarchy as a physical expression of tyranny. The *tow-tows* may seem dark-skinned now, he warrants, but once they are charged with the labours of modern agriculture and industry,

> they will grow ill-shaped, and their bones [will] become marrowless: their greater exposure to the action of a vertical sun, will blacken their skins, and they will dwindle away to dwarfs, by the more frequent prostitution of their infant

daughters to the voluptuous pleasure of the great. That pampered race [the *Arees*], on the contrary, will preserve all the advantages of an extraordinary size, of a superior elegance of form and features, and of a purer colour by indulging their voracious appetite, and living in absolute idleness. At last, the common people will perceive these grievances, and the causes which produced them; and a proper sense of the general rights of mankind awakening in them will bring on a revolution. (Forster 1777: 1.367)

Georg's criticism of domestic social inequality here is quite clear: if such corporeal horrors await the Tahitians when they achieve a polished society, it follows that the same horrors must already be upon the civilized nations of Europe. The wretched poor in England are thus portrayed as a caste still more anatomically degenerate than the Tahitian *tow-tows*, and if revolution is the inevitable consequence of degenerative inequality in Tahiti's far future, then a comparable revolution in Europe must be imminent. What is more, Georg is attacking the very basis of racialized hierarchy: he upturns the mould of climate discourse by refusing to hold the 'whiter' upper orders as an ideal from which the labouring ranks have deviated. Instead, the purity, beauty and stature so prized by civilized society are all indicted as symptoms of degeneration; this corporeal 'ideal' fed by luxury and sloth could not exist without the anatomical decline of the exploited poor.

Georg Forster's prediction of revolution in Europe was soon vindicated. He went on to become one of the founders of the Revolutionary Mainz Republic in 1793 and was exiled to Paris later in that same year when Austrian and Prussian forces seized the city. While his subsequent writings on human variety continued to be influenced by his fervent political ideology, his perspective on the social ranks of Tahiti highlights a peculiar paradigmatic shift that would become central to anti-noble sentiment at the end of the eighteenth century. One by-product of discussing noble physicality within the discourse of human-variety theory was a certain corporealization of eugeneic tradition, often bringing the language of inherited excellence uncomfortably close to that of varietal classification. If certain human varieties seemed to manifest noble qualities through their anatomy, then the tradition of eugeneic excellence could potentially be reframed as the expression of racialized type. Moreover, if human varieties could be conceived as pure genealogical units, then the noble dynasties from which this template was derived could, logically, be conceived as human varieties in miniature. For radical egalitarians like Georg Forster, human-variety literature's effective corporealization of paradigmatic nobility offered an entirely new scope for anti-noble criticism. While denunciations of noble deficiencies had existed for as long as the noble paradigm itself, the emerging model of genealogical human variety made it possible to argue that the upper orders' propensity for luxury and effeminacy had been imprinted irrevocably on their physical bodies. 'True nobility', in turn, which had traditionally been imagined as a rejection of worldly vice (using cultivation and breeding to tap into an inherent well of noble excellence that could guide one to virtuous rulership), could now be reduced to a handful of arbitrary characteristics that defined one's racial type. No more than human varieties, late-eighteenth-century nobility was losing its potential to *transform* and was instead finding itself trapped within the supposed limitations of racial lineage.

In the 1790s, arguments about the place of nobility in society very often hinged on opposing understandings of what was natural. The idea that the noble body and mind was *different* could play into both sides of this argument. For Revolutionary thinkers like Georg Forster, this conviction constituted an obvious criticism of aristocratic privilege. For others, like the Anglo-Irish statesman and infamous anti-Revolutionary Edmund Burke, the existence of distinct and unbroken noble lineages spearheaded an entire social order based on hereditary institutions. Burke's seminal argument in the *Reflections on the Revolution in France* (1790), though notoriously sentimental when it came to the *ancien régime*, was not a straightforward defence of nobility. In fact, it is often pointed out that Burke could be highly critical of noble privilege. In a rebuttal to the Duke of Bedford in 1796, for instance, he bemoaned 'those who hold large portions of wealth without any apparent merit of their own', implying that if it hadn't been for the success of the *Reflections*, the good duke might not have a title at all (1796: 15). Burke expresses this same sentiment in the *Reflections*, rehearsing the age-old apologist argument that titles represent a state of virtue rather than a badge of blood: '[y]ou do not imagine, that I wish to confine power, authority, and distinction to blood, and names, and titles' he writes, '[n]o, sir, there is no qualification for government, but virtue and wisdom' (1790: 50). Instead, Burke's argument is based above all on an idea of natural inheritance, in which institutions like nobility played a vital role. His perspective, notes Francis Canavan (1987: 166), might once again be best understood in direct contrast to Jean-Jacques Rousseau's *Discours*. Rousseau had famously declared that 'the first man, who, after enclosing a piece of ground, took it into his head to say *this is mine*, and found people simple enough to believe him, was the true founder of civil society' (1761: 97). For Burke, however, the very opposition between natural and civil society was a false premise; instead, he saw civil society as a dimension of the natural state in itself – a 'moral necessity' of natural law (Stanlis 1958:

72). According to this view, traditional institutions as they stood were anything but arbitrary. On the contrary, they had been moulded and refined since time immemorial by natural laws. They were shaped by the specific needs of the community and by the precise character of the nation, providing a model by which people had come to understand how their society worked. Society existed in a 'state of habitual social discipline', Burke explained in his *An Appeal from the New to the Old Whigs* (1791), 'in which the wiser, the more expert, and the more opulent conduct, and by conducting enlighten and protect the weaker, the less knowing, and the less provided with the goods of fortune' (1791: 107). Without this discipline upon which the proper functioning of society had become dependent, 'the multitude . . . can scarcely be said to be in civil society' (Burke 1791: 107). The continuance of traditional institutions and the civil framework of natural law, then, constituted a sort of inherited privilege – a legacy which was to be valued equally as an asset conferred by past generations as it was to be conserved and refined for generations to come. 'Society is, indeed, a contract', Burke proclaimed in the *Reflections*, and it was furthermore an intergenerational partnership between 'those who are living, those who are dead, and those who are to be born', all bound together by the 'inviolable oath which holds all physical and moral natures, each in their appointed place' (1790: 143–4). Nobility, for Burke, is thus most precious as a symbolic totem of greater hereditary order. In the *Reflections*, the genealogical paradigms of nobility provide him with an entire theoretical structure on which to build his own vision of society. No more than proponents of hereditary 'race' were borrowing from the templates of nobility to create a 'common-sense' idea of inherent racial hierarchy, Burke uses these same templates to support a 'common-sense' view of society as a great system of natural, hereditary, inequality. '[F]rom Magna Charta to the Declaration of Right', he declares,

> it has been the uniform policy of our constitution to claim and assert our liberties, as an *entailed inheritance* derived to us from our forefathers, and to be *transmitted* to our *posterity*; as an *estate*. . . . We have an *inheritable* crown; an *inheritable* peerage; and an house of commons and a people *inheriting* privileges, franchises, and liberties from a long line of *ancestors* . . . the idea of *inheritance* furnishes a sure principle of conservation, and a sure principle of *transmission*; without at all excluding a principle of *improvement*. (Burke 1790: 47–8, emphasis added)

This greater tradition of hereditary distinction, for Burke, is the natural protector of private property and the transmission of such between generations.

Nobility was representative of the hereditary system on which private property fundamentally relied and was thus representative of social and economic stability:

> the possessors of family wealth, and of the distinction which attends hereditary possession . . . are the national securities for [property] transmission. . . . For though hereditary wealth and the rank that goes with it, are too much idolized by creeping sycophants. . . . Some decent regulated pre-eminence, some preference (not exclusive appropriation) given to birth, is neither unnatural, nor unjust, nor impolitic. (Burke 1790: 75–6)

More than this, Burke explicitly links this scheme of inheritance with the order and balance of the Great Chain of Being. 'By a constitutional policy, working after the pattern of nature', he declares, 'we receive, we hold, we transmit our government and privileges. . . . Our political system is placed in a just correspondence and symmetry with the order of the world' (Burke 1790: 48). Nobles then, will inevitably have their faults, but by letting commoners rule in their place, Burke warns, one sets oneself 'at war with nature' (1790: 76).

As Hannah Arendt has suggested, Burke's view of hereditary society introduces a curiously racialized dimension to his idea of natural order. Here, that order is based entirely on the inheritance of English institutions, bestowing natural rights to Englishmen. By rejecting Rousseau's naked, unsocialized and unhistoricized 'natural man', Arendt suggests, and by replacing him with a humanity couched in terms of the 'entailed inheritance' of a nation's past, Burke implicitly dehumanizes those outside the realms of this particular hereditary scheme (1951: 300). 'A man who is nothing but a man [i.e., Rousseau's natural man]', according to this reasoning, 'has lost the very qualities which make it possible for other people to treat him as a fellow man' (Arendt 1951: 300). Essentially, Burke was portraying an Englishman's civil liberty in terms of the inherited privileges of noble tradition. Like a nobleman, an Englishman inherited his place in society, his legal rights, his title and his property, all of which characterized his natural rights as an Englishman. Viewed from another perspective, Burke's idea of the nation could be seen as an illustration of what Max Weber called 'ethnic honour' – a 'specific honour of the masses' that is 'analogous to the sense of honour of distinctive status groups' in that the subjects always understand themselves as a 'chosen people' (1978: 391). In the *Reflections*, the English resistance to 'a swinish multitude' trampling over their 'natural protectors' is posited as part of the (inherited) English national character, which is not only inherently opposed to Revolutionary egalitarianism but would itself be negated by it. Burke accordingly paints English anti-radicalism as an irrepressible characteristic of the English race and its innate love for freedom, almost harking back to the 'old spirit of Saxon liberty' that commentators like Boulainvilliers and Bolingbroke had espoused at the beginning of the century.

> Thanks to *our* sullen resistance to innovation, thanks to the cold sluggishness of *our* national character, *we* still bear the stamp of our forefathers. *We* have not as yet subtilized ourselves into savages. . . . *We* have real hearts of flesh and blood beating in our bosoms. *We* fear God; *we* look up with awe to kings; with affection to parliaments; with duty to magistrates; with reverence to priests, and with respect to nobility. Why? Because when such ideas are brought before our minds, it is *natural* to be thus affected. (Burke 1790: 127–9, emphasis added)

In this, notes Arendt, Burke's vision of social liberty is remarkable in that it perfectly protects the status quo of the arbitrarily privileged upper orders while at the same time enlarging 'the principle of these privileges to include the whole English people, establishing them as a kind of nobility among nations' (1951: 176). As Burke himself famously proclaimed:

> All this violent cry against the nobility, I take to be a mere work of art. . . . Nobility is a graceful ornament to the civil order. It is the Corinthian capital of polished society. *Omnes boni nobilitati semper favemus* ['all virtuous men naturally look with favour on noble birth', from Cicero, *Pro Sestio* 3.160]. (Burke 1790: 205)

Burke's often melodramatic descriptions of royalty and nobility in the *Reflections* provided rich fodder for Thomas Paine's infamous reply, the *Rights of Man* (1791–2). To inherit a government, Paine rebuked, was to inherit control over other people and to transmit the rights of others from father to son 'as if they were flocks and herds' (1792: 2.8). Worse still, the original ancestral claims to hereditary right had been made by conquest – establishing the ruling orders not as beacons of civilization, but constant springs of barbarity at the summit of society. 'Because . . . aristocracy is held up by family tyranny and injustice', Paine proclaimed, hereditary rulers were as preposterous as hereditary mathematicians, and served only to further 'the uncivilized principle of governments founded in conquest, and the base idea of man having property in man, and governing him by personal right' (1791: 1.34). Paine's damning portrayal of nobility in the *Rights of Man* often provides an even greater insight into contemporary noble paradigms than Burke's *Reflections*. The text's particularly derisive passage on noble titles, for instance, underlines the continuing importance of chivalric masculinity in noble tradition through its mockery of honorific titles as the capricious 'nicknames' of women and children. A peerage title, claims Paine, 'talks about its fine blue ribbon like a girl, and shews its new garter like a child'. Revolutionary France, he declares, 'has outgrown the baby-cloaths of Count and Duke, and breeched itself in manhood . . . it has put down the dwarf and set up the man' (Paine 1791: 1.32). There is more to this idea of nobility 'breeching itself in manhood' than asserting a masculine gender role: the place of noblemen in Burke's civil society is structurally patriarchal; they are figureheads of hereditary bloodlines that also represent the higher reaches of natural order, and thus the basis of institutional constructs that underpin the natural law of Man and Englishmen. By portraying nobility in terms of childishness and femininity, Paine is requisitioning its authority over a patriarchal vision of humanity, and instead assigns this authority to the 'natural' man – a figure not only devoid of inherited civil liberties but who claims the infinitely more ancient and more authoritative liberty of nature itself. By assuming the masculine role of patriarch, 'natural man' implicitly assumes the traditionally noble position of 'super-human': '[t]he artificial NOBLE shrinks into a dwarf before the NOBLE of nature'; Paine continues, 'and in the few instances . . . in whom nature, as by a miracle, has survived in the aristocracy, THOSE MEN DESPISE IT' (Paine 1791: 1.34).

Paine's dismissal of noble titles not only interrogates the spiritual and patriarchal legitimacy of noble bloodline but also questions whether titles can ever hold semiotic value. Rather than employing the standard (and at this stage, quite tired) assertion that noble rank and title are empty and dishonourable privileges without the inner virtue they represent, Paine argues that titles never meant anything in the first place – that they have always been baseless signifiers for something that does not exist. 'What are they?', he asks, '[w]hat is their worth [?] . . . through all the vocabulary of Adam, there is not such an animal as a Duke or a Count. . . . What respect can be paid to that which describes nothing?' (Paine 1791: 1.32–3). The question of whether titles refer to anything at all, rather than the question of whether those who hold them have lived up to their values, makes for an especially powerful blow to the noble paradigm. As will be remembered from Chapter 2, the idea that a title not only represented something but also represented something different from other titles was fundamental to this power strategy. Francis Nichols's carefully individualized portraits of dukes, earls and barons in the *British* and *Irish Compendiums*, for instance, each displaying the meticulously exact heraldry of each noble station, was part of a noble discourse which relied on the constant reinforcement of 'dukeness' and 'earlness' – states of being which one could live up to or not, but which existed regardless. Paine has therein targeted one of the most vulnerable flanks of paradigmatic nobility:

its reliance on abstract concepts that must constantly be performed, but whose very inconstancy of performance makes their nature impossible to define. Paine, whose writings were largely responsible for introducing the term 'aristocracy' to British debates (Goodrich 2005: 17), directly and deliberately compares noble rank with oligarchical governments so as to show that the moral pretensions of the former are meaningless: '[t]he French constitution says *there shall be no titles*', he writes, 'and of consequence, all that class of equivocal generation, in which some countries is called "aristocracy", and in others "nobility" is done away, and the peer is exalted into MAN' (Paine 1791: 1.32).

Paine consolidates his dichotomy of 'super-human' natural Man and 'sub-human' aristocrat-noble by explicitly focusing on the physical degeneration of the noble body. Such ideas might be best understood in relation to Burke's disquisition on the importance of cosmic superiority in the social elite. In the *Reflections*, Burke had justified the violent historical rise of the ruling orders as a providential resolution of spiritual order. The great conquerors of history, he writes, were not 'not so much like men usurping power, as asserting their natural place in society' (Burke 1790: 71). They justified their conquests over the centuries by consistently 'outshining' their competitors and by deploying their rightful positions in authority to 'illuminate and beautify the world' (Burke 1790: 71). Almost immediately, however, Burke warns about the inevitable degeneration that would occur should this line of conquerors be removed from their rightful positions of power. The next generation of nobles in France, he cautions, a rank which had once maintained 'a conscious dignity' and 'a noble pride' would, because of the Revolution, now be no better than the 'usurers, and Jews, who will always be their fellows, sometimes their masters' (Burke 1790: 48–9). The analogy is an interesting one, because Burke is inverting the social status of two hereditary groups – the nobility and the Jews – in order to demonstrate the danger bloodline degeneration poses to the natural order of society. Both nobility and Judaism are here seen as hereditary constituents of an inherited system of civil liberties, in which one descending line is naturally superior to the other. In the normal scheme of things, it can be inferred, one line transmits noble qualities to its descendants, while the other transmits vice. When the age-old balance of society is upset, however, the descending channels of nobility will become contaminated with vulgarity, while people of Jewish blood will gain impermissible access to their authority. Paine seizes upon this very same analogy to highlight the vulnerability of an elite governmental body that has *always* been liable to bloodline degeneration. Nobles and Jews, he suggests in his *Rights of Man*, had never stood at opposite ends of the natural order. Rather, their combined dependence on bloodline integrity meant that both groups had long since declined in a comparable way. 'Aristocracy has a tendency to degenerate the human species', he proclaims,

> by the universal œconomy of nature it is known, and by the instance of the Jews it is proved, that the human species has a tendency to degenerate, in any small number of persons, when separated from the general stock of society, and intermarrying constantly with each other. It defeats even its pretended end, and becomes in time the opposite of what is noble in man. (Paine 1791: 1.34)

The 'opposite of what is noble in man', then, is imagined in both Burke and Paine's accounts as the racially degenerate human body, though Burke applies this only to Jews while Paine applies it to Jews and nobles alike. Each theorist is also employing a very different perspective: Burke's insistence that inherited privilege forms part of the natural 'order of the world' portrays the supremacy of nobles (and hereditary elites in general) as primarily providential. Paine, on the other hand, uses a reasoning that is much more redolent of human-variety theory. His understanding of noble difference is first and foremost physiological – enshrined in a noble tradition of genealogical race that had, at this stage, thoroughly infiltrated the language of natural history. In fact, it is telling just how easy it had become in the discourse of 'aristocracy versus the people' to portray the nobility as a degenerate race, precisely because emerging concepts of race followed the template of noble tradition so conspicuously. Likewise, since noble blood had provided a discourse wherein social rank could be thought of on the same terms of animal breeding practices, it had become equally easy to point out that nobility evidently followed bad husbandry techniques, blindly 'interbreeding' rather than actively assimilating superior stock. In the latter years of the eighteenth century, in short, it had become increasingly logical to extrapolate that the noble body – following a template of race that had been established by noble tradition itself – was a degenerate body.

This intense and unprecedentedly physiological understanding of noble rank and race is everywhere to be seen in late-century Revolutionary debates on the 'aristocracy question'. The countless pamphlets that were published in response to Burke's *Reflections* and Paine's *Rights of Man* recurrently engage with the question of nobility's anatomical condition, asking if and how the historical blood isolation of a lineal race could be, or should be, considered in terms of anatomical superiority or inferiority. The anonymous author of *Considerations on Mr Paine's Pamphlet on the Rights of Man* (1791), for instance, counters Paine's example of the Jews becoming a 'degenerate race' with the evidence of noble perfectibility provided by thoroughbred horses. Paine, the writer claims, argues that the Jews have become degenerate by the same means as the nobility, namely by being 'separated from the general stock of society' and 'intermarrying with each other' (*Considerations* 1791: 39). Should this proof be admitted, the writer retorts, one would also have to accept the absurd idea that:

> the famous breed of Arabian horses, which is never suffered to mix with others, is the most degenerate race of horses. It would also prove, that . . . the Spartans . . . by constantly intermarrying in the small circle of free citizens, were become the most degenerate race of man: yet the Spartans were esteemed the bravest, the handsomest, the most virtuous men in the world, and their women the most beautiful. Does Mr. Paine seriously believe that the gallant *noblesse* of France is inferior either in moral or physical qualities to the mixed breed of his American countrymen. [?] (*Considerations* 791: 40–1)

Here, the pamphleteer is arguing directly against Paine, yet they nonetheless remain firmly rooted in a discourse of physiological race. Their argument fully recognizes that the controlled breeding practices of the nobility have rendered nobles corporeally distinct from other people, only that, in the writer's opinion, this is a superior rather than inferior distinction. More than this, while the nobility are openly compared here to thoroughbred horses, the brilliance and beauty of the Spartans are likewise attributed to the controlled breeding of a pure-blood human 'race'. In another anonymous response to Paine, *A Defence of the Constitution of England* (1791), the author asserts that the Bible made it clear that early humans had immediately clustered 'into families; some deservedly and honourably distinguished, and some reprobated and degraded', and that it was the natural hierarchy of 'good' to 'bad' families that had established ranks among men (1791: 25). 'A difference was made . . . between the families of Abel and Cain', the author declares, 'and education added to its assistance: the difference of those families may continue at this day' (*Defence* 1791: 26). Since less attention was now being lent to the genealogical purity of noble marriages, the author goes on, the nation's most magnificent families were increasingly vulnerable to a 'contamination of family principles', and this is what Paine had incorrectly interpreted as noble decline (*Defence* 1791: 28). The pamphleteer knew of one distinguished nobleman who made the mistake of marrying a common 'soldier's trull':

> The family will be infested for generations with the low and abominable vices, which are transmitted from such a wretch to her unfortunate children; and through them to future ages . . . the privileges of nobility are not only lost, but

turned against the public interest, and by being made the nurseries of vice instead of those of virtue, they are justly subjected to censure and indignation. (*Defence* 1791: 29)

Pure-blood noble race in this text, by sustaining the virtues of past generations, is identified as a function of noble rank in society, while its contamination with base blood is injurious for the community as a whole by denying the people the governance of a 'super-human' caste.

* * *

Georg Forster's *Voyage* provided an early insight into a new perspective on noble race – one that was profoundly influenced by a genealogical race model built upon the parameters of the noble paradigm. Within just a few years, the Revolutionary debates of Burke and Paine had framed nobility as a representative correlative for the very idea of heredity in society. Natural history's revolution in its understandings of human race, that is, had facilitated an ontological revolution in understandings of noble race. More than this, the role of the noble body in these debates indicates a moment of crisis not just for noble institutions but for British eugeneic tradition. The shift from a fundamentally metaphorical or providential form of race thinking to a fundamentally physiological one changed the very nature of how 'noble race' could be justified or criticized. Just like human varieties, nobility could now be hypothesized in terms of generation and degeneration – with the external influences of breeding and education echoing those of climate and civilisation and with bloodline and ancestry directly correlating with racialized descent. It might even be said that the real crisis of the British nobility in the 1790s, on the fall of their counterparts in France, was that they were recognized as a race not only in the traditional but in the modern sense of the word: as a quasi-biological entity, whose eugeneic traditions of 'high birth' had taken on a dangerous new dimension by becoming too bound up with a hierarchy of the human body, and thus could never exist again in exactly the same way.

12

Conclusion

In the opening chapter of this study, the core paradigmatic construct of noble tradition was delineated through the following six tenets:

1. Some people are naturally excellent.
2. This excellence can be transmitted genealogically.
3. Familial excellence naturally gives rise to cultural and economic dominance.
4. Inherited excellence must be re-performed in each generation.
5. The noble body is both an expression and a tool of inherited excellence.
6. Integrity of genealogical, cultural, economic, performative and corporeal excellence – called 'true nobility' – is essential for the continuance of inherited excellence in future generations.

In eighteenth-century Britain and Ireland these tenets at once underpinned the ideas of nobility as a historical tradition, nobility as a metaphysical state of virtue and nobility as an exclusive circle of elite families who stood at the summit of contemporary social hierarchy. What has been seen over the course of this study, however, is that these same tenets – by providing a conceptual link between the ideas of excellence, human anatomy and genealogical identity – informed a broad concept of 'race' in the early modern world, as well as a hierarchized system of racialized reasoning that aligned genealogically defined groups with the ranks of universal order. Let us, then, review the core construct of nobility in light of this study's investigations into nobility as a racialized entity and its influence over the development of race thinking in eighteenth-century Britain and Ireland.

The most important link between the noble paradigm and the race construct in the eighteenth century was the idea of inherent and inimitable excellence. Following the Ancient Greek model of *arete* (discussed in Chapter 2) – that is, a notion of excellence directly relative to a given context – noble excellence is not merely a natural and personal virtuosity, but an essence that is definitively appropriate for noble rank, becoming, in turn, the superlative quality of an *aristoi* caste and the basis of *aristokratia* governance. The *arete*-excellence that characterizes any given set of *aristoi* is at once based in the individual and in the nature of that individual's role in society; it is to excel within humanity by virtue of excelling within a specific (and arbitrary) social status. Through the assertion of an *arete* quality in an *aristoi* caste, that is to say, the powerful essentially justify their authority by referencing their own power. The idea of inherent and inimitable excellence, in turn, implicitly stratifies humanity into those who are excellent and those who are not; into the 'better sort' and all the rest. It necessarily constructs a lower as well as a higher field of human worth. The excellent can only become excellent through the implicit subjugation of the non-excellent, and the non-excellent can only hope to become excellent by deferring to the arbitrary social authority that defines and produces this excellence.

The racialized dimensions within this idea of inherent human excellence should not be underestimated: first, it is an idea that often supersedes even the hereditary components of noble tradition – for, it is a vision of the best members of society naturally rising to the top of that society; second, this excellence is constantly and consistently expressed through ideas of corporeal superiority, nourishing the notion that human worth is bound up with the physical human body and that better people are (literally and symbolically) stronger, more beautiful and more anatomically 'perfect' than others; and third, to recall the assertions of Étienne Balibar and Immanuel Wallerstein, noble excellence is a quintessential act of social othering by way of an arbitrary set of qualities (1991: 208–9). Race itself, claim Balibar and Wallerstein, begins with 'self-referential' race thinking – establishing those in control of the discourse as a 'race' (here, by virtue of their shared, inherited excellence) and, in the process, implicitly racializing those who do not control the discourse in terms of their ostensible deviation from the dominant racialized identity (1991: 208–9).

Crucial to this construct is the idea that inherent and inimitable excellence is manifested through superior anatomy. At its most basic level, idealized noble anatomy conveys a fantasy of military might: the true nobleman's physique is essentially presented as a warrior physique, showcasing a martial aesthetic of the human body that bespeaks strength, supremacy and the glory of the society it represents. Their form – from the tall, quick-witted parliamentarians of Cheyne's *English Malady* to the muscled Grecian heroes of the Forsters' Tahiti – is a physical expression of historical conquest; the noble body functions both as a metaphor of nation and as a very real reassurance of tangible force among the ruling caste.

Representations of noble women too are sometimes inducted into this trope: feminized versions of the 'noble warrior' physique can, for instance, be found in Boulainvilliers' Germanic women, Macpherson's Ancient Celtic women and certain 'Amazonian' descriptions of Aphra Behn's Imoinda. On another level, however, the idea that true nobles manifest a certain anatomical form – be it that of a warrior or otherwise – ostensibly provides visual evidence of that noble's *arete*-excellence, creating a self-perpetuating dynamic of hegemonic authority. If noble status is linked with a certain physical form, in other words, this physical form serves to bolster the perceived reality of noble status. The conceptual links between human excellence, physical perfection and noble rank suggest not only that nobles are anatomically superior but that, conversely, a certain anatomical form (arbitrarily named superior) bears an affinity with noble rank. The beautiful, the capable and the militarily successful manifest a *natural nobility*, independent of their social rank, that may or may not be recognized by the established authority. The social rank of nobility, that is to say, aligns itself with a perceived excellence of nature that is also understood as 'noble'.

The notion of *eugeneia*, meanwhile, asserts that noble families are much more than wealthy dynasties; their birth is, in fact, an indispensable part of their *aristoi* identity. The genealogical component of noble tradition ensures that no matter how poor or dispossessed a noble becomes, if he is well born he will always be inherently noble; and no matter how much a non-noble emulates noble lifestyle, noble functions and noble excellence, if he is low born he can never express 'true' nobility. That is, it asserts nobility, like race, to be an unchangeable (but improvable) quality of the body and blood, aligned with a certain position in the *Scala naturae*. The 'active' component of *nobilitas* was just as important as *eugeneia* to eugeneic noble identity in eighteenth-century Britain and Ireland. *Nobilitas* describes a noble quality that is part hereditary and part attained. As a long-standing element of noble tradition, it plays a fundamental role in the long-term maintenance of *eugeneia* ideals: namely, it allows the non-noble to be inducted, as needed, into a noble sphere by charging them with adherence – over successive generations – to the dominant templates of eugeneic authority. It does not contradict the genealogical paradigm of nobility but serves to enrich it, to justify it or even to account for when it is lacking. The gentry of eighteenth-century Britain and Ireland display an active *nobilitas* (being their landed income, their attention to decorum and their studied emulation of noble tradition – especially in matters of marriage and property transfer) but do not, and most likely never will, possess full eugeneic nobility (to have been directly born into a noble family). Genteel status can, albeit with difficulty, be *attained* but must subsequently be actively upheld with each coming generation; through this process, it establishes a new genealogical unit, nourishing and conceptually reinforcing the authority of the eugeneic families higher up the chain of precedence while never threatening their supremacy.

The constant interplay of *eugeneia* and *nobilitas* is at the very heart of noble race, and, in turn, at the heart of race thinking in eighteenth-century Britain and Ireland. It is through this interplay that noble race – which expounds an inherent, inimitable excellence, manifests itself through anatomical features and exists primarily as a genealogical entity – harnesses the ability to racialize other groups. By positively defining the parameters of its own 'race', nobility negatively identifies comparative racial parameters in the non-noble. In other words, all other groups, depending on their level of deviance from the master-template of race established by the noble paradigm, can (and must) be conceived in terms of 'lesser races' in order to consolidate the racial parameters that ultimately serve to protect the dominant group. Just as the gentry engage in a brand of *nobilitas* that implicitly bolsters the *eugeneia* structure of nobility, these other racialized groups can be understood to have been assigned what is essentially a lesser degree of *nobilitas*. That is to say, first, that any racialized identity must, by definition, accept the existence of 'race' itself, which is always arbitrarily defined by those who control the discourse; and second, that racialized identities thereafter depend on consistent adherence to that identity over successive generations and within genealogically confined limits. Race is passed down from one generation to the next, but each generation must 'perform' that race in order for it to exist. Just as *nobilitas* reinforces *eugeneia*, the very performance of a race within genealogical confines validates the master-template of racialized identity and necessarily validates those in control of the racialized discourse as a 'superior' race. Within noble tradition, in short, we find the three most basic elements of race thinking: first, the idea that there are naturally excellent people, that this natural excellence has a physical expression and that this state of being is transmitted genealogically; second, that this template can be transferred onto the non-excellent – that there are *non-excellent* people, that *non-excellence* has a physical expression and that *this state of being too* is transmitted genealogically; and third and most crucially, that neither of these genealogical states of being, excellent or non-excellent, can survive without the other. The noble paradigm quite simply provides a ready-made formula for racialized hierarchy.

As explored in Chapter 3, one of the most important aspects of the early-modern race concept was its sheer ambiguity and subsequent capacity for contradiction. Racialized understandings of the exotic other were not, in eighteenth-century Britain, clearly distinct from racialized understandings of religious groups, national groups nor indeed different social ranks, and the genealogical basis of racialized groupings was, partly at least, a case of inheritance rather than heredity. Nations, then, were racialized because they transmitted their traditions, language and culture genealogically; different social orders, likewise, were racialized because they genealogically transmitted the status and identity of their particular order. The ambiguity of racialized identity, furthermore, reflects the inherent relativity of the Great Chain of Being world view. The Neoplatonic template of universal order was not only dependent on arbitrary cultural context but had the power to reframe this context as an inevitable aspect of Creation. Thus, just as self-referential race thinking began with those in charge of the discourse defining the limits of race, the Great Chain model of universal order allowed those who controlled the discourse to decide who sat atop the scale of precedence, while the rest of society was automatically graded according to its proximity to that paradigm of a dominant elite. In this way, the Chain model also allowed multiple and contradictory signifiers of superior or inferior social order to be considered in relation to one another. Any quality deemed deviant in relation to the established authority – poverty, incivility, heathenism, skin colour or linguistic difference, for example – could, through the idea of a Great Chain of Being, be considered in relation to any other deviant quality, thus establishing a shared dimension of 'natural' subjugation. Laziness, for instance, could thus seamlessly be aligned with stupidity or barbarism (as in Hottentot mythology), while sexual laxity could be 'rationally' aligned with non-standard clothing or mode of life (as in Oliver Goldsmith's descriptions of Asian populations). Since any deviant quality indicated a naturally low position in the universal order, these qualities could be variously combined to characterize the racialized identity of lower echelons of human hierarchy.

The Great Chain of Being world view not only favoured and promoted the idea that universal hierarchies were fixed in the scheme of creation but also that they remained constant by way of genealogy: lesser beings, this philosophy assumed, gave rise to lesser beings and higher beings gave rise to higher beings. In this respect, the very act of hierarchical subjugation in early modern Britain and Ireland can itself be understood in terms of racialization, delineating arbitrary qualities in certain groups that are expected to be passed down from one generation to the next, thereby limiting these groups in terms of spiritual worth. The Curse of Ham tradition is a case in point: this myth, referenced in Chapter 3, was initially deployed to rationalize the social oppression of serfs during the early medieval period, before subsequently serving as a common explanation for the anatomical otherness of Black Africans, then being utilized to assert the natural inferiority the Jews, and even, as demonstrated in Maurice Shelton's *True Rise of Nobility*, being revived to demonstrate the superior 'Japhetic' legacy of the British nobility. The consistent premise of the Curse of Ham tradition is genealogy – it identifies its arbitrary groups, be they serfs, Black Africans, Jews or nobles, in terms of temporal and lineal continuity; they not only become real and coherent groups by existing over successive generations within a genealogical limitation but are therefore automatically associated with a certain cosmic rank.

Race thinking, as established by noble tradition, actively functioned in conjunction with the Great Chain of Being world view. Nobility provided eighteenth-century race thinking with a crucial dimension: the eugeneic principle of blood. The isolation of genealogical groups in terms of lineal purity, as for example in the reasoning of Boulainvilliers, ultimately forged one of the most binding links between 'noble race' and eighteenth-century human-variety theory. Boulainvilliers' texts provide a prime example of self-referential race thinking in action: his Germanic nobles form a 'race' because they can be understood in terms of direct lineal legacy; through this legacy, accordingly, their inherent and inimitable excellence (a natural talent for just governance and military success) can be linked to their distinct physical appearance (blond, tall and beautifully proportioned) and their ethnic provenance (descent from Frankish conquerors). Boulainvilliers, indeed, exploits the noble tradition of blood purity – which usually served to limit and fortify noble status – in order to racialize an entirely new eugeneic unit and to characterize this unit in terms of natural superiority. Blood purity, in other words, enables Boulainvilliers to construct a 'race' across borders, languages, cultures and centuries of history. More than this, it allows him to 'prove' that this race of French and English nobles reflect a dominant rank in the Great Chain of Being: their purity of blood incontrovertibly testifies to their descent from historical and providential conquerors.

These three structural supports of noble race – (1) the 'top-down' system of human stratification (relating all subordinate groups to a dominant paradigm), (2) the identification of genealogical groups with precise social ranks and (3) the use of blood to define the limits of a racialized identity – can all be seen to inform the development of human-variety theory in the eighteenth century. If contemporary critics worried that Carolus Linnaeus had not adequately asserted the *Homo sapiens*' superiority over the rest of the Animal Kingdom in his *Systema Naturae*, they could certainly rest assured that the *Homo sapiens europeanus albus* was, in every one of his given attributes, innately and inimitably superior to his fellow human varieties. As explored in Chapter 5, Buffon's and Goldsmith's development of a 'race' construct that can only exist in a state of temporal constancy, as well as their refinement of a climate theory that emphasized the effect of environmental influences within genealogical groups, lent the older, well-established notions of genealogical identity an entirely new significance in the experimental field of human-variety theory. When the idea of true nobility is imposed upon the discourse of human variety, as in Johann Reinhold Forster's *Observations Made on a Voyage Round the World*, the two ideas are often difficult to distinguish: Forster's *Arees* manifest a white European physical type as a direct consequence of their nobility, intimating that white Europeans, as a group, and owing to the very same combination of *eugeneia* and *nobilitas*, are a kind of nobility among mankind.

Most of all, human-variety theory reflects noble tradition in its underlying desires. In the modern Western world, the concept of 'human race' as a biological or scientific reality has been all but entirely debunked – a development which highlights more than ever one of the central questions in the history of race: What kind of society would put so much effort into discovering the precise borders of racialized human groups where, by all available evidence, they did not exist? By understanding the hegemonic functions of noble race, its capacity to racialize other groups in order to fortify its own reality and its relationship with a lineal Chain of Being world view, we can come one step closer to finding a response to this question. Ultimately, human-variety theory was just one, 'scientific' manifestation of the vast hierarchical systems that underpinned the concept of humanity in eighteenth-century Britain and Ireland. The noble paradigm informed human-variety theory precisely because it had established itself as the dominant template of corporeal (and indeed socio-economic) excellence, and, by consequence, the entire hierarchy that was built around this template, descending, in a plenitudinous, gradational and continuous manner, through various levels of deviance.

This study ultimately argues that, when investigating the history of 'human races', it is crucial to appreciate that the older conception of race which prevailed in Britain and Ireland throughout the eighteenth century did not merely concern the identification of human groups who ostensibly looked and acted a certain way, who practised an exotic religion or culture or who existed as a colonial other. It was, in fact, a mode of understanding humanity itself, which had existed long before the emergence of immutable human types, and which, in many ways, continued to exist alongside later templates of major human races. It was a mode of understanding humanity, furthermore, that underpinned every relationship between every social and spiritual rank in eighteenth-century Britain and Ireland, because it was the basis of rank itself; it was an idea of race that Thomas Paine rallied against in his *Rights of Man* and that Edmund Burke clung to so dearly as the foundation of everything he understood about a functioning society; it was an idea of race that allowed Lord Monboddo to assert the idea of nobility, super-human anatomy and natural rulership as a foil to the quasi-humanity of anthropoid apes; it was an idea of race, indeed, that allowed Aphra Behn's Oroonoko and Anna Maria Mackenzie's Prince Adolphus to be 'white' and 'Black' at the same time, because it engaged with the entire system of social signifiers around them in order to vindicate a certain understanding of their position in the natural order of things.

Nobility, it might be said, bears so many similarities to race theory because they both recognized, on some level, what we now understand as the mechanics of genetics and biological heredity. Yet, far more important than this is the fact that both nobility and race thinking, on recognizing these vague and mysterious patterns in the general scheme of human generation, automatically interpreted them in terms of superiority and inferiority. As mentioned in Chapter 11, many late-eighteenth-century commentators found it easy to racialize nobility, because race thinking follows the same hierarchical structures as noble tradition. To this, it might be added that it was easy to racialize nobility because both nobility and race thinking expressed a similar desire to control the limits of humanity: by defining themselves according to a precise set of qualities and by insisting that these qualities exist within certain genealogical parameters, the elites of both functioned as touchstones for an entire system of human interaction that always privileged one dominant group above all others. Nobility is inseparable from race – both in the older and the newer senses of the word – because, by its very nature, it expresses a hierarchy of human value which is inextricable from graded excellence, graded anatomy and graded genealogy, and because, during the eighteenth century, this structure ultimately became the prime methodology for ranking human types in a hierarchy of worth which was thereafter proclaimed part of the natural order of things. The eighteenth-century British and Irish nobilities existed within the same power paradigm as emerging human races and for the same reasons. At the close of the eighteenth century, and at the dawn of a new era wherein global humanity would be subjected to a brutal new order of pseudo-biological stratification, nobility stood as one of Britain and Ireland's most conspicuous expressions of a 'better sort' of human being – an ancient standard of hegemonic elitism that insidiously shaped the very future of Western humanity. While the great towering wigs, the shimmering waistcoats and the looming paniers would fall into decline at the end of the century, the ancient tenets of the noble paradigm were yet rushing forth into the modern era, permeating the very foundations of human value at every level and redefining who, exactly, was born to rule.

References

A Defense of the Constitution of England (1791), London: R. Baldwin.
'American Anthropological Association Statement on Race' (1998), *American Anthropologist*, 100 (3): 712–13.
'An Act Abolishing the House of Lords' ([1649] 1899), in Samuel Rawson Gardiner (ed.), *The Constitutional Documents of the Puritan Revolution 1625–1660*. Oxford: Clarendon Press.
Addison, Joseph (1709), *The Tatler*, no. 75, Glasgow: Robert Urie.
Agnew, Vanessa (2003), 'Pacific Island Encounters and the German Invention of Race', in Rod Edmond and Vanessa Smith (eds), *Islands in History and Representation*, 81–94, London: Routledge.
Allen, Richard (2018), 'Slavery in a Remote but Global Place: The British East India Company and Bencoolen, 1685–1825', *Social and Education History*, 7 (2): 151–76.
Appiah, Kwame Anthony (1989), 'The Conservation of "Race"', *Black American Literature Forum*, 23 (1): 37–60.
Appiah, Kwame Anthony and Henry Louis Gates Jr, eds (2005), *The Encyclopaedia of the African and the African-American Experience*, Oxford: Oxford University Press.
Aquinas, Thomas ([c. 1264] 1905), *Of God and His Creatures: An Annotated Translation of the Summa Contra Gentiles of St. Thos. Aquinas*, trans. Joseph Rickaby, London: Burns and Oates.
Aravamudan, Srinivas (1999), *Tropicopolitans: Colonialism and Agency, 1688–1804*, Durham: Duke University Press.
Arendt, Hannah ([1951] 1973), *The Origins of Totalitarianism*, New York: Harvest.
Aristotle ([c. 335-323 BCEa] 1921), 'Politica', trans. Benjamin Jowett, in W. D. Ross (ed.), *The Works of Aristotle*, vol. 10, Oxford: Clarendon Press.
Aristotle ([c. 335-323 BCEb] 1931), 'De Anima', trans. J. A. Smith, in W. D. Ross (ed.), *The Works of Aristotle*, vol. 3, Oxford: Clarendon Press.
Aristotle ([c. 335-323 BCEc] 1928), 'Metaphysica', trans W. D. Ross, in W. D. Ross (ed.), *The Works of Aristotle*, vol. 8, Oxford: Clarendon Press.
Augstein, Hannah Franziska (1996), *Race: The Origins of an Idea 1760–1850*, Bristol: Thoemmes.
Augustine, Saint ([c. 412-426 CE] 1871), *The City of God against the Pagans*, trans. Marcus Dods, Edinburgh: T&T Clark.
Augustodunensis, Honorius ([1110–1139] 1895), 'De imagine Mundi', in J.-P. Migne (ed.), *Patrologiae cursus completus sive biblioteca universalis, integra, uniformis, commoda, oeconomica, omnium SS*, 119–86, Paris: Garnier.

Baldry, H. C. (1965), *The Unity of Mankind in Greek Thought*, Cambridge: Cambridge University Press.

Balibar, Étienne and Immanuel Wallerstein (1991), *Race, Nation, Class: Ambiguous Identities*, trans. Chris Turner, London: Verso.

Ballexserd, Jacques (1762), *Dissertation sur l'éducation physique des enfans*, Paris: Vallat-La-Chapelle.

Bancel, Nicholas, Thomas David and Dominic Thomas, eds (2014), *The Invention of Race: Scientific and Popular Representations*, New York: Routledge.

Banks, Joseph (1768–1771), 'Endeavour journal, 25 August 1768–12 July 1771', in *Sir Joseph Banks Papers*, The State Library of New South Wales. Available online: https://www.sl.nsw.gov.au/banks/section-02 (accessed 1 September 2022).

Banton, Michael (1998), *Racial Theories*, second edn, Cambridge: Cambridge University Press.

Barnard, Tony (2003), *A New Anatomy of Ireland: The Irish Protestants 1649–1770*, Yale: Yale University Press.

Bartlett, Thomas (2014), 'The Emergence of the Irish Catholic Nation: 1750–1850', in Alvin Jackson (ed.), *The Oxford Handbook of Modern Irish History*, 517–43, Oxford: Oxford University Press.

Bartlett, Thomas, ed. (2004), *Revolutionary Dublin, 1795–1801: The Letters of Francis Higgins to Dublin Castle*, Dublin: Four Courts Press.

Bartlett, Thomas, Kevin Dawson and Dáire Keogh, eds (1998), *Rebellion: A Television History of 1798*, Dublin: Gill and Macmillan.

Barzun, Jacques (1938), *Race: A Study in Modern Superstition*, London: Metheun.

Baum, Bruce (2006), *The Rise and Fall of the Caucasian Race*, New York: New York University Press.

Beaglehole, J. C., ed. (1967), *The Journals of Captain James Cook on His Voyages of Discovery: The Voyage of the Resolution and Discovery 1776–1780*, Cambridge: Cambridge University Press.

Beck, Hans (2022), 'Republican Elites: Patricians, *Nobiles*, Senators and Equestrians', in Valentina Arena and Jonathan Prag (eds), *A Companion to the Political Culture of the Roman Republic*, 347–61, Hoboken: Wiley.

Bede the Venerable ([*c.* 731 CE] 1907), *Bede's Ecclesiastical History of England*, trans. A. M. Seller, London: George Bell.

Behn, Aphra (1688), *Oroonoko; or, the Royal Slave*, London: Will Canning.

Bernasconi, Robert (2009), 'Who Invented the Concept of Race?', in Les Back and John Solomos (eds), *Theories of Race and Racism: A Reader*, Second edn, 83–103, London: Routledge.

Bernasconi, Robert, ed. (2001), *Bernier, Linnaeus and Maupertuis*, Bristol: Thoemmes Press.

Bernier, François (1684), 'Nouvelle division de la terre', in *Le Journal des Scavans*, 135–40, Paris: Jean Cusson.

Bethencourt, Francisco (2013), *Racisms: from the Crusades to the Twentieth Century*, Princeton: Princeton University Press.
Bewick, Thomas ([1790] 1804), *A General History of Quadrupeds*, New York: G. and R. Waite.
Bindman, David (2002), *Aesthetics and the Idea of Race in the Eighteenth Century*, Ithaca: Cornell University Press.
Bindman, David and Henry Louis Gates Jr, eds (2011), *The Image of the Black in Western Art: From the 'Age of Discovery' to the 'Age of Abolition'*, Cambridge, MA: Harvard University Press.
Black, Jeremy (2008), *Eighteenth-Century Britain, 1688–1783*, Basingstoke: Palgrave.
Blackstone, William (1765), *Commentaries on Laws of England*, Oxford: Clarendon Press.
Blower, Elizabeth (1785), *Maria; a Novel*, London: T. Cadell.
Blumenbach, Johann Friedrich ([1775] 1865), 'On the Natural Variety of Mankind', first edn, trans. Thomas Bendyshe, in Thomas Bendyshe (ed.), *The Anthropological Treatises of John Friedrich Blumenbach*, 65–144, London: Longman.
Blumenbach, Johann Friedrich (1781), *De generis humani varietate nativa*, Gottingen: Viduam and Vandennosk.
Blumenbach, Johann Friedrich ([1795a] 1865), 'On the Natural Variety of Mankind', third edn, trans. Thomas Bendyshe, in Thomas Bendyshe (ed.), *The Anthropological Treatises of John Friedrich Blumenbach*, 145–276, London: Longman.
Blumenbach, Johann Friedrich (1795b), *De generis humani varietate nativa*, Gottingen: Vandenhoek and Ruprecht.
Blumenbach, Johann Friedrich ([1806a] 1865), 'Contributions to Natural History', trans. Thomas Bendyshe, in Thomas Bendyshe (ed.), *The Anthropological Treatises of John Friedrich Blumenbach*, 277–340, London: Longman.
Blumenbach, Johann Friedrich (1806b), *Beyträge zur Naturgeschichte*, vol. 1, Göttingen: Heinrich Dieterich.
Blumenbach, Johann Friedrich (1810), *Abbildungen naturhistorischer Gegenstände*, Göttingen: Heinrich Dieterich.
Boas, Franz (1912), 'Changes in the Bodily Form of Descendants of Immigrants', *American Anthropologist*, 14 (3): 530–62.
Boas, Franz (1937), 'Race Prejudice from the Scientist's Angle', *Forum and Century*, 98 (2): 90–4.
Bolingbroke, Henry St John ([1730–1731] 1768), 'Remarks upon the History of England', in *The Miscellaneous Works of the Late Right Honourable Lord Bolingbroke*, 43–290, Edinburgh: A. Donaldson.
Bontius, Jacobus ([1631] 1658), *Historiae naturalis et medicae Indiae orientalis*, in Guliemi Pisonis, *De Indiae utriusque re naturali et medica* (annex), 40–160, Amsterdam: Ludovic and Daniel Elzevirios.

Bougainville, Louis Antoine de (1771), *Voyage autour du monde*, Paris: Saillant.
Bougainville, Louis Antoine de (1772), *A Voyage Round the World*, trans. J. R. Forster, Dublin: J. Exshaw.
Boulainvilliers, Henri de (1728), *État de la France*, London: W. Robert.
Boulainvilliers, Henri de (1732), *Essais sur la noblesse de France*, Amsterdam: n.p.
Boulainvilliers, Henri de (1739), *An Historical Account of the Ancient Parliaments of France*, trans. Charles Forman, London: J. Brindley.
Boulukos, George (2008), *The Grateful Slave: The Emergence of Race in Eighteenth-Century British and American Literature*, Cambridge: Cambridge University Press.
Braude, Benjamin (1997), 'The Sons of Noah and the Construction of Ethnic and Geographical Identities in the Medieval and Early Modern Periods', *The William and Mary Quarterly*, 54 (1): 103–42.
Brion Davis, David (1966), *The Problem of Slavery in Western Culture*, Ithaca: Cornell University Press.
Brown, John ([1778] 1831), *The Self-Interpreting Bible*, Edinburgh: Thomas Ireland.
Brown, Laura (2001), *Fables of Modernity: Literature and Culture in the English Eighteenth Century*, Ithaca: Cornell University Press.
Brown, Laura (2010), *Homeless Dogs and Melancholy Apes: Humans and Other Animals in the Modern Literary Imagination*, Ithaca: Cornell University Press.
Brown, Peter (2012), *Through the Eye of a Needle: Wealth, the Fall of Rome, and the Making of Christianity in the West, 350–550 AD*, Princeton: Princeton University Press.
Brown, Richard (1991), *Society and Economy in Britain, 1700–1850*, London: Routledge.
Browne, Thomas (1643), *Religio Medici*, London: A. Crooke.
Brunt, P. A. (1982), 'Nobilitas and Novitas', *Journal of Roman Studies* 72: 1–17.
Buchan, William ([1769] 1828), *Domestic Medicine; or, a Treatise of the Prevention and Cure of Diseases, by Regimens and Simple Medicines*, Exeter: J. Williams.
Buffon, Comte de [Georges Louis Leclerc] (1749–1788), *Histoire naturelle*, Paris: L'Imprimerie Royale.
Buffon, Comte de [Georges Louis Leclerc] (1777), 'Addition à l'article des variétés de l'espèce humaine', in *Histoire naturelle*, Paris: L'Imprimerie Royale.
Buffon, Comte de [Georges Louis Leclerc] (1780–1785), *Natural History, General and Particular, by the Count de Buffon*, trans. William Smellie, London: W. Strahan and T. Cadell.
Buranelli, Vincent (1957), 'The Historical and Political Thought of Boulainvilliers', *Journal of the History of Ideas*, 18 (4): 475–94.
Burke, Edmund (1790), *Reflections on the Revolution in France*, London: J. Dodsley.
Burke, Edmund (1791), *An Appeal from the New to the Old Whigs in Consequence of Some Late Discussions in Parliament Relative to the Reflections on the Revolution in France*, London: J. Dodsley.

Burke, Edmund (1796), *Letter to a Noble Lord on the Attack made on Mr. Burke and His Pension, in the House of Lords*, London: T. Williams.

Burney, Frances ([1774] 1889), 'Letter to Samuel Crisp, 1 September 1774' in Annie Raine Ellis (ed.), *The Early Diary of Frances Burney 1768-1778*, 321–6, London: Bell.

Burns, William E. (2001), *The Scientific Revolution: An Encyclopedia*, Santa Barbara: ABC-CLIO.

Camper, Petrus (1779), 'Account of the Organs of Speech of the Orang-Outang', *Philosophical Transactions of the Royal Society*, 69 (1): 139–59.

Camus, Antoine le (1753), *Médecine de l'esprit*, vol. 1, Paris: Ganeau.

Canavan, Francis (1987), *Edmund Burke: Prescription and Providence*, Durham: Carolina Academic Press.

Cannadine, David (1994), *Aspects of Aristocracy Grandeur and Decline in Modern Britain*, London: Yale University Press.

Cannon, John (1982), 'The Isthmus Repaired: The Resurgence of the English Aristocracy, 1660–1760', *Proceedings of the British Academy*, 68: 432–4.

Cannon, John (1987), *Aristocratic Century: The Peerage of Eighteenth-Century England*, Cambridge: Cambridge University Press.

Carey, Brycchan (2006), 'Slavery and Romanticism', *Literature Compass*, 3 (3): 397–408.

Cartledge, Paul (2009), *Ancient Greek Political Thought in Practice*, Cambridge: Cambridge University Press.

Cat, Nicolas le (1765), *Traité de la couleur de la peau humaine*, Amsterdam: n.p.

Cavendish, William (1658), *La méthode et invention nouvelle de dresser les chevaux*, Antwerp: Jacques Van Meyrs.

Cavendish, William (1667), *A New Method and Extraordinary Invention of Dressing Horses*, London: Thomas Milbourn.

Cavendish, William (1743), *A General System of Horsemanship in all its Branches*, London: J. Brindley.

Chambers, Ehpraim (1741), *Cyclopedia, or Universal Dictionary of Arts and Sciences*, fifth edn, London: D. Midwinter.

Chaplin, Joyce (2009), 'Race', in D. Armitage and M. J. Braddick (eds), *The British Atlantic World 1500–1800*, 173–90, Basingstoke: Palgrave.

Charron, Pierre, ([1612] 1751), *Of Wisdome*, trans. Samson Lennard, London: Luke Fanne.

Chater, Kathleen (2009), *Untold Histories: Black People in England and Wales during the period of the British Slave Trade, c.1660-1807*, Manchester: Manchester University Press.

Chesterfield, Philip Dormer Stanhope (1774), *Letters Written by the Late Right Honourable Philip Dormer Stanhope, Earl of Chesterfield, to His Son Philip Stanhope*, Dublin: G. Faulkner.

Cheyne, George (1733), *The English Malady*, London: G. Strahan.

Chisholm, Colin (1799), *An Essay on the Malignant Pestilential Fever introduced into the West Indian Islands*, Philadelphia: Thomas Dobson.

Church, Arthur Herbert (1886), *English Porcelain*, London: Chapman and Hall.
Cicero, Marcus Tullius ([56 BCE] 1891). 'Pro Sestio', in *The Orations of Marcus Tullius Cicero*, 151–224, trans. C. D. Yonge, London: George Bell.
Clark, J. C. D. (1985), *English Society 1688–1832*, Cambridge: Cambridge University Press.
Clarkson, Thomas (1788), *An Essay on the Impolicy of the African Slave Trade*, London: J. Phillips.
Considerations on Mr Paine's Pamphlet on the Rights of Man (1791), Edinburgh: William Creech.
Constitution de la République française, du 5 Fructidor, An III (1795), Lyon: Frères Perisse.
Cook, James (1784), *A Compendious History of Captain Cook's First and Second Voyages*, London: G. Kearsely.
Cook, James (1821), *The Three Voyages of Captain James Cook Round the World*, London: Longman.
Corbey, Raymond (2005), *The Metaphysics of Apes: Negotiating the Animal-Human Boundary*, Cambridge: Cambridge University Press.
Cunningham, Bernadette (2001), 'Geoffrey Keating's Foras Feasa ar Éireann', *History Ireland*, 9 (1): 14–17.
Curran, Andrew S. (2011), *The Anatomy of Blackness*, Baltimore: John Hopkins Press.
Darwin, Erasmus (1804), *The Temple of Nature*, Baltimore: M. Conrad.
Davidson, Jenny (2004), *Hypocrisy and the Politics of Politeness: Manners and Morals from Locke to Austen*, Cambridge: Cambridge University Presss.
Davidson, Jenny (2009), *Breeding: A Partial History of the Eighteenth Century*, New York: Colombia Press.
Davies, John (1612), *A Discouerie of the True Causes Why Ireland was neuer Entirely Subdued, nor brought vnder Obedience of the Crowne of England*, London: John Jaggard.
Delany, Mary ([1729] 1861), 'Letter from Mrs Pendarves to Mrs Anne Granville', in *Autobiography and Correspondence of Mary Granville, Mrs Delany*, 223–5, London: R. Bentley.
Devyver, André (1973), *Le sang épuré: les préjugés de race chez les gentilshommes français de l'ancien régime, 1560–1720*, Brussels: Éditions de l'université.
Diderot, Denis and Jean Le Rond d'Alembert (1765), *Encyclopédie ou Dictionnaire raisonné des sciences, des arts et des métiers*, vol. 8, Neufchâtel: Samuel Faulche.
Dodd, William (1749a), 'The African Prince, now in England, to Zara at His Father's Court', *The Gentleman's Magazine*, 19: 323–5.
Dodd, William (1749b), 'Zara at the Court of Annamaboe, to the African Prince now in England', *The Gentleman's Magazine*, 19: 372–3.
Donlon, Walter (1999), *The Aristocratic Ideal and Selected Papers*, Wauconda: Bolchazy.

Doron, Claude-Olivier (2012), 'Race and Genealogy: Buffon and the Formation of the Concept of Race', *Humana Mente Journal of Philosophical Studies*, 22: 75–109.

Douglas, Bronwen and Chris Ballard (2008), *Foreign Bodies: Oceania and the Science of Race 1750–1940*, Sydney: Australian National University Press.

Edmondson, Joseph and William Segar (1764–1784), *Baronagium Genealogicum: Or the Pedigrees of the English Peers*, vol. 5, London: Fletcher.

Egenolf, Susan B. (2009), *The Art of Political Fiction in Hamilton, Edgeworth and Owenson*, Burlington: Ashgate.

Ellis, Harold A. (1988), *Boulainvilliers and the French Monarchy: Aristocratic Politics in Early Eighteenth-Century France*, Ithaca: Cornell University Press.

Elyot, Thomas ([1531] 1834), *The Book of the Governor*, London: Arthur Turberville Elliot.

Encyclopaedia Britannica (1788–1797), eds Colin MacFarquhar and George Gleig, third edn, Edinburgh: A. Bell and C. Macfarquhar.

Encyclopaedia Britannica (1810), ed. James Millar, fourth edn, Edinburgh: Vernor.

Encyclopaedia Britannica (1968), revised fourteenth edn, London: Encyclopaedia Britannica Inc.

Encyclopaedia Britannica: A Survey of Universal Knowledge (1929), fourteenth edn, London: The Encyclopaedia Britannica Company.

Encyclopaedia Britannica, Micropaedia: Ready Reference (1989), London: Encyclopaedia Britannica.

Encyclopaedia Britannica, Micropaedia: Ready Reference (2007), revised fifteenth edn, London: Encyclopaedia Britannica.

Estwick, Samuel (1773), *Considerations on the Negro Cause*, London: J. Dodsley.

Feerick, Jean E. (2010), *Strangers in Blood: Relocating Race in the Renaissance*, London: University of Toronto Press.

Ferrier, John (1788), *The Prince of Angola: A Tragedy, Altered from the Play of Oroonoko*, Manchester: J. Harrop.

Festa, Lynn (2005), 'Personal Effects: Wigs and Possessive Individualism in the Long Eighteenth Century', *Eighteenth-Century Life*, 29 (2): 47–90.

Feuer, Lewis S. (1977), 'Arthur O. Lovejoy', *The American Scholar*, 46 (3): 358–66.

Fielding, Henry (1749), *The History of Tom Jones, a Foundling*, London: A. Millar.

Firth, Charles Harding (1910), *The House of Lords During the Civil War*, London: Longman.

Florio, Giovanni (1611), *Queen Anna's New World of Words*, London: Bradwood.

Floyd-Wilson, Mary (2003), *English Ethnicity and Race in Early Modern Drama*, Cambridge: Cambridge University Press.

Fludd, Robert (1617), *Utriusque cosmi maioris scilicet et minoris metaphysica*, Oppenheim: Johann Theodore de Bry.

Formigari, Lia ([1968] 1973), 'Chain of Being', in Philip P. Wiener (ed.), *Dictionary of the History of Ideas*, vol. 1, 325–35, New York: Charles Scribner's Sons.

Forster, Georg (1777), *A Voyage Round the World*, London: B. White.
Forster, Georg ([1786] 1894), 'Noch etwas über die Menschenraßen', in Albert Leitzmann (ed.), *Ausgewählte kleine schriften von Georg Forster*, 26–57, Stuttgart: G.J. Göschensch Verlagshandlung.
Forster, Johann Reinhold (1778), *Observations Made During a Voyage Round the World*, London: G. Robinson.
Foster, R. F. (1988), *Modern Ireland, 1600–1972*, Harmondsworth: Penguin.
Four Statements on the Race Question (1950), Paris: UNESCO.
Fox, Christopher (1995), 'How to Prepare a Noble Savage: The Spectacle of Human Science', in Christopher Fox, Roy Porter and Robert Wokler (eds), *Inventing Human Science: Eighteenth-Century Domains*, 1–30, Los Angeles: University of California Press.
Fredrickson, George M. (2002), *Racism: A Short History*, Princeton: Princeton University Press.
Funnell, William and William Dampier (1707), *A Voyage round the World*, London: W. Botham.
Gallagher, Catherine (1996), 'Oronooko's Blackness', in Janet Todd (ed.), *Aphra Behn Studies*, 235–58, Cambridge: Cambridge University Press.
Galton, Francis (1883), *Inquiries into the Human Faculty*, London: Macmillan.
Gascoigne, John (1994), *Joseph Banks and the English Enlightenment: Useful Knowledge and Polite Culture*, Cambridge: Cambridge University Press.
Gentleman's Magazine (1749), vol. 19, London: Edward Cave.
Gentleman's Magazine (1761), vol. 31, London: D. Henry.
Gibbon, Edward (1787), *The History of the Decline and Fall of the Roman Empire, Volume the Third*, Basil: J.J. Tourneisen.
Glanvill, Joseph ([1681] 1726), *Sadducismus triumphatus*, London: A. Bettlesworth.
Glasgow, Joshua (2008), 'On the Methodology of the Race Debate: Conceptual Analysis and Racial Discourse', *Philosophy and Phenomenological Research*, 76 (2): 333–58.
Godwin, Joscelyn (1991), *Robert Fludd: Hermetic Philosopher and Surveyor of Two Worlds*, London: Phanes Press.
Goldenberg, David (2003), *The Curse of Ham*, Princeton: Princeton University Press.
Goldsmith, Oliver (1774), *A History of the Earth and Animate Nature*, London: J. Nourse.
Goldstein, Jurgen (2019), *Georg Forster: Voyager, Naturalist, Revolutionary*, trans. Anne Janusch, Chicago: University of Chicago Press.
Goodrich, Amanda (2005), *Debating England's Aristocracy in the 1790s: Pamphlets, Polemics and Political Ideas*, Woodbridge, Suffolk: Boydell Press.
Gordon, James (1808), *History of the Rebellion in Ireland in the Year 1798*, London: T. Hurst.
Goring, Paul (2002), '"John Bull, Pit, Box and Gallery, said No!": Charles Macklin and the Limits of Ethnic Resistance on the Eighteenth-Century London Stage', *Representations*, 79: 61–81.

Grant, William (1779), *Some Observations on the Origins, Progress and Method of Treating the Atrabilious Temperament and Gout*, London: T. Cadell.

Grieg, Hannah (2013), *The Beau Monde: Fashionable Society in Georgian London*, Oxford: Oxford University Press.

Grieg, Hannah (2015), 'Faction and Fashion: The Politics of Court Dress in Eighteenth-Century England', in Isabelle Paresys and Natacha Coquery (eds), *Se vêtir à la cour en Europe 1400-1815*, 1–33, Villeneuve d'Ascq: l'Institut de recherches historiques du Septentrion. Available online: https://doi.org/10.4000/apparences.1311 (accessed 1 September 2022).

Grotius, Hugo ([1642] 1884), *De origine gentium americanarum dissertatio*, trans. Edmund Goldsmid, Edinburgh: Unwin Brothers.

Guest, Harriet (2004), 'Ornament and Use: Mai and Cook in London', in Kathleen Wilson (ed.), *A New Imperial History: Culture, Identity and Modernity in Britain and the Empire, 1660–1840*, 317–44, Cambridge: Cambridge University Press.

Hall, Stuart (1996), 'New Ethnicities', in David Morley and Kuan-Hsing Chen (eds), *Stuart Hall: Critical Dialogues*, 442–51, London: Routledge.

Hanley, Ryan (2002), 'The Royal Slave: Nobility, Diplomacy and the "African Prince" in Britain, 1748–1752', *Itinerario*, 39: 329–47.

Hannaford, Ivan (1996), *Race: The History of an Idea in the West*, London: John Hopkins Press.

Hart, W. A. (1964), 'Africans in Eighteenth-Century Ireland', *Irish Historical Studies*, 33 (129): 19–32.

Harvey, William (1628), *Exercitatio anatomica de motu cordis et sanguinis in animalibus*, Frankfurt: Guiliemi Fitzeri.

Hawkesworth, John [and Thomas Southerne] (1759), *Oroonoko: A Tragedy, as it is now Acted at the Theatre-Royal in Drury Lane, by Thomas Southerne with Alterations*, London: C. Bathurst.

Henry, Maura A. (2002), 'The Making of Elite Culture', in H. T. Dickenson (ed.), *A Companion to Eighteenth-Century Britain*, 311–28, Oxford: Blackwell.

Hippocrates ([c. 300-200 BCE] 1734), *Hippocrates upon Air, Water and Situation*, trans. Francis Clifton, London: J. Watts.

Hoare, Michael, ed. (1982), *The Resolution Journal of Johann Reinhold Forster*. London: The Hakluyt Society.

Hoffheimer, Michael H. (1982), 'Maupertuis and the Eighteenth-Century Critique of Preexistence', *Journal of the History of Biology*, 15 (1): 119–44.

Hogarth, William (1753), *The Analysis of Beauty*, London: J. Reeves.

Hudson, Nicholas (1996), 'From "Nation" to "Race": The Origin of Racial Classification in Eighteenth-Century Thought', *Eighteenth-Century Studies*, 29 (3): 247–64.

Hudson, Nicholas (2005), 'Social Rank, "the Rise of the Novel" and Whig Histories of Eighteenth-Century Fiction', *Eighteenth-Century Fiction*, 17 (4): 563–98.

Huigen, Siegfried (2007), *Knowledge and Colonialism: Eighteenth-Century Travellers in South Africa*, Leiden: Brill.

Hunt, Margaret (1993), 'Racism, Imperialism and the Traveller's Gaze in Eighteenth-Century England', *Journal of British Studies*, 32 (4): 333–57.
Hunter, John ([1775] 1865), 'Inaugural Disputation on the Varieties of Man', in Thomas Bendyshe (ed.), *The Anthropological Treatises of John Friedrich Blumenbach*, 357–94, London: Longman.
Hunter, John ([1786–1787] 1839), *Principles of Surgery*, ed. James F. Palmer, Philadelphia: Haswell.
Isaac, Benjamin (2004), *The Invention of Racism in Classical Antiquity*, Princeton: Princeton University Press.
Iwanisziw, Susan B., ed. (2006), *Oroonoko: Adaptations and Offshoots*, Burlington: Ashgate.
Jaadla, Hannaliis, Leigh Shaw-Taylor and Romola Davenport (2021), 'Height and Health in Late Eighteenth-Century England', *Population Studies*, 75 (3): 381–401.
Jacob, François (1993), *The Logic of Life: A History of Heredity*, trans. Betty E. Spillman, Princeton: Princeton University Press.
Jaeger, Werner (1944–1945), *Paideia: The Ideals of Greek Culture*, trans. Gilbert Highet, New York: Oxford University Press.
James, F. G. (1979), 'The Active Irish Peers in the Early Eighteenth Century', *Journal of British Studies*, 18 (2): 52–69.
James, F. G. (1995), *Lords of the Ascendancy: The Irish House of Lords and its Members 1600–1800*, Michigan: Catholic University of America Press.
James, Lawrence (2004), *Warrior Race: A History of the British at War*, New York: St. Martin's Press.
James, Lawrence (2009), *Aristocrats: Power, Grace, Decadence*, London: Abacus.
Johnson, Samuel ([1755] 1756), *A Dictionary of the English Language*, vol. 2, London: J. Knapton.
Johnson, Samuel ([1779] 1787), 'Life of Pope', in *The Works of Samuel Johnson*, vol. 4, London: J. Buckland.
Jones, Clyve, ed. (1989), *A Pillar of the Constitution: The House of Lords in British Politics, 1640–1784*, London: Hambeldon.
Jordan, Winthrop J. (1968), *White Over Black: American Attitudes Toward the Negro, 1550–1812*, Kingsport: North Carolina Press.
Jouanna, Arlette (1981), *L'idée de race en France au XVIe et au début du XVIIe siècle: 1498–1614*, Montpellier: Atelier de reproduction des thèses Montpellier III.
Juvenal ([*c*. 100 CE] 1745), 'Satire 8', in Thomas Sheridan (ed.), *The Satires of Juvenal*, 216–43, London: D. Browne.
Kames, Henry Home (1774), *Sketches of the History of Man*, Edinburgh: W. Creech.
Kant, Immanuel ([1777] 2000), 'Of the Different Human Races', trans. Jon Mark Mikkelsen, in Robert Bernasconi and Tommy L. Lott (eds), *The Idea of Race*, 8–22, Indianapolis: Hackett.
Karian, Stephen (2002), 'The Texts of *Gulliver's Travels*', in F. Boulaire and D. Carey (eds), *Les voyages de Gulliver: Mondes lointains ou mondes proches*. Presses

universitaires de Caen. Available online: http://books.openedition.org/puc/341 (accessed 1 September 2022).

Keating, Geoffrey ([1634] 1723), *The General History of Ireland*, trans. Dermod O'Connor, Dublin: James Carson.

Kidd, Colin (1999), *British Identities before Nationalism: Ethnicity and Nationhood in the Atlantic World 1600–1800*, Cambridge: Cambridge University Press.

Kidd, Colin (2004), 'Ethnicity in the British Atlantic World, 1688–1830', in Kathleen Wilson (ed.), *A New Imperial History: Culture, Identity and Modernity in Britain and the Empire, 1660–1840*, 260–77, Cambridge: Cambridge University Press.

Knight, William (1900), *Lord Monboddo and Some of His Contemporaries*, London: John Murray.

Knox, Vicesimus (1793), *Personal Nobility; or, Letters to a Young Nobleman on the Conduct of His Studies and the Dignity of the Peerage*, London: Charles Dilly.

Koerner, Lisbet (1999), *Linnaeus: Nature and Nation*, Cambridge, MA: Harvard University Press.

Kreuger, Christine L. (2010), *Reading for the Law: British Literary History and Gender Advocacy*, Charlottesville: University of Virginia Press.

Krischer, André (2011), 'Noble Honour and the Force of Law', in Jörn Leonhard and Christian Wieland (eds), *What Makes the Nobility Noble?*, 67–89, Göttingen: Vandenhoek and Ruprecht.

Lamb, Jonathan (2001), *Preserving the Self in the South Seas 1680–1840*, Chicago: University of Chicago Press.

Landry, Donna (2009), *Noble Brutes: How Eastern Horses Transformed English Culture*, Baltimore: John Hopkins University Press.

Lavene, Mark (2005), *Genocide in the Age of the Nation State: The Rise of the West and the Coming of Genocide*, vol. 2, London: I.B. Taurus.

Lawrence, Richard (1682), *The Interest of Ireland*, Dublin: Joseph Ray.

Lecky, William Hartpole (1878), *A History of England in the Eighteenth Century*, London: Longmans.

Lecky, William Hartpole (1892), *A History of Ireland in the Eighteenth Century*, London: Longmans.

Leibniz, Gottfried Wilhelm ([1714] 1867), 'Monodology', trans. Frederick Henry Hedge, *The Journal of Speculative Philosophy*, 1 (3): 129–37.

Leonhard, Jörn and Christian Weiland, eds (2011), *What Makes the Nobility Noble? Comparative Perspectives from the Sixteenth to the Twentieth Century*, Göttingen: Vandenhoek.

Liceti, Fortunio (1634), *De Monstrorum causis, natura et differentiis libri duo*, Padua: Paumum Frambottum.

Lieberman, Leonard, Katarzyna A. Kaszycka, Antonio J. Martinez Fuentes, Leonid Yablonsky, Rodney C. Kirk, Goran Strkalj, Qian Wang and Li Sun (2004), 'The Race Concept in Six Regions: Variation Without Consensus', *Colegium Anthropologicum*, 28 (2): 907–21.

Linnaeus, Carolus (1735), *Systema naturae sive regna tria naturae*, First edn, Leiden: Joannis Wilhelmi de Groot.
Linnaeus, Carolus (1758), *Systema naturæ per regna tria naturæ*, Tenth edn, Stockholm: I. Salvii.
Linnaeus, Carolus (1788), *Systema naturæ per regna tria naturæ*, Thirteenth edn, Leipzig: Gmelin.
Linnaeus, Carolus (1806), *A General System of Nature through the Three Grand Kingdoms*, trans. William Turton, London: Lackington and Allen.
Lithgow, William (1632), *The Totall Discourse of the Rare Adventures and Painefull Peregrinations of Long Nineteene Years Travayles from Scotland to the most Famous Kingdoms in Europe, Asia* and *Africa*, Lyon: n.p.
Locke, John ([1690] 1836), *An Essay Concerning Human Understanding*, London: T. Tegg.
Long, Edward (1774), *The History of Jamaica*, London: T. Lowndes.
López-Beltrán, Carlos (1994), 'Forging Heredity: from Metaphor to Cause, a Reification Story', *Studies in History and Philosophy of Science, Part A*, 25 (2): 211–35.
Lovejoy, Arthur Onken ([1936] 1971), *The Great Chain of Being: A Study of the History of an Idea*, Cambridge, MA: Harvard University Press.
Lower, Richard ([1669] 1740), *Tractus de corde item de motu, colore sanguinis*, n.p: Jacobum Willeke and Jacobum de Beunje.
Lytton Sells, Arthur (1977), *Les sources françaises de Goldsmith*, Geneva: Slatkine.
Mackenzie, Anna Maria (1792), *Slavery: Or, the Times*, London: J. Robinsons.
Macklin, Charles ([1759] 1793), *Love à la Mode, a Farce*, London: John Bell.
Macklin, Charles ([1762] 1783), *The True-Born Irishman; or, Irish Fine Lady*, Dublin: The Booksellers.
Macpherson, James (1763), *Temora: An Ancient Epic Poem*, London: T. Beckett.
Macpherson, James (1771), *Introduction to the History of Great Britain and Ireland*, London: Becket and de Hondt.
Malcomson, A. P. W. (1978), *John Foster: The Politics of the Anglo-Irish Ascendancy*, Oxford: Oxford University Press.
Malcomson, A. P. W. (2000), 'The Irish Peerage and the Act of Union, 1800–1971', *Transactions of the Royal Historical Society*, 10: 289–327.
Mallon, Ron (2004), 'Passing, Traveling and Reality: Social Constructionism and the Metaphysics of Race', *Noûs*, 38 (4): 644–73.
Marks, Jonathan (2002), *What it Means to be 98% Chimpanzee: Apes, People and Their Genes*, Berkeley: University of California Press.
Maupertuis, Pierre-Louis Moreau de ([1745] 1768), 'Vénus Physique', in *Œuvres de Maupertuis*, 3–135. Lyon: Jean-Marie Bruyset.
Maupertuis, Pierre Louis de (1752), *Lettres de M. de Maupertuis*, Dresden: George Conrad Walther.
McCahill, Michael W. (1981), 'Peerage Creations and the Changing Character of the British Nobility, 1750–1830', *The English Historical Review*, 96: 259–84.

McCahill, Michael W. (1998), 'Open Elites: Recruitment to the French Noblesse and the English Aristocracy in the Eighteenth Century', *Albion*, 30 (4): 599–629.

McCahill, Michael W. (2009), *The House of Lords in the Age of George III (1760–1811)*, Oxford: Wiley Blackwell.

McCormick, Eric H. (1977), *Omai*, Auckland: Auckland University Press and Oxford University Press.

McCracken, J.L. (1986), 'The Social Structure and Social Life: 1714–1760', in T. W. Moody and W. E. Vaughan (eds), *A New History of Ireland IV: Eighteenth-Century Ireland, 1691–1800*, 31–56, Oxford: Clarendon Press.

Meara, Dermutio de [Diarmuid Ó Méadhra] ([1619] 1667), 'Pathologia hereditaria generalis', in Edmund de Meara, *Examen diatribæ Thomæ Willisii*, 183–233, Amsterdam: Gerardum Schagen.

Meijer, Miriam Claude (1999), *Race and Aesthetics in the Anthropology of Petrus Camper*, Amsterdam: Rodopi.

Meiners, Christoph (1785), *Grundriss der Geschichte der Menschheit*, Lemgo: Meyerischen Buchhandlung.

Middleton, Charles R (1985), 'Irish Representative Peerage Elections and the Conservative Party, 1832–1841', *Proceedings of the American Philosophical Society*, 129 (1): 90–111.

Millar, John ([1771] 1806), *On the Origin of the Distinction of Ranks in Society*, London: Blackwood.

Millar, Monica L. (2009), *Slaves to Fashion: Black Dandyism and the Styling of Black Diasporic Identity*, Durham: Duke University Press.

Miller, Genevieve (1962), '"Airs, Waters and Places" in History'. *Journal of the History of Medicine and Allied Sciences*, 17 (1): 129–40.

Mingay, G. E. (1963), *English Landed Society in the Eighteenth Century*, London: Routledge.

Miramon, Charles de and Maaike van der Lugt, eds (2008), *L'hérédité entre moyen âge et époque moderne*, Florence: Sismel.

Molineux, Catherine (2012), *Faces of Perfect Ebony: Encountering Atlantic Slavery in Imperial Britain*, Cambridge, MA: Harvard University Press.

Monboddo, Lord [James Burnett] (1774), *The Origin and Progress of Language*, Edinburgh: J. Balfour.

Monboddo, Lord [James Burnett] (1779–1799), *Ancient Metaphysics; or, the Science of Universals*, Edinburgh: Bell and Bradfute.

Montagu, Ashely ([1942] 1946), *Man's Most Dangerous Myth: The Fallacy of Race*, New York: Columbia University Press.

Montesquieu [Charles Louis de Secondat] ([1748] 1784), 'De l'esprit des lois', in *Œuvres complètes de Montesquieu*, 1.3–1.216, Paris: Sanson.

Morning, Ann (2011), *The Nature of Race: How Scientists Think and Teach about human Difference*, Berkeley: University of California Press.

Moryson, Fynes ([1617] 1904), 'The Manners and Customs of Ireland', in *Illustrations of Irish History and Topography*, 310–25, ed. C. Litton Falkiner, London: Longmans.

Müller-Wille, Staffan and Hans Jörg Rheinberger (2012), *A Cultural History of Heredity*, Chicago: Chicago University Press.
Müller-Wille, Staffan and Hans Jörg Rheinberger, eds (2007), *Heredity Produced: At the Crossroads of Biology, Politics and Culture, 1500–1870*, Cambridge, MA: MIT Press.
Myers, Norma (1996), *Reconstructing the Black Past: Blacks in Britain 1780-1830*, London: Frank Cass.
Nash, Richard (2005), '"Honest English Breed": The Thoroughbred as Cultural Metaphor', in Karen L. Raber and Treva J. Tucker (eds), *The Culture of the Horse: Status, Discipline and Identity in the Early-Modern World*, 245–72, Basingstoke: Palgrave Macmillan.
Nichols, Francis (1726), *The British Compendium or, Rudiments of Honour, Containing the Descents, Marriages, Issues, Titles, Posts and Seats of All the Nobility of England*, London: R. Nutt.
Nichols, Francis (1729), *The British Compendium or, Rudiments of Honour, Containing an Origin of the Scots and Succession of their Kings for Above 2000 years*, London: R. Nutt.
Nichols, Francis (1735), *The Irish Compendium, Containing the Descents, Marriages, Issues, Titles, Posts and Seats of All the Nobility of Ireland*, London: Bettlesworth and Hitch.
Novak, Maximillian E. and David Stuart Rodes, eds (1976), *Oroonoko*, Lincoln: University of Nebraska Press.
Nussbaum, Felicity A. (2003), *The Limits of the Human: Fictions of Anomaly, Race and Gender in the Long Eighteenth Century*, Cambridge: Cambridge University Press.
Ó hÓgáin, Dáithí (2006), *The Lore of Ireland: An Encyclopaedia of Myth, Legend and Romance*, Woodbridge, England: Boydell Press.
O'Conor, Charles ([1753] 1766), *Dissertations on the History of Ireland*, Dublin: G. Faulkner.
O'Gorman, Frank (2016), *The Long Eighteenth Century: British Political and Social History 1688–1832*, London: Bloomsbury Academic.
O'Keefe, John (1785), *Omai, or a Trip around the World*, London: T. Cadell.
O'Keefe, John (1786), *Omai, or a Trip around the World, Set to Music by William Shield*, London: Longman and Broderip.
Oldfield, J. R. (1995), *Popular Politics and British Anti-Slavery: The Mobilisation of Public Opinion against the Slave Trade 1787–1807*, Manchester: Manchester University Press.
Oliver, Douglas (1974), *Ancient Tahitian Society*, Honolulu: University of Hawai'i Press.
Osmer, William (1756), *A Dissertation on Horses*, London: T. Waller.
Osmer, William ([1760] 1766), *A Treatise on the Diseases and Lameness of Horses*, London: T. Waller.
Ovington, John (1696), *A Voyage to Suratt in the Year 1689*, London: Jacob Tonson.

Oxford English Dictionary, 'breeding, n.3.' OED Online, Oxford: Oxford University Press. Available online: www.oed.com/view/Entry/23024 (accessed 28 September 2021).

Oxford English Dictionary, 'race, n.6.' OED Online, Oxford: Oxford University Press. Available online: www.oed.com/view/Entry/157031 (accessed 28 September 2021).

Paine, Thomas (1791), *Rights of Man* [Part 1], Dublin: P. Byrne.

Paine, Thomas (1792), *Rights of Man* [Part 2], Dublin: P. Byrne.

Paley, Ruth, Paul Seaward, Beverly Adams, Robin Eagles and Charles Littleton, eds (2010), *Honour, Interest and Power: An Illustrated History of the House of Lords 1660–1715*, Woodbridge, England: Boydell Press.

Palmer, Caroline (2008), 'Brazen Cheek: Face-Painters in Late Eighteenth-Century England', *Oxford Art Journal*, 31 (2): 197–213.

Paresys, Isabelle (2018), 'The Body', in Peter McNeil (ed.), *A Cultural History of Dress and Fashion in the Age of Enlightenment*, 63–86, London: Bloomsbury Academic.

Patrick, F. C. (1797), *The Irish Heiress, a Novel*, London: Minerva Press.

Patterson, Orlando (1982), *Slavery and Social Death*, Cambridge, MA: Harvard University Press.

Pauw, Cornélius de (1768), *Recherches philosophiques sur les américains*, Berlin: Georges Jacques Decker.

Perkin, Harold James (1968), 'The Social Causes of the British Industrial Revolution', *Transactions of the Royal Historical Society*, 18: 123–43.

Perkin, Harold James (1985), 'An Open Elite' (review), *Journal of British Studies*, 24 (4): 496–501.

Pettigrew, William (2013), *Freedom's Debt: The Royal African Company and the Politics of the Atlantic Slave Trade 1672–1752*, Chapel Hill: University of North Carolina Press.

Pinto-Correia, Clara (1997), *The Ovary of Eve: Egg and Sperm and Preformation*, Chicago: University of Chicago Press.

Plato ([c. 380 B.C.E] 1908), *The Republic of Plato*, trans. Benjamin Jowett, Oxford: Clarendon.

Pliny ([1601] 1847–1848), *Natural History*, trans. Philemon Holland, London: George Barclay.

Poczai, Péter and Jorge A. Santiago-Blay (2021), 'Principles and Biological Concepts of Heredity before MENDEL', *Biology Direct*, 16 (19): 1–17. Available online: https://biologydirect.biomedcentral.com/articles/10.1186/s13062-021-00308-4 (accessed 5 October 2022).

Pope, Alexander (1734), *Essay on Man*, London: John Wright and Lawton Gilliver.

Pope, Thomas ([1628] 1866), 'Original Letters to Sir Thomas Pope', *Miscellanies of the Philobiblon Society*, 9: 6.2–6.18.

Porter, Roy (1982), *English Society in the Eighteenth Century*, London: Penguin.

Prichard, James Cowles (1813), *Researches into the Physical History of Man*, London: John and Arthur Arch.

Prum, Michel, ed. (2012), *Racialisations dans l'aire anglophone*, Paris: Harmattan.
Quinlan, Sean M. (2006), 'Inheriting Vice, Acquiring Virtue: Hereditary Disease and Moral Hygiene in Eighteenth-Century France', *Bulletin of the History of Medicine*, 80 (4): 649–76.
Quinlan, Sean M. (2010), 'Heredity, Reproduction, and Perfectibility in Revolutionary and Napoleonic France, 1789–1815', *Science Direct*, 34 (4): 142–50.
Raber, Karen (2005), 'A Horse of a Different Colour: Nation and Race in Early Modern Horsemanship Treatises', in Karen L. Raber and Treva J. Tucker (eds), *The Culture of the Horse: Status, Discipline and Identity in the Early-Modern World*, 225–44, Basingstoke: Palgrave Macmillan.
Ray, John (1693), *Historia Plantarum Generalis*, vol. 1, London: Samuel Smith and Benjamin Walford.
Real Academia Española (1734), *Diccionario de la lengua castellana*, vol. 4, Madrid: Real Academia Española.
Reardon, Jenny (2005), *Race to the Finish: Identity and Governance in an Age of Genomics*, Princeton: Princeton University Press.
Records of the General Conference of the United Nations Educational, Scientific and Cultural Organisation (1949), Fourth Session, Paris: UNESCO.
'Researches into the Physical History of Man. By J. Cowles Prichard' (1814), *The Monthly Review, or Literary Journal Enlarged*, 75: 127–34.
Ribeiro, Aileen (1984), *Dress in Eighteenth-Century Europe 1715–1789*, London: B.T. Batsford.
Richardson, Samuel ([1740] 1780), *Pamela; or Virtue Rewarded*, London: W. Strahan.
Robertson, George (1948), *The Discovery of Tahiti: A Journal of the Second Voyage of HMS Dolphin Round the World*, ed. Hugh Carrington, London: The Hakluyt Society.
Ross, Ian Campbell (1985), 'Review of "Pope's *Essay on Man*" by A.D. Nutall', *Hermathena*, 138: 77–9.
Roumy, Franck (2008), 'La naissance de la notion canonique de consanguitas et sa reception dans le droit civil', in Charles de Miramon and Maaike van der Lugt (eds), *L'hérédité entre Moyen Age et Époque moderne*, 41–66, Florence: Sismel.
Rousseau, G. S. (1974), *Goldsmith: The Critical Heritage*, London: Padstow.
Rousseau, Jean-Jacques (1755), *Discours sur l'origine et les fondements de l'inégalité parmi les hommes*, Amsterdam: Marc Michel.
Rousseau, Jean-Jacques (1761), *A Discourse upon the Origin and Foundation of the Inequality among Mankind*, London: J. Dodsley.
Sallust ([41–40 BCE] 1756), *Sallust's History of the Cataline Conspiracy and the War with Jugurtha*, trans. John Mair, Edinburgh: W. Sands.
Schaub, Jean-Frédéric (2015), *Pour une histoire politique de la race*, Paris: Seuil.
Schiebinger, Londa (2004), *Nature's Body: Gender in the Making of Modern Science*, New Brunswick: Rutgers University Press.
Scully, Denys (1812), *A Statement of the Penal laws which Aggrieve the Catholics of Ireland: With Commentaries*, Part 1, Dublin: H. Fitzpatrick.

Sebastiani, Silvia (2000), 'Race as a Construction of the Other: "Native Americans" and "Negroes" in the 18th-Century Editions of the Encyclopaedia Britannica', in Bo Stråth (ed.), *Europe and the Other and Europe as Other*, 195–228, Brussels: P.I.E. Peter Lang.
Sebastiani, Silvia (2015), 'Challenging Boundaries: Apes and Savages in Enlightenment', in Wolf D. Hund, Charles W. Mills and Silvia Sebastiani (eds), *Simianization: Apes, Gender, Class and Race*, 105–37, Berlin: Lit Verlag.
Seth, Suman (2018), *Difference and Disease: Medicine, Race and the Eighteenth-Century British Empire*, Cambridge: Cambridge University Press.
Seymour, Susanne and Sheryllynne Haggerty (2010), *Slavery Connections of Bolsover Castle (1600 - c.1830)*, Swindon: English Heritage.
Shelton, Maurice (1718), *An Historical and Critical Essay on the True Rise of Nobility, Political and Civil*, London: C. Rivington.
Sheppard, F. H. W., ed. (1957), 'The Wood-Mitchell Estate: Fournier Street', in *Survey of London 27: Spitalfields and Mile End New Town*, 199–225, London: London County Council. Available online: https://www.british-history.ac.uk/survey-london/vol27 (accessed 1 August 2014).
Siena, Kevin (2019), *Rotten Bodies: Class and Contagion in Eighteenth-Century Britain and Ireland*, New Haven: Yale University Press.
Sloan, Phillip (1995), 'The Gaze of Natural History', in Christopher Fox, Roy Porter and Robert Wokler (eds), *Inventing Human Science: Eighteenth-Century Domains*, 112–51, Los Angeles: University of California Press.
Smith, Samuel Stanhope (1787), *An Essay on the Causes and Variety of Complexion and Figure in the Human Species*, first edn, Philadelphia: Robert Aitken.
Smith, Samuel Stanhope (1810), *An Essay on the Causes and Variety of Complexion and Figure in the Human Species*, second edn, New Brunswick: J. Simpson.
Smith, Thomas ([1583] 1906), *De Republica Anglorum: A Discourse on the Commonwealth of England*, Cambridge: Cambridge University Press.
Smollett, Tobias ([1771] 1784–1785), *The Expedition of Humphry Clinker*, Dublin: W. Sleater.
Southerne, Thomas ([1696] 1699), *Oroonoko: A Tragedy*, London: C. Hitch.
Spenser, Edmund ([1596] 1840), 'The View of the Present State of Ireland', in *The Works of Edmund Spenser*, 479–530, London: Walter Spiers.
Sprat, Thomas (1667), *History of the Royal Society of London*, London: J Martyn.
Spring, David and Eileen Spring (1985), 'The English Landed Elite 1540–1879: A Review', *Albion* 17: 149–66.
Spurr, Stephen (2014), 'Patricians', in Simon Hornblower and Anthony Spawforth (eds), *The Oxford Companion to Classical Civilization*, 576–77, second edn, Oxford: Oxford University Press.
Stanlis, Peter (1958 [2017]), *Edmund Burke and the Natural Law*, London: Routledge.
Starr, Chester G. (1992), *The Aristocratic Temper of Greek Civilization*, New York: Oxford University Press.

Stehelin, John Peter [and Johann Andreas Eisenmenger] (1748), *Rabbinical Literature; or, the Traditions of the Jews*, London: J. Robinson.

Stibbs, Bartholomew and Francis Moore (1738), *Travels into the Inland Part of Africa*, London: Edward Cave.

Stock, Paul (2011), '"Almost a Separate Race": Racial Thought and the Idea of Europe in British Encyclopaedias and Histories 1771–1830', *Modern Intellectual History*, 8 (1): 3–29.

Stone, Lawrence (1965), *The Crisis of the Aristocracy 1558–1641*, Oxford: Clarendon Press.

Stone, Lawrence and Jean Fawtier Stone (1984), *An Open Elite? England 1540–1880*, Oxford: Clarendon Press.

Swaminathan, Srividhya (2009), *Debating the Slave Trade: Rhetoric of British National Identity 1759–1815*, Farnham: Ashgate.

Swatland, Andrew (1996), *The House of Lords in the Reign of Charles II*, Cambridge: Cambridge University Press.

Swift, Jonathan (1724–1725), *A Letter to the Whole People of Ireland* [*Drapier's Letters IV*], Dublin: Harding.

Swift, Jonathan (1726), [Gulliver's Travels] *Travels into Several Remote Nations of the World*, London: Benjamin Motte.

Swift, Jonathan (1735), [Gulliver's Travels] 'The Travels of Captain Lemuel Gulliver', in *The Works of J. S, D.D, D.S.P.D.*, Dublin: George Faulkner.

Sydenham, Thomas ([1683] 1742), 'A Treatise on the Gout and Dropsy', in *The Entire Works of Thomas Sydenham MD*, 416–87, London: Edward Cave.

Sypher, Wylie (1942), *Guinea's Captive Kings: British Anti-Slavery Literature of the Eighteenth Century*, Chapel Hill: North Carolina University Press.

Temple, William ([1695] 1708), *An Introduction to the History of England*, London: Richard and Ralph Simpson.

Thompson, E. P. (1976), 'The Grid of Inheritance: A Comment', in Jack Goody, Joan Thirsk and E. P. Thompson (eds), *Family and Inheritance: Rural Society in Western Europe 1200–1800*, 320–60, Cambridge: Cambridge University Press, 1976.

Tillyard, Stella (1998), *Citizen Lord: The Life of Edward Fitzgerald, Irish Revolutionary*, New York: Farrar.

Tocqueville, Alexis de (1856), *The Old Regime and the Revolution*, trans. John Bonner, New York: Harper and Brothers.

Todorov, Tzvetan (1993), *Nationalism, Racism and Exoticism in French Thought*, trans. Catherine Porter, Cambridge, MA: Harvard University Press.

Turner, Richard (1779), *A View of the Earth*, London: J. Dodsley.

Tyson, Edward (1699), *Orang-outang, sive homo sylvestris*, London: Thomas Bennet.

Universal Magazine (1749), vol. 4, London: J. Hinton.

Van Duzer, Chet (2012), 'Hic Sunt Dracones: The Geography and Cartography of Monsters', in Asa Simon Mittman and Peter J. Dendle (eds), *The Ashgate Research Companion to Monsters and the Monstrous*, 387–438, Farnham: Ashgate.

Vandermonde, Charles Augustin (1756), *Essai sur la manière de perfectionner l'espèce humaine*, vol. 1, Paris: Vincent.
Vassa, Gustavus ([1789] 1794), *The Interesting Narrative of the Life of Olaudah Equiano*, London: Gustavus Vassa.
Veblen, Thorstein ([1899] 1912), *The Theory of the Leisure Class*, New York: Macmillan.
Vincent, Susan J. (2009), *The Anatomy of Fashion: Dressing the Body from the Renaissance to Today*, Oxford: Berg.
Voegelin, Eric ([1933] 1997), *Race and State*, trans. Ruth Hein, ed. Klaus Vondug, Baton Rouge: Louisiana State University Press.
Voltaire (1733), *Letters Concerning the English Nation*, London: C. Davies.
Wahrman, Dror (1995), *Imagining the Middle Class: The Political Representation of Class in Britain c.1780–1840*, Cambridge: Cambridge University Press.
Wahrman, Dror (2004), *The Making of the Modern Self: Identity and Culture in Eighteenth-Century England*, New Haven: Yale University Press.
Wall, Richard (1758), *A Dissertation on the Breeding of Horses upon Philosophical and Experimental Principles*, London: G. Woodfall.
Walpole, Horace ([1776] 1866), 'Letter to Mann, 16 July 1776', in Peter Cunningham (ed.), *The Letters of Horace Walpole*, 6.356–6.358, London: Henry G. Bohn.
Warburton, William (1756), *A View of Lord Bolingbroke's Philosophy*, London: A. Miller.
Weatherby, James ([1791] 1839), *The General Stud Book*, Brussels: C. Muquart.
Weber, Max (1978), *Economy and Society: An Outline of Interpretive Sociology*, eds Guenther Roth and Claus Wittich, Berkeley: University of California Press.
Weller, Barry (1992), 'The Royal Slave and the Prestige of Origins', *The Kenyon Review*, 14: 65–78.
Wellesley, Richard ([1800] 1862), 'Letter from Marquis Wellesley to Mr. Pitt, April 28, 1800', in Philip Henry Stanhope, *Life of Pitt*, vol. 3, 3.222–3.233, London: John Murray.
Wells, Andrew (2015), 'Race and Racism in the Global European World before 1800', *History Compass*, 13 (9): 435–44.
Westminster Magazine; or, the Pantheon of Taste (1774), vol. 2, August 1774, London: W. Goldsmith.
Wheeler, Roxann (2000), *The Complexion of Race: Categories of Difference in Eighteenth-Century British Culture*, Philadelphia: University of Pennsylvania Press.
White, Charles (1799), *An Account of the Regular Gradation in Man*, London: C. Dilly.
Willis, Thomas ([1664] 1666), *Cerebri anatome cui accesit nervorum descripto et usus studio*, Amsterdam: G. Schagen.
Wilson, Kathleen (2003), *The Island Race: Englishness, Empire and Gender in the Eighteenth Century*, London: Routledge.
Wilson, Richard G. (2002), 'The Landed Elite', in H. T. Dickinson (ed.), *A Companion to Eighteenth-Century Britain*, 158–71, Malden: Blackwell.
Wolff, Caspar Friedrich (1759), *Theoria Generationis*, Halle: Hendel.

Woodard, Helena (1999), *African-British Writings in the Eighteenth Century: The Politics of Race and Reason*, London: Greenwood.
Worrall, David (2007), *Harlequin Empire: Race, Ethnicity and the Drama of the Popular Enlightenment*, London: Pickering and Chatto.
Young, Arthur ([1776] 1780), *A Tour in Ireland*, London: T. Cadell.

Index

1767 porcelain figure group 37, 38
1798 Rebellion 154

Abolitionism 185
Abolition of the Slave Trade 175, 186
Account of the Regular Gradations in Man (White) 71
Acts of Union 10, 27
Addison, Joseph 58
aequaliter complexionatum (equal temperament) 61
Agnew, Vanessa 197
Air, Water and Places (Hippocrates) 73
ambivalent human taxonomy 5
American Anthropological Association (AAA) 47, 48
American revolutionary wars 145
ancien régime 22, 201
Ancient Metaphysics (Monboddo) 88, 103
Anderson, Hans Christian 9
anglomaniac 104
Anthropomorpha 50
anti-Abolitionists 192
An Appeal from the New to the Old Whigs (Burke) 202
Appiah, Kwame Anthony 3
Aquinas, Thomas 61
Arab stallions 98, 99
Arderon, William 77
Arendt, Hannah 4, 203, 204
arete 17, 211, 212
arete-excellence 212, 213
arii/aree 163, 166, 167, 169–71, 198–200, 217
aristocracy 22, 196, 206
aristocrate 196
aristocratic racism 6
aristoi 17, 18, 212, 213
aristos 17
Aristotle 17, 53, 60, 61
Ascendancy 142, 143, 154
Augustine, St. 61

Augustodunensis, Honorius 52
Austin, William 181

Baartman, Saartjie 78, 79
Bakewell, Robert 101
Baldry, H. C. 8
Balibar, Étienne 6, 56, 212
Ballard, Chris 172
Ballexserd, Jacques 114
Bancel, Nicholas 4
Banks, Joseph 160–2
Banton, Michael 4
barbarous nations, clothes of 92
Barbary horse 85, 99
Barnard, Tony 144
Bartlett, Thomas 140, 141
Barzun, Jacques 45
Baum, Bruce 129
Beaglehole, J. C. 163
beau monde 33
Behn, Aphra 175, 182
Bernard, Henri 104
Bernasconi, Robert 5
Bernier, François 5, 80
Bethencourt, Francisco 5, 130
Bewick, Thomas 119
Bickerstaff, Isaac (editorial persona) 58
Bickerstaff, Isaac (playwright) 169
Bindman, David 37, 38, 131, 132, 170, 187, 188
biological race 46
Black, Jeremy 32
Black servants 39, 177–9
Black slave 175
Blackstone, William 26, 30
Blayney, Lord 144
blood hierarchy 2, 48, 150
blood purity 11, 109, 216
  medicalization of 118
Blower, Elizabeth 152
Blumenbach, Johann Friedrich 2, 44, 77, 79, 91–3, 123, 130–4, 141, 196

Boas, Franz   45
bodily potential   2
Bolingbroke, Henry St. John   66, 108
Bontius, Jacobus   76, 83, 86
Book of the Governor (Elyot)   28
Bougainville, Louis Antoine de   88, 159, 160, 166, 198
Boulainvilliers, Henri de   104–7, 118, 216
Boulukos, George   176
breeding   6, 10, 57–8, 101
Brion Davis, David   76, 177, 184
British aristocracy   16, 24
British Compendium (Nichols)   39, 53, 72
British court
    artistic tradition   37
    attendees' choice of clothing   33
    costumes   33
    dress   34
    fashion   33
    garments, impact of   34
    hairpieces   35
    high heels   36
    make-up   35
    mantua dress   34
    processions   31
    sections of   31
British Royal African Company (RAC)   187
Brown, John   53
Brown, Laura   168, 182, 185
Browne, Thomas   64, 65
Buchan, William   117
Buffon, Comte de   83–6, 89, 91, 123, 125–7, 131, 176
    law of common propagation   128
Buranelli, Vincent   106
Burke, Edmund   201–4, 206, 207
Burnett, James   87
Burney, Frances   168
Byrne, Charles   78

Camper, Petrus   86, 136
Camus, Antoine Le   114
Canavan, Francis   201
Cannadine, David   16, 23, 196
Cannon, John   23–5
Cape of Good Hope   79
Cartledge, Paul   17
casta system   5

Caucasians   132, 133
Cavendish, William   98, 99
Celt   109, 110, 113
Chambers, Ephraim   111
Chaplin, Joyce   4
Charron, Pierre   50
Chater, Kathleen   177–9
Chesterfield, Phillip Dormer Stanhope   30, 31
Cheyne, George   113
Chisholm, Colin   115
City of God (Augustine)   61
civility   93
    corporeal effect of   85
    matrix of   73
civilized behaviour   73, 92, 172
Clark, J. C. D.   22, 23
Clarkson, Thomas   177
climate theory   73–6, 84, 95, 111, 124
Coan, John   77
Coke, Edward   100
Colman, George   169
Commentaries on the Laws of England (Blackstone)   26
Commons (House of)   26, 36
complexion   6
Condon dynasty of Waterford   147
Considerations on the Negro Cause of 1773 (Estwick)   71
conspicuous consumption   30, 32
Cook, James   79, 158
Corbey, Raymond   86
corporeal inequality   95
country houses   32
Curse of Ham   51, 215, 216
Cyclopedia (Chambers)   111

d'Alembert, Jean le Rond   97
Dampier, William   79
Dapper, Olfert   88
Darwin, Charles   45
Darwin, Erasmus   118
Davidson, Jenny   6, 31, 57, 58
Davies, John   147
De generis humani varietate nativa (Blumenbach)   2, 44, 77, 91, 92, 196
de Meara, Dermutio   111
Deniker, Joseph   45

de Pauw, Cornelius Franciscus   131, 133, 135
Derby Porcelain Factory   37
descent-based hierarchy   1
Devyver, André   106, 108
Diderot, Denis   97
Discours sur l'origine et les fondements de l'inégalité parmi les hommes (Rousseau)   201
Disputatio Inauguralis (Hunter)   80, 111
Dissenting Protestants   139, 140, 165
Dissertation on the Origin of the Native Races of America (Grotius)   74
Dissertations on the History of Ireland (O'Conor)   148
distinction of rank   29, 66, 107
Dodd, William   188
Domestic Medicine (Buchan)   117
domestic slaves   94
Donlon, Walter   18
Doron, Claude-Olivier   7, 49
Douglas, Bronwen   172
Duke of Bedford in 1796   201
Dukes of Argyll   7

Earee ra hie   161
Earls of Seaforth   7
Edmundson, Joseph   53
Egenolf, Susan   155
Eisenmenger, Johann Andreas   52
Elliot, C. H.   57
Elyot, Thomas   28
Emerson Hall   59
Encyclopaedia Britannica   24, 47, 93, 108, 114, 134, 135
encyclopaedic programme   63
Endeavour   158, 160
English Malady (Cheyne)   113, 118, 212
environmental influences   74, 217
Esprit des lois (Montesquieu)   74
Essais sur la Noblesse de France (Boulainvilliers)   104–6, 118
Essay on Man (Pope)   60, 66, 67
Essay on the Causes of Variety of Complexion and Figure in the Human Species (Stanhope Smith)   8, 79, 93
Estwick, Samuel   71
ethnic honour   203

ethno-cultural patchwork   139
ethno-historical discourses   110
ethno-histories   104, 118, 119, 148
eugeneia   17, 18, 30, 69, 101, 102, 145, 214
   of inimitable bloodline   20
   noble tradition of   103, 181
   notion of   213
eugeneic patriciate   19, 20
Eupatridai   17
Eurocentric political hierarchy   158
extreme environments   74, 95
extrinsic racism   3

Faulkner, George   102
fecundity principle   87
Feerick, Jean   6, 54
'Feral Man'   82
Ferrier, John   186, 187
Fielding, Henry   149
field slaves   94
Fitzgerald, Lord Edward   153, 154
Florio, John   50
Floyd-Wilson, Mary   75
Fludd, Robert   62
Forman, Charles   104
Formigari, Lia   63
Forster, Georg   125, 163, 169, 197–200, 209
Forster, Johann Reinhold   159, 160, 165–7, 169, 171, 172
Foster, R. F.   143
Fredrickson, George   4
Funnell, William   80

Gaelic lineage   146, 151, 152
Gaelic nobility   146, 150, 151
Gaelic rebellion of 1641   141
Gallagher, Catherine   183
Galton, Frances   45
Gates Jr, Henry Louis   37, 38, 131
genealogical bloodlines   118
genealogical purity   11, 117, 134, 208
genealogical race theory   122, 136, 137, 209
Gentleman's Magazine   31, 178
geohumouralism   75
Germains   107, 109, 113, 121
Germanist theory of noble origin   106

Gibbon, Edward   19
Gillray, James   149
Glanvill, Joseph   64, 65
Glasgow, Joshua   4
Godolphin Arabian   100
Goldenberg, David   51
Goldsmith, Oliver   89–92, 95, 117, 127, 130, 141, 167, 176
Goldstein, Jurgen   199
Goodrich, Amanda   13, 22, 195, 196
Gordon, James Bentley   142
Gordon, Robert   79
Grant, William   115–17, 141
Great Chain of Being   47, 59, 60, 62
   chain model of creation   61, 64, 71
   idea of universe as   63
   infinite building blocks of   84
   unfinished map, human society   64
   world view   215, 216
Great Commoner   38
Grieg, Hannah   33
Grotius, Hugo   74
Gulliver's Travels (Swift)   102

ha'apori   162, 163
haereditarii morbi   111
Haggerty, Sheryllynne   99
Hall, Stuart   4
Haller, Albrecht von   81
Hanley, Ryan   187
Hannaford, Ivan   6, 51
Hart, W. A.   142
Harvey, William   112
Hawkesworth, John   186
hegemonic elitism   218
Henry, Maura   32
heredar   97
hereditary   111
   degeneration   114
   diseases   103, 112, 114, 115, 117, 131
   dynamics of nobility   103
   elites   1, 2, 16, 17, 73, 121, 160
   governance   9
   nobility   1, 56, 157, 193
   power   14, 65, 118, 152
   principles   112, 127
   privilege   19, 20, 56, 152
   society   203
   trait transmission   48, 98

'Hereford map' of 1300   77
Hiberniores Hibernis ipsis   147, 152, 153
Hiberno-Norman elite   140
hierarchical symbolism   41
Hippocrates   73, 74, 77
Historiae naturalis et medicae Indiae orientalis (Bontius)   76, 86
History of Jamaica (Long)   87, 135
History of the Earth and Animated Nature (Goldsmith)   89
Hogarth, William   131
Homeric poetry   8
Homo   2, 6, 50, 81
   H. africanus niger   83
   H. americanus   83
   H. asiaticus   83
   H. europeanus   83
   H. monstrosus   35
   H. nocturnus   83
   H. sapiens (knowing man)   82
   H. troglodytes (cave-dwelling man)   82
horses of blood   100, 121
'Hottentot apron'   78
Hottentot body   86
'Hottentot Venus'   78
House of Lords   26, 27, 30, 36, 65, 144
Houyhnhnms   102
Hudson, Nicholas   5, 6, 23, 51, 105, 125
human-ape hybrids   87, 88
human being, principal varieties of   89–90
human diversity   1, 75, 123
human hybridization   127
humanity   65, 81, 132
human race   43, 82, 121, 217
human-variety theory   6, 43, 68, 73, 75, 78, 84, 89, 95, 119, 122, 123, 127, 130, 176, 217
   hybrid system of   90
   racialized discourse of   175
humoural discourse   75
humoural theory   75, 112
Hunter, John   80, 111, 112, 127
hybridity   129

'Idea of the Good'   60
Independent Whig   56
inimitable excellence   211, 212, 214, 216
Inquiries into the Human Faculty (Galton)   45

Integrae naturae speculum artisque imago 62, 63
intergenerational property transfer 11, 98
intergenerational trait transmission 97, 123, 127
intrinsic racism 4
Irish Catholics 139–41
Irish Compendium 39
'Irish Giant' 78
The Irish Heiress (Patrick) 151
Irish nation 142, 151, 154
Irish nobility 139, 143, 144, 147, 155
Irish Patriot Party 151
Irish peerage 23, 144, 145
Isaac, Benjamin 5

Jaadla, Hannaliis 8
Jacob, François 48
James, F. G. 145
James, Lawrence 8
Johnson, Samuel 49, 50, 66, 104
Jordan, Winthrop 86
Jouanna, Arlette 7, 16, 54

Kames, Henry Home 124, 176
Kant, Immanuel 44, 127–9, 133, 176
Keating, Geoffrey 147
Kidd, Colin 51, 122, 141
knowledge regime, biological identity 51
Knox, Vicesimus 31
Krischer, André 37
Kurentsi, Eno Baisie 187

Lamb, Jonathan 163
landed elite 22, 23
Landry, Donna 102
la Peyrère, Isaac de 124
Lavater, Johann Kasper 136
law of common propagation 128
Law of the Twelve Tables 19
Lawrence, Richard 141
Lecky, William Hartpole 21
Leibniz, Gottfried Wilheim 61
Lennard, Samson 50
Letters Concerning the English Nation of 1733 (Voltaire) 21
Liceti, Fortuno 77
Lieberman, Leonard 48

limpieza de sangre 56
Linnaeus, Carolus 2, 35, 49, 75, 81–3, 126, 175
Lithgow, William 79
Locke, John 86
Long, Edward 87, 115, 124, 129, 135, 183, 184
López-Beltrán, Carlos 97, 111, 112
Lovejoy, Arthur Onken 59, 60, 68
Lower, Richard 112
Ludwig, Gottlieb 132

McCahill, Michael W. 22, 23, 145
McCormick, Eric H. 170
Mackenzie, Anna Maria 175, 189, 192, 193
Macklin, Charles 149, 151
Mac Maioge 147
Macpherson, James 108–10, 118, 119
Macrocepheli 77
magnate class 24
Malcomson, A. P. W. 143, 144
Mallon, Ron 3
Malpighi, Marcello 131
Manahounies 161
Marks, Jonathan 47
martial equestrianism 98
Mathias, Gabriel 187
Maupertuis, Pierre Louis Moreau de 122
Meiners, Christoph 132, 133
mental and moral superiority 18
Millar, John 75
modern race thinking 2
Molineux, Catherine 37, 39
Monboddo, Lord 87–9, 95, 103
mongrel ancestry 69
monogenist climate theory 125
monogenists/monogenism 123–5
'Monstrous Man' 82
monstrous races 76, 77, 83
Montagu, Ashley 44, 46
Montesquieu 74
Morning, Ann 48
Moryson, Fynes 79, 141
Motte, Benjamin 103
mountain-dweller deformity 109
Müller-Wille, Staffan 5, 49, 51, 130
Myers, Norma 179

Nash, Richard 104
native nobility 53
native prince 168, 181, 185
natural historians 1, 7, 9, 43, 157
Natural History (Pliny) 76
natural philosophy 63
natural states 54
New English 140, 147
Nichols, Francis 39, 53, 72, 205
nobiles 19, 20
nobilitas 17–20, 213, 214
nobility 7–9, 20, 24, 29, 66, 101, 203, 218
  hereditary dynamics of 103
  historiographical label of 16
  of Ireland 139 (*see also* Irish nobility)
  social rank of 213
noble blood 6, 10, 28, 103, 128, 155
noble excellence 15, 211, 212
noble identity 16
noble intensification 41
noble lineage 2
noble paradigm 9, 11, 14, 43, 73, 137, 197, 214
  core stratagem of 28
  elemental building block of 18–19
  ostensible truisms 15
  power strategies of 137
noble physique 157, 175
noble race 54, 197, 209
  hegemonic paradigm of 155
  structural supports of 216
noble savage tropes 39
noble tradition 16, 112, 216
  genealogical component of 213
noble virtue 106
Nomenclature des singes (Buffon) 86
non-noble 15, 16, 18
Norfolk Pygmy 77
Nouvelle Division de la Terre (Bernier) 5, 80
Novak, Maximillian E. 184
novus homo 28
Nussbaum, Felicity 179, 185

Observations Made during a Voyage Round the World (Forster) 165
O'Conor, Charles 147, 148
O'Flaherty, Augusta 151

O'Gorman, Frank 32, 36
O'Keefe, John 169
Old English 140, 143, 146, 147, 155
Oliver, Douglas 162, 163
Omai 168–71
open aristocracy 13, 22
  myth of 21, 23
orang-outangs 76, 83, 86–8, 124
ordo 61
Origin and Progress of Language (Monboddo) 88
Origin of the Distinction of Ranks in Society (Millar) 75
Origin of the Species (Darwin) 45
Oroonoko (Behn) 175, 181, 186
Oroonoko effect 184, 188
Osmer, William 101
Ossian poems 108, 110
ostensible truism 15
outbreeding method 99, 103
Ovington, John 78, 79

Paine, Thomas 204–8, 218
Pamela (Richardson) 68, 71
parental traits 49
Paresys, Isabel 34, 35
parliamentary robes 40
part-symbolic-part-literal vector 41
Patricians 19, 28
Patrick, F. C. 151
Patterson, Orlando 177
peerage 24–8
peerage class 24
Perkin, Harold 13, 14, 22
petite noblesse 20, 22
Phasians 74
Pinto-Correia, Clara 122
Pitt, William 37, 38
plebeian orders 31
Plebeians 19
Plenitude 60
Pliny 76
polygenists/polygenism 123, 124, 135
'poor Indian' 68
Pope, Alexander 60, 66–8, 89
Pope, William 144
Porter, Roy 24, 36
Praeadamitae (la Peyrère) 124
Prichard, James Cowles 157, 158, 172

Prince of Angola: A Tragedy (Ferrier)   186
'Prince of Annamaboe'   187
principle of continuity   61
principle of gradation   60–1
pro-slavery racialism   87
Protestant Reformation   51, 122
proto-racism   6
Prum, Michel   5
pseudo-scientific framework   44

Quakers   176
quasi-mystical allusions   16

Raber, Karen   99
race   1, 6, 10, 43, 50, 54, 59, 85, 125
   definition   47, 49
   discourse   6
   folk belief of   48
   folk theory of   4
   genealogical reasoning of   7
   as line of descent   51
race inférieure   56
'race of coxcombs'   56
race supérieure   56
Race: The History of an Idea in the West (Hannaford)   6
race theory   44, 45, 91, 121, 195
race thinking   5, 216
   elements of   214
racial categories   5
racial filiation   122
racialism   3
racialized body   39
racialized determinism   71
racial pseudoscience   5, 44, 46, 48
rank symbolism   39
Rare Adventures and Painefull Peregrinations (Lithgow)   79
Ray, John   126
razza   50
Recherches philosophiques (Pauw)   131
Reflections on the Revolution in France (Burke)   201–3, 206
Reinhold, Johann   197
Religio Medici (Browne)   64
Remarks upon the History of England (Bolingbroke)   108
Republican Refuted (Elliot)   57
Resolution   158, 164, 165

Revolutionary egalitarianism   203
Revolutionary France   22, 192, 205
Reynold, Joshua   170
Rheinberger, Hans Jörg   5, 49, 51, 130
Richardson, Samuel   68
Rights of Man (Paine)   207, 218
right to freedom of speech   27
Ripley, William Z.   45
Robertson, George   159
Rodes, David Stuart   184
Rolls of Parliament of 1454   25
Ross, Ian Campbell   66
Roumy, Franck   97
Rousseau, Jean-Jacques   88, 201
Royal Anthropological Society   45
Royal Slave   37, 184
   cultural fantasy of   181
   trope   175, 187, 188, 193

Saducismus Triumphatus (Glanvill)   64
Scala naturae   60, 61, 72
Scandalum magnatum   27
Schaub, Jean-Frédéric   4
scholarship   22
Scully, Denys   140
Sebastiani, Silvia   76, 86, 93, 114
Segar, William   53
Self-Interpreting Bible (Brown)   53
self-referential race thinking   212, 215
Sessarakoo, William   39, 187
Seth, Suman   92, 124
Seymour, Susanne   99
Sharp, Granville   176
Shelton, Maurice   29, 53, 66
Sheppard, F. H. W.   190
Siena, Kevin   97, 112, 114, 115
Sketches of the History of Man (Kames)   124
skin colour   57
   bodily mechanics of   131
Slavery (McKenzie)   175
Sloan, Phillip   126, 127
Smith, Thomas   17
Smollett, Tobias   148
social alterization   5
social conservatism   65
social elites   23, 93
Somerset, James   176
Southerne, Thomas   184

South Seas   157
   three voyages to   158
Spenser, Edmund   141
Sprat, Thomas   63
stadial theory   75, 161
Stanhope Smith, Samuel   8, 79, 93–5, 130, 172
Starr, Chester G.   18
Stehelin, John Peter   52
Stibbs, Bartholomew   57
Stock, Paul   5
Stone, Jeanne Fawtier   22
Stone, Lawrence   22
Stuart monarchy   25
substantial gentry   25
Summa Contra Gentiles (Aquinas)   61
super-human caste   209
superior race   214
Swift, Jonathan   102, 103, 140
Sydenham, Thomas   115
Sypher, Wylie   185, 192
Systema naturae (Linnaeus)   49, 81, 123

Tahitian society   158
taint   114
tapu (taboo)   162, 163
Tatler (Addison)   58
Temora (Macpherson)   109
temperate environments   74
Temple, William   108
Thompson, E. P.   197
thoroughbred nobles   103
thoroughbreds   100, 102, 104
thorough-breeding craze   104
Tocqueville, Alexis de   21
Todorov, Tzvetan   5
Tom Jones (Fielding)   149
Toutous   161, 162
tow-tows   169, 170, 198, 199
traditional race discourse   125
trait transmission   49, 112, 121
transatlantic slave trade   5, 142, 158
Treatise on the Diseases and Lameness of Horses (Osmer)   101
Treatise on the Gout (Sydenham)   115
true nobility   15, 18, 28, 30, 201
True Rise of Nobility (Shelton)   29, 53, 66
Turk, Byerly   100
Turkish horses   99

Turner, Richard   70
Turton, William   83
Tyson, Edward   76, 86

uncomplicated childbirth   117
UNESCO   46
   Statement on Race   44, 46, 47
United Irishman, Society of   154
Universal Magazine (1749)   52, 53
untainted blood   121

Vandermonde, Charles-Augustin   114
varietal diversification   158
varietal racism   191
varietates   82, 83
Variétés dans l'espèce humaine (Buffon)   84
Vassa, Gustavus   188
View of the Earth (Turner)   70
Voegelin, Eric   3, 45
Voltaire   21, 22
Voyage Round the World (Dampier and Funnell)   80, 197
Voyage to Suratt (Ovington)   78

Wahrman, Dror   88, 196
Wall, Richard   101
Wallerstein, Immanuel   6, 56, 212
Walpole, Horace   145
Webber, James   164
Weber, Max   203
Wedgwood, Josiah   175, 177
Weller, Barry   181
Wells, Andrew   4, 74
Westminster   26, 32, 141
Wheeler, Roxann   6, 57, 75
White, Charles   71, 124, 130, 135, 136
Wilberforce, William   177
Willis, Thomas   112
Wilson, Kathleen   51, 105, 158
Wilson, R. G.   24, 32
Wingfield family, pedigree of   55
witchcraft legislation   65
Wolff, Caspar Friedrich   122
woman   116, 185
   of fashion   117
   of savage nations   92
Woodard, Helena   68, 70
Worrall, David   169

www.ingramcontent.com/pod-product-compliance
Lightning Source LLC
Chambersburg PA
CBHW070723020526
44116CB00031B/1408